RESTORING REAL REPRESENTATION

RESTORING REAL REPRESENTATION

Robert C. Grady

UNIVERSITY OF ILLINOIS PRESS
Urbana and Chicago

This book is printed on acid-free paper.

Library of Congress Cataloging-in-Publication Data
Grady, Robert C. (Robert Cowan), 1945–
  Restoring real representation / Robert C. Grady.
     p.   cm.
  Includes index.
  ISBN 0-252-01967-9 (cl)
  1. Representative government and representation.   I. Title.
JF1051.G68   1993
324.6'3—dc20   92-18273
                                                   CIP

CONTENTS

PREFACE

American politics revolves around representation: *who* represents *whom* and with *what* consequences. Conflicts about individual opportunity and group equality, interest group and corporate power, the consent of the people in opposition to the dominance of the powerful, the proper relationship between the public interest and private interests—these and others involve claims on public authority, and representation is the vehicle par excellence for advancing the contending claims. The constitutional founders believed they had discovered in popular representation the fulcrum for republicanism; James Madison called it the "pivot" of the Constitution. In the late twentieth century, their optimism seems curiously distant. "We the people" collectively do not hold public institutions in very high esteem, as the abundance of polls eliciting widespread dissatisfaction with their performance seems to suggest. This state of affairs should not be surprising; citizens seem to have grasped the proposition that the founders' commitment to popular representation has been attenuated, that the practice of representation is the practice of *interest group* representation.

The displacement of popular representation in favor of interest group representation is attributable to many factors in America's political history. Most of these factors are beyond the scope of this book. Political scientists cannot claim credit for change or for the sources of change, but they can, or should, take credit for explaining it. This book is about the latter sort of credit: the efforts of political scientists to explain politics—and, ultimately, to rationalize it. It is a revisionist undertaking in three ways.

First, the book makes a case for Madison the democrat, not Madison the elitist, antimajoritarian proponent of factional accommodation. The displacement of popular representation in favor of interest representation is not attributable to the elitist commitments of the founders, notably Madison's, which somehow preordained a politics of interest representation, notwithstanding scholarly acceptance of the elitist characterization as though it were a truism. The argument is that Madisonian constitutional principles are designed to enhance popular representation and several subsidiary principles encompassed by that concept, chiefly civic equality and civic responsibility, or civic virtue. Pluralism and its heirs discount these; proponents of real representation require them.

Second, it examines the liabilities of pluralism and its more recent incarnations as interest group liberalism and corporatism. Singly and together, they undercut the grounds for real representation in favor of representation for the organized and well-placed. They are also explanatory theories, however, and they cannot be disregarded in the third aspect of revisionism undertaken here: an argument to help revive popular representation and buttress the now largely symbolic electoral connection between citizen and government with meaningful, democratic functional jurisdictions for participation and representation.

This part of the argument draws heavily on participatory theory and the descriptive elements of corporatism to make a case for democratic functional constituencies. The foray into the Madisonian past provides a baseline. Many critics of contemporary politics have proposed reforms that inadequately account for constitutional principles. The sometimes not-so-implicit assumption of the reformers is that past principles are irrelevant, inadequate, or wrongheaded or that reform can be accomplished without regard for the historical or theoretical antecedents of contemporary pathologies. In reverting to Madison, this book attempts to effect a synthesis between past principles and contemporary practices. Like any such effort, it requires compromises between the sometimes airy views of past ideals and the alleged realism of contemporary practices. The argument for democratic functional constituencies is, in the end, an argument for a reordering of priorities, both political and intellectual. Some of the prescriptions appear tentative but the criticisms from which they derive are to the point.

Acknowledgments

Four chapters previously appeared in journals in substantially different form. For permission to reprint them, grateful acknowledgment is given to the editors of *American Politics Quarterly, Journal of Politics, Political Science Quarterly,* and *Polity.* An Eastern Michigan University faculty research fellowship and a sabbatical leave supported much of the work.

Several individuals have influenced the shape of the arguments here with their criticisms of earlier versions of the articles or chapters: Charles Anderson, Alfonso Damico, George Graham, Scarlett Graham, Edward Greenberg, Frank Hearn, Lawrence Joseph, Michael Lienesch, Theodore Lowi, and Eric Nordlinger. Jack Gunnell and Jeffrey Lustig provided extensive and penetrating analyses of the entire manuscript. Thanks to Richard Goff for stylistic nagging and to James Johnson, my former department head, for practicing a supportive version of interest group liberalism in parceling out certain scheduling benefits. Needless to say, the arguments here would have been better had I only paid more heed to their criticisms. Richard Martin, an executive editor at the University of Illinois Press, provided gentle but effective prodding, and Jane Mohraz, the manuscript editor, made the painstaking job of editorial revisions less painful than expected. They, Theresa Sears, and the rest of the press staff have my gratitude for seeing this through the production process—and for deadlines I usually could meet. Editorial revisions to the manuscript were undertaken after I had been appointed to the Ann Arbor city council to fill an unexpired term and subsequently elected to a full term; my experiences as a "representative" only reinforce the direction of the arguments.

Finally, but in many ways first, thanks to Debbie and the kids— Ben, Owen, Nathan, and Marshall—for putting up with it all and for the nonacademic sort of support that we all need. One's work habits are largely a function of one's rearing, and that responsibility goes to the people to whom the book is dedicated: to the memory of my mother, to Dad, and to "Unc."

CHAPTER 1

The Eclipse of Real Representation

Ratification of the Constitution ushered in a new order. Henceforth, the measure of political legitimacy for the United States—indeed, for the world in the eyes of the Federalists—would be the consent of the people exercised through popular representation. In *The Federalist Papers,* James Madison proclaimed that the "principle of representation" served as the "pivot on which" the constitutional system would "move." At the Pennsylvania ratification debates, James Wilson enthusiastically hailed the Constitution's foundation: "the world has left to America the glory and happiness of forming a government where representation shall at once supply the basis and the cement of the superstructure. For representation . . . is the true chain between the people and those to whom they entrust the administration of government."[1]

History provided the founders with numerous examples of the fragility of republics in the face of factional conflicts. Their republican experiment with popular representation required limitations on power and its potential for abuse at the hands of faction. Their experiment also, and more fundamentally, presupposed some degree of civic virtue—the quality of a responsible, active, and effective citizenry. Civic virtue did not connote an abstract moral quality of subordinating individual interests to the common good, however. The founders were realists, and contemporary politics reinforced their unquestioning, but not uncritical, acceptance of the role of "possessive individualism" in social life (to borrow C. B. Macpherson's illuminating term). They recognized, therefore, that civic virtue had to be predicated on self-interest and the stakes held by citizens in the political process.[2] They assumed, perhaps simplistically by twentieth-century standards, that the essential qualities of the citizenry were served best by the government that governed least, to paraphrase Jefferson. A more or less minimal or "nightwatchman" role for government was taken for granted. Since constitutional ratification, however, political practices have changed, and the consequences for the founders' "pivot" of the Constitution have been substantial.

A preference for minimal government intrusion into society and the economy did not mean that the founders were unconcerned about economic issues, particularly those that might prove divisive, such as export taxes and commercial and navigation laws that might benefit northern interests at the expense of the southern states. These sorts of issues were understood, however, in the context of factional conflicts that might undercut national unity and constitutional supremacy; that is, they were not generally viewed as normative issues affecting the proper objectives and "scope" of government.[3] In the nineteenth century, however, the United States underwent unprecedented economic and industrial development, and toward the end of the nineteenth and into the twentieth century, government was faced with demands to regulate and sustain the economy. Initially in state and local jurisdictions and then at the national level, especially from the 1930s on, governments increasingly assumed responsibility for regulating business practices, providing social welfare, making economic policy, and the like to maintain the U.S. form of free enterprise capitalism. How could governmental intervention be justified? The ideals of the minimal state provided little guidance. As governments undertook their regulatory endeavors, frequently at the behest of organized interests to support their objectives or to control other interests, a symbiotic relationship between the state and organizations of private power developed.

Recent scholarship has stressed the gradual development of an "administrative" or "corporate" state, one that emerged through a series of negotiations, accommodations, and trade-offs to integrate the national capitalist economy and traditional liberal values within the framework of the positive state.[4] Popular values of individual initiative and free enterprise, symbolized by the Horatio Alger stories and reinforced by a belief in the sanctity of private property, helped justify governmental acquiescence to economic interests in determining the nature of regulations and subsidies. Much popular and scholarly literature reflected the widely held assumption that business and interest group activities could achieve societal objectives that might have fallen within the province of the state in earlier mercantilist theories of political economy. Government intervention in support of these activities could be rationalized as an extension of the minimal state when the acknowledged alternatives were a bygone mercantilism or contemporary European socialism. The historian Louis Hartz explained the public's acceptance of state "promotionalism" of business interests by stressing how the Alger myth was adapted to the requirements for state-aided economic development in the name of individual initiative and opportunity.[5] These beliefs remain pervasive, as evidenced by their resurgence in the rhetoric, if not the realities, of domestic politics in the 1980s. To critics of the administrative state, however, governments have abandoned any pretext of promoting the individualism of the Alger myth.

Pluralism and the Madisonian Model

The upshot of the transition from the minimal state of the Constitution's republican government to the supportive administrative state of the twentieth century is that *interest group representation,* not popular representation "derived from the great body of society" (*Federalist 39*)—the citizens—became the predominant theme in contemporary theories of American politics. A theory of the "group basis of politics" emerged that rationalized the modern state and avoided a confrontation between requirements for government's regulatory activities and the constitutional principles of the founders. Accompanying the ascendancy of interest group politics was an emphasis on social consensus about the proper relationships between the public and the private spheres. This value consensus was frequently associated with the philosophy of John Locke. To many contemporary scholars, American politics embodied the principles of Lockean liberalism. Even so able a historian as Hartz could describe, apparently without recognizing the hyperbole, "the national acceptance of the Lockian creed, ultimately enshrined in the Constitution."[6] By mid-twentieth century, *pluralism* was the generally accepted label for the new theory. Pluralism all but abandoned the requirements for popular representation in favor of group representation, and it rationalized the decline of civic equality and the ascent of corporate power by pleading for the virtues of consensus and a mythic "potential group" that would presumably allay concerns with excessive institutional power and inequality.

Most pluralists have characterized the constitutional theory of the founders as Madison's theory, and they have found it to be defective. They have focused primarily on Madison's apparent preoccupation with faction and his prescriptions for alleviating the problem of majority faction, and they have downplayed or ignored his justifications of popular representation and the role of popular majorities. This is partly because of the availability of *The Federalist Papers* for pedagogical and scholarly work designed to explain Madison's relevance, or irrelevance, for contemporary politics but chiefly because of the influential work of Charles A. Beard, who set the tone for pluralist scholars. Beard popularized the notion that *Federalist 10* provides simply a mechanistic formula for limiting popular majorities.[7] The mechanistic, antimajoritarian motif became an article of faith and the *Madisonian model* its disparaging caricature as pluralist theory developed into the prevailing explanatory framework for political scientists.[8]

Several historians attempted to downplay the pluralists' portrayal of Madison's theory. Douglass Adair argued that Beard's account was too narrow and misrepresented Madison, and Adrienne Koch concluded that the Madisonian model caricature is simply misleading.[9] Subsequently, other scholars challenged, directly or indirectly, pluralist theory by criticizing the status of Madisonian liberalism. These later critics claim to have discovered the influence of "classical republican" or, somewhat more narrowly, "civic humanist" traditions on the founding. Their revisions have spawned an ongoing debate among political theorists over the respective influence and roles of Lockean liberalism, classical republicanism, Madisonian theory, and even prerepublican ancient virtue and neoliberal Calvinist moralism.[10] These revisions are important, and they reinforce the attempt to look beyond the obvious in Madison, the institutional framework of *Federalist 10,* and examine (see chapter 2) not only his concern with faction but also his arguments for popular representation and its corollaries—civic equality and civic responsibility, the latter sometimes called civic virtue—that he develops in his other essays and writings and that are downplayed in versions of the Madisonian model. Notwithstanding these revisionist efforts, and no matter how misrepresentative or misleading the elitist and overly mechanistic portrayal of Madison may be, it is the Madisonian model caricature that continues to influence political scientists.[11]

The Argument

"Voters are not fools," V. O. Key, Jr., wrote three decades ago, reflecting on the shared responsibilities of scholars for influencing candidates' and political leaders' images of the electorate: "Fed a steady diet of buncombe, the people may come to expect and to respond with highest predictability to buncombe."[12] Dietary maladies and their cures are now ritualized. Each election season begins with renewed efforts to bring the voters back in; each election season ends with marginal reductions in participation, or status quo maintenance, but never higher levels of participation that signal a long-term trend; and each election season produces poll after poll that elicits widespread disaffection from elective institutions. For a discipline whose raison d'être is the public realm, political science remains curiously detached. Pluralist theory has devalued the citizens' civic roles, esteemed by the founders, and helped reduce elections to symbolic exercises in the minds of many eligible voters. Critics of pluralism have had an important impact on the discipline, and it is no longer dominated by pluralism. Outside the academy, however, pluralist accommodation continues, and citizens respond appropriately to ersatz venues for participation. A case for the restoration of real representation must address those features of contemporary scholarship and politics that citizens recognize, however dimly, as the cause of disaffection and the source of change.

The argument of this book is critical, prescriptive, and therefore polemical: how citizen representation can be restored to its "pivotal" role in politics; what is to be done. To revivify real representation, scholars and citizens must acknowledge the changes incurred since the founding era and attempt to buttress the now largely symbolic electoral connection between citizen and government with meaningful, *democratic functional jurisdictions* for participation and representation. This is a revisionist claim that appears superficially to be incompatible with the principles of the constitutional founders. The case for democratic functional constituencies is based on the proposition that meaningful citizen participation is contingent on citizens' having a stake or interest in politics and that citizens can realize and act on these interests in their associational capacities, not as isolated persons with only symbolically expressive outlets, which popular elections have become for many people. The argument must show how these functional jurisdictions can be reconciled with constitutional values to make participation, public consent, and popular representation once again central to governance. The case for restoring real representation necessarily begins with the source of its decline, pluralism and its critics.

Alternatives to Pluralism: An Overview

Dissenters from mainstream political science have challenged the inadequacies of pluralism. They argue that the major sorts of groups valued by pluralists are involuntary and undemocratic, not simply voluntary associations. The beneficiaries of the group process are not ordinary citizens but those who happen to belong to well-organized institutions that hold disproportionate resources relative to other associations and, principally, those who constitute the leadership of such organizations. The growth of the positive or administrative state figures prominently in these criticisms. Whether it is cause or consequence of private interests' excessive power is disputed. For some of the critics, these organizations have privileged positions in or privileged access to the policy-making process. For others, they conduct policy for the state based on legislative or administrative delegations of authority to them.[13]

An implication of the criticisms is that pluralism is not simply an empirical theory but a not-so-veiled normative theory. It justifies not only the provision of benefits to well-organized, undemocratic interest organizations but also a policy-making process of legislative abdication to the desires of such groups and their administrative and committee clientele or allies in government. This has produced, in the words of Grant McConnell, a "reformulation and redistribution of authority" from elective institutions to "private governments" without, at the same time, any coherent rationale for it: "the persistence and growth of private power have posed an embarrassing problem for all who are involved in exercising it. The problem is authority. What justifies the existence of power; by what principle is it rightful? For, if it is not justifiable, power is properly open to attack and, if possible, destruction."[14] That the reallocation of authority to private entities creates, in reality, a vacuum of public authority is a central theme of *interest group liberalism's* critique of pluralism, which is the focal point of chapter 3.

Critics of interest group liberalism return to the central premises of Madisonian theory in advocating constitutionalism, or the rule of law.[15] Adherence to the rule of law is designed to revitalize the separation of powers, segregating legislative deliberation from executive decision making yet ultimately forcing cooperation between the two branches. Each branch must appeal to its constituents—the electorate—to buttress its claims rather than abdicate its constitutional role to the wishes of organized interests. These objectives, presented as a proposal for reform, have significant liabilities (see chapters 4 and 10). It is up to Congress to restore its deliberative role and public accountability, and on purely instrumental grounds, the likelihood of implementing long-term congressional reform is slim. The case for the rule of law, however, articulates basic constitutionalist principles that can serve as important criteria or ground rules for the effort to justify and utilize democratic functional constituencies within the liberal framework.

Understanding pluralism as interest group liberalism provides a baseline for two other alternatives: *corporatism* and *participatory theory*. Corporatist theoreticians are concerned less with interest group liberalism's democratic shortcomings than with its inefficiencies as a framework for policy-making.[16] Their remedies are explored in chapter 5 under the rubric of neoliberal industrial policy, which is designed to institutionalize tripartite bargaining arrangements among the positive, interventionist state and the leadership of key sectors of the economy (industry, labor, and banking). Corporatists are unabashedly elitist, aiming to attain increased "governability" and stability through the abilities of functional organizations to control member demands and thereby to reduce demands on government, as the assessment in chapter 6 makes clear. It is an antidemocratic solution to the democratic problem of restoring real representation. This does not trouble corporatist theoreticians. Although few of them pay attention to the factors shaping contemporary pluralism (unlike the other pluralist critics), they believe their European model is applicable to American politics and is preferable to traditional liberal practices. The corporatists' emphasis on functional representation, however, is not incompatible with the participationists' view of the appropriate organizational jurisdictions for politics. If its elitist, managerial bias can be mitigated, the important role it assigns to functional interests can be used constructively, with important modifications suggested by participatory theory.

Participatory democrats observe virtually the same "data" that the critics of interest group liberalism do, but they tend to stress their effects on citizens rather than the decline of authority. Both, for example, recognize that effective interest representation is the state-sponsored representation of organized or "vested" interests and that representation through popular elections and legislative deliberation is largely symbolic. Although the pluralists' justification for these arrangements appears to be straightforward (based on the views that citizens are deficient and that ideals of an earlier age are unrealistic), it confuses cause with effect. The incorporation of private interest representatives within the governmental process undermines the grounds citizens have for taking an interest in politics. As a result, pluralism, as interest group liberalism, does not describe the role of civic apathy so much as it provides a basis for it, and it encourages public cynicism toward the responsibilities of elected officials.

The participatory theorists' label for pluralism—the elitist theory of democracy, or democratic elitism—follows their criticism.[17] Diverging from the rule of law proponents, however, many of them attribute the group domination of American politics to elitist commitments of the founders that thereby, they believe, preordained the pluralist politics of elite representation and interest accommodation; for example, C. B. Macpherson attributes Madison's elitism to possessive individualist premises undergirding his preoccupation with protecting the "opulent against the majority."[18] This detracts from their criticism of pluralism, inasmuch as they accept at face value rather than question the pluralist dismissal of civic virtue, but not from their reform alternatives. These are explored and evaluated in chapters 7 and 8: first, that the ideals of participatory democracy can be adapted to contemporary politics to enhance participation in the workplace and local community jurisdictions; second, that these can serve as the groundwork for an egalitarian system of democracy and stimulate change in the political system. Participatory objectives are constrained by the prevailing interest group liberal or corporatist modes of organizing participation and representation in the political system. They are not, however, merely unrealistic panaceas, and the last two chapters (9 and 10) develop a case for their realization.

Restoring Real Representation: A Preview

In advocating workplace, industrial, and local democracy, participationists propose to democratize functional constituencies on the grounds that functional units have largely displaced traditional democratic constituencies. On this point, participatory theory converges with corporatism in a way that suggests a viable alternative to interest group liberalism. However much these two schools of thought differ, it is possible, because of their common assumptions about the locus of political life, to envision a hybrid produced by combining corporatist functional jurisdictions, which interact with public officials and complement the roles of elected legislatures, and participatory practices within such jurisdictions. In other words, it is possible to retain the policy-making structural or institutional format of corporatism but replace its elitist and antidemocratic functions with democratic organizations. The proposal, in brief, is that the participatory requirements of workplace democracy can be used to democratize functional constituencies; that is, workplace democracy and functional jurisdictions together can contribute to a revived form of democracy and democratic representation.

How well would such a hybrid support the values of traditional liberalism, particularly the Madisonian and constitutionalist perspectives? Indeed, how does one reconcile democratic functional constituencies with traditional democratic ideals of popular representation? Superficially, not very well. An attempt to reconcile functional jurisdictions, even democratic ones, with traditional liberal ideals about popular representation appears problematic. The problem is somewhat analogous to concerns of Madison and Jefferson, in their Virginia and Kentucky resolutions, to force the national government to conform to their principles of constitutional democracy based on their claims about the appropriate roles for state and local democracies. (Their arguments about interposition differed from John C. Calhoun's later arguments, which are more analogous to our usual views of elite corporatism.) Moreover, an obvious criticism is that the hybrid would create nothing more than "democratic corporatism." Because of the connotations associated with corporatism—not so much its earlier syndicalist, fascist, and authoritarian associations but its current elitist and managerial ones—*democratic corporatism* is an inappropriate label. The proposal encompasses far more than a corporatist framework, and the preferred term, *democratic functional constituencies,* conveys its distance from corporatism.

The need to consider democratic functional constituencies as the basis for representation was anticipated by Andrew Hacker, who articulated the issues well in advance of the interest group liberal criticism of pluralism and the efforts by neoliberals and corporatists to mitigate the consequences of interest group liberalism. He recognized the substantial dependence of the employee on the corporate organization. Madisonian-like notions of local, regional, and ethnic interests had become, he believed, "superficial characteristics" rather than meaningful grounds for civic participation. In place of these, "the transient employee of a national corporation must find a substitute attachment to give him communal roots." Hacker concluded that it is "necessary to stand Madison on his head" and seriously consider the alternatives to traditional venues for representation, since in them citizens lack any real "interest to defend in the political arena" and politics is therefore "meaningless." He recognized then, as participationists and corporatists more recently acknowledge, that "functional, or corporate, citizenship is arising to replace local or regional citizenship."[19]

Hacker's insights, as well as the positions taken by corporatists and participatory theorists, do not suggest that economic or functional jurisdictions can totally displace traditional geographic ones. The workplace is used here as an exemplar of functional jurisdictions because it is where so much of the emphasis on small-scale democracy is placed. To focus on the workplace is not to exclude other arenas. Although functional jurisdictions are principally corporate units, the argument can be extended to the other interest associations (ethnic, religious, geographic) that provide the wherewithal for people's interests and through which they can define their civic roles. The focus on the workplace provides an appropriate vehicle for working out the conditions and prerequisites for democratic functional constituencies. Some individuals may be better adept at sustaining, or better situated to sustain, traditional venues of civic enfranchisement. But others—many others—are better "enfranchised" through their functional interest organizations (and disenfranchised from traditional jurisdictions). These latter mandate a rethinking of whether and how traditional liberal democratic values about participation and representation can have relevance and a reconsideration of possible roles for functional interest associations, *at least those organized democratically.*

Functional representation has a long association with liberal theory—an association of persistence, returning time and again after its detractors had presumably discredited it.[20] The discrediting of functional representation usually proceeds along the following lines: (1) functional representation violates the liberal standard of individualism: the rational, unencumbered, autonomous individual who is the best judge of his or her own interests; (2) it undermines a corollary of individualism: that individual interests can be governed only through elective legislative bodies, ideally designed around the juridical norm of "one person, one vote" (a norm that acknowledges the equality of autonomous individuals); (3) it entails the political equivalent of an infinite regress in search of the most fundamental interest(s) informing the individual and his or her associational membership. It is implied that ever more narrowly defined communities of interests have the right to veto interests articulated through elections of popular representative bodies—a standard criticism of Calhoun's theory of nullification.

The first two criticisms are hardly separable. The conflict between functional representation and liberal individualism is clearly enunciated with the notion of *faction.* Factional interests not only disrupt the public interest but also make claims on individual interests that are incompatible with liberal ideals. Charles W. Anderson underscores the two problems in an essay addressed to corporatists: "The most fundamental premises of liberal democracy stand against any effort *to prefigure the interests that individuals ought to endorse.*"

Accordingly, he cautions, "This is the flaw in any corporate theory of representation. How can one legitimate the legislative authority of powerful and contending interests over popular consent?"[21] The third criticism is that there are simply no a priori grounds for defining the most basic functional unit for representation, such as the individual in the case of popular representation, and for the "scope" of its jurisdiction. Reflecting on the European experience with functional representation, Norberto Bobbio summarizes this problem in two ways, first, with respect to the failure to identify appropriate constituencies, and, second, with respect to the failure to identify appropriate jurisdictions for their activities and responsibilities: "any shortcomings in the functioning of [corporatist] democracy are not due to the representation being sectional [functional], but to its not being sectional enough. . . . [However, w]hat is open to criticism is not sectional representation as such, but sectional representation which has been extended outside its proper sphere."[22]

The criticisms are well-taken, and they will be dealt with in the penultimate chapter. To briefly anticipate the argument there, functional organizations must practice internal democracy, and their political authority must be sanctioned under public interest criteria established by an elective legislature. It will not suffice to *assume* that functional organizations represent their members and that functional elites have decision-making authority based on pluralist assumptions of informal representation through overlapping memberships and the like. For those policy arenas in which functional interests are authorized to exert influence, requirements for democratic functional constituency representation must be imposed and adhered to.

The third criticism implies the right of veto, even secession. Such an implication, however, requires a theory of group rights to justify a veto role for functional interests or their right to secede. The argument for the legitimate role of democratic functional constituencies does not confuse function with right; it sustains the case for vigorous support of individual and associational interests—their "voice"—rather than their grounds for "exit."[23]

The dilemma for contemporary American liberalism is that, notwithstanding these criticisms of functional representation, the representation of functional interests and their exercise of authority, both over the members in their jurisdictions and through authority delegated to them by government, are alive and well. They arise from ongoing political processes that show no evidence of decline but, to the contrary, show all the marks of increasing their roles to the exclusion of the traditional venues for governance, popular elections, and popular representation through elective legislatures. Liberals may criticize this state of affairs, but for all intents and purposes, they—at least *interest group* liberals—seem to have accommodated themselves to the realities of functional representation and authoritative decision making by functional bodies as though these are *merely* theoretical inconveniences. Democratic workplaces can be exemplars of democratized functional constituencies, but to create ongoing workplace democracies and extend their participatory values to the state, it is necessary to accommodate participatory theory to the requirements of institutional practices, not the institutional practices that undermine democracy—interest group liberalism and corporatism—but those that support democracy—the powerful and complementary normative principles of participatory theory and the rule of law.

NOTES

1. Wilson's remarks are from John Bach McMaster and Frederick D. Stone, eds., *Pennsylvania and the Federal Constitution, 1787–1788*, vol. 1 (New York: Da Capo Press, 1970; reprint of 1888 ed.), 273; Madison's, from Alexander Hamilton, James Madison, and John Jay, *The Federalist Papers*, ed. Clinton Rossiter (New York: New American Library, 1961), no. 63; see no. 14, par. 4, and cf. no. 39, par. 4, and no. 37, par. 6. Hereafter, citations to *The Federalist Papers* are given in the text by number.
2. The problem of faction and the role of civic virtue and other conditions for representation are discussed in chapter 2.
3. For a thoughtful assessment, see Scarlett G. Graham, "Government and the Economy," in *Founding Principles of American Government*, rev. ed., ed. George J. Graham, Jr., and Scarlett G. Graham (Chatham, N.J.: Chatham House Publishers, 1984), 305–30.
4. This and the preceding paragraph illustrate some salient points of an otherwise complex and controversial history. See R. Jeffrey Lustig, *Corporate Liberalism* (Berkeley: University of California Press, 1982); Stephen Skowronek, *Building a New American State* (New York: Cambridge University Press, 1982), esp. chaps. 7–8. See also Elizabeth Sanders, "Business, Bureaucracy, and the Bourgeoisie: The New Deal Legacy," in *The Political Economy of Public Policy*, ed. Alan Stone and Edward J. Harpham (Beverly Hills, Calif.: Sage Publications, 1982), 115–40; James Q. Wilson, "The Politics of Regulation," in *The Politics of Regulation*, ed. Wilson (New York: Basic Books, 1980), 357–94. For compatible but somewhat different treatment, see Edward S. Greenberg, *Capitalism and the American Ideal* (Armonk, N.Y.: M. E. Sharpe, 1985), chap. 5. For earlier work exploring these issues, see Avery Leiserson, *Administrative Regulation* (Chicago: University of Chicago Press, 1942).

5. Louis Hartz, *The Liberal Tradition in America* (New York: Harcourt, Brace and World, 1955). For the views of critical and traditional scholars respectively, cf. Kenneth M. Dolbeare, *Democracy at Risk,* rev. ed. (Chatham, N.J.: Chatham House Publishers, 1986), chap. 2, and Alpheus T. Mason and Richard H. Leach, *In Quest of Freedom,* 2d ed. (Englewood Cliffs, N.J.: Prentice-Hall, 1972).

6. Hartz, *Liberal Tradition in America,* 9.

7. Charles A. Beard, *An Economic Interpretation of the Constitution of the United States* (New York: Macmillan, 1935; orig. pub. 1913), chap. 6, esp. 152–68. Beard focused almost solely on the institutional relationships described in *Federalist 10* in his "economic" interpretation of the Constitution.

8. Robert A. Dahl, *A Preface to Democratic Theory* (Chicago: University of Chicago Press, 1956), underscored the deficiencies of Madison's institutional analysis; James MacGregor Burns, *The Deadlock of Democracy* (Englewood Cliffs, N.J.: Prentice-Hall, 1963), popularized the caricature.

9. Douglass Adair, *Fame and the Founding Fathers,* ed. Trevor Colbourn (New York: St. Martin's Press, 1974), 75–77; Adrienne Koch, *Madison's "Advice to My Country"* (Princeton, N.J.: Princeton University Press, 1966), xi–xv, chap. 2. See the brief overview of Madison caricatures in Robert J. Morgan, "Madison's Analysis of the Sources of Political Authority," *American Political Science Review* 75 (Sept. 1981): 613–25, at 613–14.

10. Robert E. Shalhope, "Toward a Republican Synthesis," *William and Mary Quarterly,* 3d ser. 29 (Jan. 1972): 49–80, reviews the earliest work; J. G. A. Pocock, *The Machiavellian Moment* (Princeton, N.J.: Princeton University Press, 1975), presses the civic humanist theme; Thomas L. Pangle, *The Spirit of Modern Republicanism* (Chicago: University of Chicago Press, 1988), defends the importance of ancient virtue; John P. Diggins, *The Lost Soul of American Politics* (Chicago: University of Chicago Press, 1984), laments the decline of Calvinist influence. The enthusiasm for classical republicanism has waned somewhat. For second thoughts, see Isaac Kramnick, *Republicanism and Bourgeois Radicalism* (Ithaca, N.Y.: Cornell University Press, 1990), esp. chaps. 1, 6, 8.

11. See *Mr. Madison's Constitution and the Twenty-first Century* (Washington, D.C.: American Historical Association and American Political Science Association, 1988).

12. V. O. Key, Jr., *The Responsible Electorate* (Cambridge, Mass.: Belknap Press of Harvard University Press, 1966), 7.

13. Henry S. Kariel, *The Decline of American Pluralism* (Stanford, Calif.: Stanford University Press, 1961); Theodore J. Lowi, *The End of Liberalism,* 2d ed. (New York: W. W. Norton, 1979); Grant McConnell, *Private Power and American Democracy* (New York: Alfred A. Knopf, 1966); Michael Reagan, *The Managed Economy* (New York: Oxford University Press, 1963); E. E. Schattschneider, *The Semisovereign People* (New York: Holt, Rinehart and Winston, 1960); James Q. Wilson, "The Rise of the Bureaucratic State," *Public Interest* 41 (Fall 1975): 77–103. The most popular account of cor-

porate-government interdependence is John Kenneth Galbraith, *The New Industrial State* (New York: Houghton Mifflin, 1968).

14. McConnell, *Private Power,* 164, 51–52; see also 153–54.

15. Chiefly Lowi, *End of Liberalism,* 2d ed. See also the related criticism and alternative emphasis on constitutionalism in Kariel, *Decline of American Pluralism,* and the criticism of the "franchise" state and the argument for "repoliticization" in Alan Wolfe, *The Limits of Legitimacy* (New York: Free Press, 1977), chaps. 4, 5, 10. McConnell, *Private Power,* calls for a restoration of publicly shared values to reaffirm the institutional basis of public authority, but his recommendation to strengthen the presidency predated the public's and scholarly community's concern with the imperial presidency and seems to run aground on the shoals of the personalized or "plebiscitary" presidency. On the latter, see Theodore J. Lowi, *The Personal President* (Ithaca, N.Y.: Cornell University Press, 1985). Party responsibility and neoconservative antidotes to interest group liberalism are also briefly discussed in chapter 3; for reasons made clear there, they are not as consistent or compelling as the interest group liberalism critique and its rule of law alternative.

16. Cf. Raymond M. Seidelman, "Pluralist Heaven's Dissenting Angels: Corporatism in the American Political Economy," in *The Political Economy of Public Policy,* ed. Alan Stone and Edward J. Harpham (Beverly Hills, Calif.: Sage Publications, 1982), 49–70.

17. Perhaps the best elitist critique remains Peter Bachrach, *The Theory of Democratic Elitism* (Boston: Little, Brown, 1967), see esp. 71–79.

18. C. B. Macpherson, *The Life and Times of Liberal Democracy* (New York: Oxford University Press, 1977), 15, n. 6, quoting Madison. Macpherson and other participationists tend to assume without critical examination that founding principles are antithetical or at least irrelevant to contemporary politics. Many of the founders were political elitists—and slave owners and men who believed that women were possessions. But as societal values have changed over two centuries and principles of egalitarianism, social welfare, and the positive state have emerged, it is inappropriate to discount their eighteenth-century perspectives from the vantage point of twentieth-century values. (Few advocates of participatory democracy would discount Rousseau's principles on the grounds that he was a misogynist.) It is appropriate instead to consider how their principles can be adapted to the twentieth century without the ideological baggage that their critics deploy ad hominem.

19. Andrew Hacker, "Politics and the Corporation," in *The Corporation Take-Over,* ed. Hacker (Garden City, N.Y.: Doubleday, 1964), 239–62, esp. 246ff. (quotations from 247, 256).

20. For a particularly good survey, see Leiserson, *Administrative Regulation,* chaps. 1, 10. See also Charles A. Beard and John D. Lewis, "Representative Government in Evolution," *American Political Science Review* 32 (Apr. 1932): 223–40; Norberto Bobbio, *The Future of Democracy,* trans. Roger Griffin, ed. Richard Bellamy (Minneapolis: University of Minnesota Press, 1987), chap. 2; Lustig, *Corporate Liberalism.*

21. Charles W. Anderson, "Political Design and the Representation of Interests," *Comparative Political Studies* 10 (Apr. 1977): 127–52, at 148 (italics added), 143.

22. Bobbio, *Future of Democracy*, 51.

23. For an interesting attempt to ground a right of secession in group rights, see Allen Buchanan, *Secession* (Boulder, Colo.: Westview Press, 1991). Exit *or* voice is never a zero-sum option. See Albert O. Hirschman, *Exit, Voice, and Loyalty* (Cambridge, Mass.: Harvard University Press, 1970).

CHAPTER 2

Representation, Faction, and Civic Virtue: Madison's Paradoxical Legacy

During the constitutional ratification debates, James Madison asserted that the principle of popular representation distinguished the Constitution from those of earlier republics. Representation was "neither unknown to the ancients nor wholly overlooked in their political constitutions," he explained, but the Greek constitutions limited the principle to "*representing* the people in their *executive* capacity" only (*Federalist 63*). The legislative assemblies of the ancients were "wholly popular," a form of "pure democracy," and these were fraught with "instability, injustice, and confusion"—the "violence of faction" that the Constitution was intended to minimize (*Federalist 14, 10*). Nor were the experiments of "modern Europe," which had introduced the principle of representation to legislative assemblies, based solely on popular representation. In Europe, "no example is seen of a government wholly popular and founded, at the same time, wholly on that principle" (*Federalist 14*).

European governments were "mixed" governments, some modeled, in Madison's eyes, on classical republican ideals and others influenced by "some celebrated authors, whose writings have had a great share in forming the modern standard of political opinions" (*Federalist 14*). During the constitutional convention and the ratification debates, however, the prerequisites for classical republicanism were scrutinized and found to be inappropriate for the new nation. Pure democracies were rife with factionalism, and mixed republics had to be limited to relatively small territorial jurisdictions.[1] In the territory encompassed by the United States, popular representation, and only popular representation, could serve as the "pivot" upon which the Constitution was to be based. For this reason, Madison asserted,

"America can claim the merit of making the discovery the basis of unmixed and extensive republics" (*Federalist 14*) and thereby can provide a new definition of republican government: "a government in which the scheme of representation takes place" (*Federalist 10*).

But how, or on what basis, would the "scheme of representation" take place, particularly in a society characterized in part by a multiplicity of interests, that is, factions? In *Federalist 39*, Madison stipulated the necessary and sufficient conditions for the Constitution's republican form of government. It is one

> which derives all its powers directly or indirectly from the great body of the people, and is administered by persons holding their offices during pleasure for a limited period, or during good behavior. It is *essential* to such a government that it be derived from the great body of the society, not from an inconsiderable proportion of a favored class of it. . . . It is *sufficient* for such a government that the persons administering it be appointed, either directly or indirectly, by the people.[2]

Madison's conditions are highly general, not specific, formulas. He acknowledged the tension between them and the development of political stability in his well-known discussion, in *Federalist 37*, of the tension between the "genius of republican liberty" on the one hand and the need for "stability" and "energy in government" on the other. The tension would be ameliorated somewhat by the division of responsibilities in government, the provision of different terms of office for the executive and the two legislative houses, and mixed modes of elections and appointments—devices designed to ensure governmental continuity across elections and to minimize the chances that the government would fall under the sway of faction. (The executive in particular, as Alexander Hamilton made clear in *Federalist 70*, was to be the key institution for energetic government.) But chiefly Madison recurred to the principle of representation as the key to both liberty and stability.

Representation was appropriate not only because of the size of the United States, which precluded "pure democracy" (and its attendant factionalism), but also because it would enhance republican liberty and the likelihood of good—effective and stable—government. In his frequently cited consideration of the optimal size of an electoral constituency and the proportion of candidates to electors in *Federalist 10*, Madison asserted that popular representation would "refine and enlarge the public views by passing them through the medium of a chosen body of citizens, whose wisdom may best discern the true interest of their country and whose patriotism and love of justice will be least likely to sacrifice it to temporary or partial considerations." Several important propositions can be derived from this brief claim and the elaboration Madison provides for it:[3] (1) the conduct of elections in large jurisdictions will minimize the influence of factions; (2) factional influence will further be minimized by many geographic jurisdictions (as opposed to one jurisdiction from which a number of representatives would be chosen); (3) citizens will tend to elect the best representative from the array of candidates in their jurisdiction; and (4) as a result, the elected body, as a whole, will be more likely to seek the public good even though, individually, some representatives may represent factious interests.

Numerous commentators have charged that Madison sought to elevate government by elites over government by the people when he stressed the need to refine and enlarge public opinion. The charge has some merit if one acknowledges that a particular system of representation may tend to produce representatives from one class more frequently than from others (Madison and Hamilton recognized that lawyers played disproportionate roles). But it is also beside the point in view of Madison's argument, in *Federalist 39,* that the eligible electorate be composed of equal citizens and that the electoral process should thus reflect "the great body of the society, not . . . an inconsiderable proportion of a favored class." (Madison's insistence on not only the desirability but also the necessity of politically equal citizens is further discussed later in this chapter.) Even Madison's collaborator in *The Federalist Papers,* Hamilton, more given to overt elitism in his caricature of the electorate as a "great beast," acknowledged the importance of basing representation on civic equality. He cautioned that "the people commonly *intend* the PUBLIC GOOD" but that they do not "always *reason right* about the *means* of promoting it" (*Federalist 71*). Representation, he hoped, would alleviate these doubts, in part because an electorate of equals would not produce a system of class-based representation: "Where the qualifications of the electors are the same, whether they have to choose a small or a large number, their votes will fall upon those in whom they have most confidence; whether these happen to be men of large fortunes, or of moderate property, or of no property at all" (*Federalist 35*). In effect, popular elections would serve to "filter out" the factious extremes and to "filter up" the ablest representatives—Jefferson's "natural aristoi" rather than the "artificial aristocracy" that he attributed to John Adams.[4]

Notwithstanding their hopes for republican liberty and good government, the founders did not believe that representation was unproblematic. They realized that the liberties of equal citizens, upon which they justified popular representation, would also facilitate the emergence of factions. As Madison noted in an oft cited remark, "Liberty is to faction what air is to fire, an aliment without which it instantly expires" (*Federalist 10*). Consent and popular representation would consequently further encourage individuals to mobilize into the sorts of self-interested groups that might undermine republican government. Since factions, or interest associations, would develop out of the very individual interests upon which people are expected to make their electoral choices, Madison recognized that the "factious spirit" must be both regulated *and relied on* in representative government: "The regulation of these various and interfering interests forms the principal task of modern legislation and involves the spirit of party and faction in the necessary and ordinary operations of government" (*Federalist 10*).

Representation, Virtue, and Constitutionalism

Madison saw governmental institutions as mediating structures for individuals and groups actively engaged in the pursuit of their interests. In correspondence with Washington before the constitutional convention, he had stressed the desirability of having government serve as a "disinterested & dispassionate *umpire*" in interest conflicts rather than having it take one side or another. At that time, finalizing his *Vices of the Political System of the United States* in preparation for the convention, Madison seemed more concerned about avoiding *mis*representation than promoting representation: "The great desideratum in Government is such a modification of the Sovereignty as will render it sufficiently neutral between the different interests and factions, to controul one part of the Society from invading the rights of another, and at the same time sufficiently controuled itself, from setting up an interest adverse to that of the whole Society."[5] Madison appears to echo Hume: "A constitution is only so far good, as it provides a remedy against maladministration."[6]

Later during the Virginia ratifying convention, however, Madison argued that no constitutional mechanisms could prevent maladministration and factional governance in the absence of "sufficient virtue and intelligence in the community": "I go on this great republican principle, that the people will have virtue and intelligence to select men of virtue and wisdom. Is there no virtue among us? If there be not, we are in a wretched situation. No theoretical checks—no form of government can render us secure. To suppose that any form of government will secure liberty or happiness without any virtue in the people, is a chimerical idea."[7] Elected officials, he responded to critics, would neither be irresponsible nor have "exalted integrity and sublime virtue." "I consider it reasonable to conclude, that they will as readily do their duty, as deviate from it." The qualities of the citizenry—their "virtue and intelligence"—are thus essential to sustain responsible behavior on the part of public officials. They are not, however, sufficient conditions for good government.[8]

Although republican government presupposes civic "virtue and intelligence in the community," it is unlikely that these qualities will displace self-interest. Earlier, in *Federalist 51*, Madison posed the rhetorical question, "But what is government itself but the greatest of all reflections on human nature?" He prefaces his answer with two illustrative disclaimers: "If men were angels, no government would be necessary. If angels were to govern men, neither external nor internal controls on government would be necessary." Citizens are neither angels nor governed by angels, but Madison rejects the notion, shared by some contemporaries and opponents, that they are therefore devils, rendering self-government impossible and making tyranny the likely result of popular experiments with government:

> As there is a degree of depravity in mankind which requires a certain degree of circumspection and distrust, so there are other qualities in human nature which justify a certain portion of esteem and confidence. Republican government presupposes the existence of these qualities in a higher degree than any other form. Were the pictures which have been drawn by the political jealousy of some among us faithful likenesses of the human character, the inference would be that there is not sufficient virtue among men for self-government; and that nothing less than the chains of despotism can restrain them from destroying and devouring one another. (*Federalist 55*)

Ultimately Madison's hopes for republicanism remain with the people. To realize these hopes, however, institutional arrangements—arrangements that combine the advantages of an extensive territory with a multiplicity of interests—must be utilized to tap and direct individuals' drives and proclivities, both positive *and* negative.

Madison thus can answer his question about government being a reflection on human nature in the following way: "In framing a government which is to be administered by men over men, the great difficulty lies in this: you must first enable the government to control the governed; and in the next place oblige it to control itself. A dependence on the people is, no doubt, the primary control on the government; but experience has taught mankind the necessity of auxiliary precautions" (*Federalist 51*). The auxiliary precautions reinforce the primary or popular control on government. They also effect "different modes of elections and different principles of action" (*Federalist 51*); that is, they qualify how the people serve as the primary control of government. The institutional arrangements divide the citizenry into separate electorates. They help stimulate public deliberations among the diverse electorates, since the same citizens choose representatives to the House of Representatives and to the state legislatures, which select (in the original constitutional provisions) the states' senators. They are also effective by relying on precisely the sorts of behavioral motivations to make republicanism workable that lead to the "factious spirit" in the first place (see especially *Federalist 10*). This is why the *regulation* of faction must in fact *involve* the spirit of faction in ordinary governmental activities. The necessary auxiliary precautions, then, are partly the function of institutional constraints and partly the outgrowth of social cleavage and conflicts of interest.

The Problem of Faction

How is it possible both to regulate and control the effects of factions and to incorporate them in the day-to-day administrative and legislative activities of government—particularly a government whose election should have helped refine and enlarge the interests of the electorate? Up through the ratification debates, the founders believed that factional activities in the governmental process would not detract from their primary objective of securing a regime based on popular representation and that these activities might even help provide a broad-based representation of citizens.

Shortly after defending the Constitution's basis in popular representation in his *Federalist Papers* essays, Madison suggested the value of certain types of property qualifications for electors. In his comments on Jefferson's "Draught of a Constitution for Virginia," Madison contrasted the consequences of governments that imposed property qualifications on the electorate, or subjected the rights of persons to the rights of property, with the consequences of abandoning all forms of voter qualifications: "Give all power to property; and the indigent [will] be oppressed. Give it to the latter [indigent] and the effect may be transposed. Give a defensive share to each and each will be secure." He thus acknowledged the value of a "freehold or equivalent" qualification for voters but cautioned against extremes that favored the propertied at the expense of the "indigent" or vice versa.[9]

Madison argued that to support narrow qualifications or to reject all qualifications would pit the propertied against the propertyless and exacerbate factional divisions:

> In all the Governments which were considered as beacons to republican patriots & lawgivers, the rights of persons were subjected to those of property. The poor were sacrificed to the rich. In the existing state of American population, & American property[,] the two classes of rights were so little discriminated that a provision for the rights of persons was supposed to include of itself those of property, and it was natural to infer from the tendency of republican laws, that these different interests would be more and more identified. Experience and investigation have however produced more correct ideas on this subject. It is now observed that in all populous countries, the smaller part only can be interested in preserving the rights of property. . . . It is well understood that interest leads to injustice as well when the opportunity is presented to bodies of men, as to individuals; to an interested majority in a republic, as to the interested minority of any other form of Government.[10]

Madison hoped that constitutional ratification would institutionalize the basis for citizens' responsibilities as electors because they had interests in their rights. The workings of the Constitution, he thought, should minimize the likelihood of factional conflicts that reflected class divisions (with respect to Jefferson's constitution for Virginia, he recommended, "The time to guard agst. this danger is at the first forming of the Constitution").[11]

Notwithstanding these hopes, Madison feared that mere constitutional formalities could be used to serve as a cover for government by a factious minority, or to "mask" minority rule as Robert J. Morgan aptly describes it.[12] Within a few short years, Madison found that his fears were coming to pass. During the administrations of Washington and Adams, it became apparent that the Constitution's grounding in popular representation was being undercut by efforts to promote, in his view, class interests. The former *Federalist Papers* collaborators found themselves at odds over various proposals made by Hamilton to support economic development. Madison, joined by Jefferson, believed that these proposals, and later the Adams administration's Alien and Sedition Acts, would bring government under the control of a faction, a minority faction. Madison reacted to them by further developing the requirements for citizen participation. While not denying his earlier endorsement of the utility of a "freehold or equivalent" electoral qualification, he now seemed to believe that this qualification would be appropriate only within a broader, "Lockean" notion of property. This included the rights people have in their persons to "life, liberty and estate"—that is, their political and civil liberties and their faculties and abilities—not simply their rights as possessors of land or wealth.

In a series of essays in the *National Gazette* that complemented his other writings at the time, Madison made it abundantly clear that the people's stake or vested interest in society was not limited to material possessions but that these goods presupposed their basic political or civil liberties. He invoked Lockean parlance to defend the proposition that "government is instituted to protect property of *every sort*," that is, "lives" and "liberties," not principally "estate":

> If there be a government then which prides itself in maintaining the inviolability of property; which provides that none shall be taken *directly* even for public use without indemnification to the owner, and yet *directly* violates the property which individuals have in their opinions, their religion, their persons, and their faculties; nay more, which *indirectly* violates their property, in their actual possessions, in the labor that acquires daily subsistence, and in the hallowed remnant of time which ought to relieve their fatigues and soothe their cares, the influence will have been anticipated, that such a government is not a pattern for the United States.[13]

Madison believed that policies favoring one class over another or material possessions over people's liberties and faculties fundamentally distorted the Constitution and reduced the people's real "stake" in society: "That is not a just government, nor is property secure under it, where arbitrary restrictions, exemptions, and monopolies deny to part of its citizens that free use of their faculties, and free choice of their occupations, which not only constitute their property in the general sense of the word; but are the means of acquiring property strictly so called."[14]

When he saw such distortions, which he believed were encouraged in Hamilton's mercantilism, Madison reacted much as he had when he feared the Alien and Sedition Acts used the Constitution to support minority control over the public. Madison argued that several countermeasures would be appropriate. These could be undertaken, inter alia:

1. By establishing a political equality among all. 2. By withholding *unnecessary* opportunities from a few, to increase the inequality of property, by an immoderate, and especially an unmerited, accumulation of riches. 3. By the silent operation of laws, which, without violating the rights of property, reduce extreme wealth towards a state of mediocrity, and raise extreme indigence towards a state of comfort. 4. By abstaining from measures which operate differently on different interests, and particularly such as favor one interest at the expence of another.[15]

Madison thus found himself balancing his own partisan reactions against his principles. He responded to administration policies as though they were factious. As indicated by the countermeasures he enumerated, however, he attempted to ground his own arguments in constitutional principles rather than self-interest. He viewed Hamilton's proposals as part of a larger design to govern by faction, and he feared, in the case of the Adams administration's Alien and Sedition Acts, that constitutional formalities were being used to cover or "mask" minority rule.[16] At least later in his life, he made it clear that governmental accountability hinged on respecting the wills of legitimate majorities rather than those of factions, whether minority or majority, when he complained to Jefferson that critics of the "general Welfare" clause nonetheless found constitutional support to subsidize primarily local endeavors (roads and canals).[17]

Madison's Paradoxical Legacy

Madison's concerns about Hamilton's policies and the Adams administration underscore a fundamental paradox that follows the solutions to the problem of faction. Given the very nature of faction, claims on behalf of legitimate public authority would understandably be scrutinized by other citizens as the claims of factious interests. Even if government by faction could be avoided, a hope that Madison came to realize had been belied, different interest groups in society would tend to believe that the governmental directives with which they disagree are factious. When the exercise of power is disadvantageous or directed specifically against someone's interests, as inevitably it is, factional influence over the decisions would be suspected precisely because the groups adversely affected would attempt to attain their own objectives under the "mask" of majority rule and representation when similarly situated.[18]

Madison's preoccupation at the time of constitutional ratification with the "violence of faction" (*Federalist 10*) in the republican experiments of the states testifies to this problem. Indeed, prior to the convention he had advocated "a negative [by the national government] in all cases whatsoever on the Legislative Acts of the States" because he realized the state factions would respond to federal directives in kind.[19] From the convention until late in his life, Madison continually reverted back to the principle of representation and its attendant civic virtue when he grappled with the problem of faction. He believed that popular representation would sustain republican liberty, enhance effectiveness and stability in government, and serve as the "check" of last resort, so to speak, on faction. In his commentary in *Federalist 10* about the relationship between constituency size and the selection of able representatives, Madison explained how popular representation would "refine and enlarge the public views" in both the electoral process and the deliberations of the representatives. Individual citizens could be expected to vote for candidates representing their interests, and factional interests would find a voice in the legislative process in the form of these elected officials. The necessary compromises and accommodations hammered out in legislative deliberations were expected to blunt the effect of the factious spirit, producing legislation that would benefit some interests at the expense of others but, on the whole, would ameliorate rather than intensify factional divisions and distributions of resources (wealth and power). Late in his life, his communications with Jefferson and others echoed his stance during the Virginia ratifying convention. If anything, he had become more adamant about the importance of majority rule in sustaining the principle of representation: "the vital principle of republican government is the *lex majoris partis,* the will of the majority. . . . if the will of a majority cannot be trusted where there are diversified and conflicting interests, it can be trusted nowhere, because such interests exist everywhere."[20]

Madison's commitment to popular representation was predicated on the proposition that the citizens, at least in their capacity as electors, would evince a measure of civic virtue, as his later comments indicate. This commitment was evident early in Madison's promotion of a bill of rights. When he introduced the Bill of Rights before the first Congress, it was obvious, he asserted, "That all power is originally vested in, and consequently derived from the people. That Government is instituted, and ought to be exercised for the benefit of the people. That the people have an indubitable, unalienable, and indefeasible right to reform or change their government, whenever it be found adverse or inadequate to the purposes of its institution."[21] Madison's defense of the Bill of Rights was predicated not so much on the formal protections it vouchsafed as on its educative functions.

A bill of rights is designed to protect individual rights from governmental or factional intrusions. Madison supported it also, and more strongly, because it would have a salutary effect on public opinion and political behavior. A bill of rights would serve a symbolic role. Its principles would be incorporated within public opinion, which serves as the chief constraint on government, or as its "real sovereign." In an essay for the *National Gazette,* published in December 1791, Madison stressed that:

> Public opinion sets bounds to every government, and is the real sovereign in every free one.
>
> As there are cases where the public opinion must be obeyed by the government; so there are cases, where not being fixed, it may be influenced by the government.
>
> In proportion as government is influenced by opinion, it must be so [influenced], by whatever influences opinion. This decides the question concerning a *Constitutional Declaration of Rights,* which requires an influence on government, by becoming a part of the public opinion.[22]

A bill of rights would support civic virtue in the citizenry and in that sense serve to constrain factional excesses by government. In his earlier speech supporting adoption of the Bill of Rights before Congress, Madison argued that while opponents believed that "all paper barriers against the power of the community [faction], are too weak to be worthy of attention," nevertheless the Bill of Rights would constrain both governmental excesses and factious majorities because it would be upheld by public opinion: "yet, as they have a tendency to impress some degree of respect for them, to establish the public opinion in their favor, and rouse the attention of the whole community, it may be one mean[s] to controul the majority from those acts to which they might be otherwise inclined."[23] In contemporary parlance, the Bill of Rights would tend to uphold civic virtue because it would become engrained in the political culture and would be transmitted through the socialization process. The power of these "paper barriers" lies in their "political truths" acquiring "by degrees the character of fundamental maxims of free Government, and as they become incorporated with the national sentiment, counteract the impulses of interest and passion."[24]

Circumstances might not always be optimal to sustain public responsibility and civic virtue, however. In his essay for the *National Gazette,* Madison acknowledged that the basis for a citizen's sense of public responsibility might erode, just as he feared that constitutional forms could be used to mask minority rule: "The larger a country, the less easy for its real opinion to be ascertained, and the less difficult to be counterfeited; when ascertained or presumed, the more respectable it is in the eyes of individuals. This is favorable to the authority of government. For the same reason, the more extensive a country, the more insignificant is each individual in his own eyes. This may be unfavorable to liberty."[25]

Madison's remarks seem to anticipate Alexis de Tocqueville's conclusions. Tocqueville warned that a society of atomistic individuals would breed apathy and quiescence and encourage social conformity. This process, he feared, would detract from civic responsibility and ultimately produce a tyranny of public opinion molded by elite manipulation.[26] Like Tocqueville later, who held out hope that free associations, a free press, enlightenment, and the "mores" of the American people might counteract these tendencies, Madison concluded the essay with these remarks about the value of open communication and a free press: "Whatever facilitates a general intercourse of sentiments, as good roads, domestic commerce, a free press, and particularly a *circulation of newspapers through the entire body of the people,* and *Representatives going from, and returning among every part of them,* is equivalent to a contraction of territorial limits, and is favorable to liberty, where these may be too extensive."[27] Subsequent history, however, at least as interpreted by twentieth-century political scientists, seems to have confirmed the concerns Madison and Tocqueville shared, about these matters at least.

Interpretations of Madison's Legacy

The problematic or paradoxical character of Madison's solutions to factional politics and his prescriptions for invigorating civic virtue have left his theory open to diverse and often critical interpretations. For many commentators—perhaps most—the situation in which Madison found himself during the early administrations was not paradoxical at all but an outgrowth of his efforts to link popular and interest group representation within the "necessary and ordinary operations of government." Many of these, who have adopted the theoretical framework known as pluralism, have decried what, in their view, is an overreliance on institutional or mechanistic "checks" in the "Madisonian model" (as they characterize *Federalist 10*). They see positive advantages in a political process of interest group accommodation and elite representation, particularly when it is contrasted with a largely apathetic and uninformed electorate. Pluralists, in effect, acknowledge their Madisonian heritage but disparage its presumed mechanistic formula for a divided government, which, they believe, is outmoded in the twentieth century.

Critics of pluralism frequently attribute its deficiencies precisely to its alleged Madisonian lineage. One author's claim that "the passionate pursuit of interest" is incorporated in the Constitution's operative assumptions as though it were "natural, an expression of tendencies latent in all human associations," presages the later elitist criticisms that pluralism and Madisonianism discount the egalitarian underpinnings of democracy in favor of "possessive individualism."[28] Madison, however, warned against the consequences of unfettered individualism and believed that government had a positive responsibility to promote the conditions for civic virtue. These concerns, expressed during the first administrations and late in his life, are not out of line with the objectives he articulated during ratification. It simply does not follow from Madison's stance during ratification or in his later years that the citizen, as one recent commentator observed, "is essentially a passive character whose disposition to support the state amounts to little more than a habit of obedience."[29] To conclude that the founders promoted the abandonment of political roles in favor of economic roles and passivity and civic deference instead of public responsibilities is too extreme and reflects not Madison's position but a view of Madison influenced by the portrait of a quiescent public caricatured in twentieth-century pluralist theory.

These positions—both the pluralists' and their critics'—raise contentious issues from the perspective of Madison's constitutional theory. They are issues that must be reckoned with, and this task is taken up in the next chapter. There it is argued that the pluralists all but abandoned the constitutional founders' ideal that popular representation would serve as the pivot of the Constitution. Instead they have embraced a theory of group accommodation, the upshot of which is that interest group representation, not popular representation "derived from the great body of society" (*Federalist 39*)—the citizens—has become the predominant theme in contemporary theories of American politics.

NOTES

1. The importance of classical republican ideals and their shortcomings are developed in Bernard Bailyn, *The Origins of American Politics* (New York: Vintage Books, 1970); Bailyn, *The Ideological Origins of the American Revolution* (Cambridge, Mass.: Harvard University Press, 1967); Gordon S. Wood, *The Creation of the American Republic, 1776–1787* (New

York: W. W. Norton, 1972). For a variation on their themes, see J. G. A. Pocock, *The Machiavellian Moment* (Princeton, N.J.: Princeton University Press, 1975).

2. See also the debates in the early sessions of Congress exerpted in Charles S. Hyneman and George W. Carey, eds., *A Second Federalist* (Columbia: University of South Carolina Press, 1970), 211–22.

3. See also Madison's comments on Jefferson's provision for the election of the state senate in "Observations on [Jefferson's] 'Draught of a Constitution for Virginia,'" ca. Oct. 15, 1788, in *The Papers of James Madison*, vol. 11, 286–87. Subsequent citations are to *Papers of James Madison* followed by the volume number. Volumes 1–10 are edited by William T. Hutchinson, William M. E. Rachal, Robert A. Rutland, Charles F. Hobson et al. (Chicago: University of Chicago Press, 1962–1977); volumes 11–on, by Rutland, Hobson, Thomas A. Mason et al. (Charlottesville: University Press of Virginia, 1977–on).

4. Representation as a "filter" for factions and ability is stressed in Wood, *Creation*, 506–18. For a Madisonian interpretation of Hamilton's *Federalist 35*, see Jean Yarbrough, "Representation and Republicanism: Two Views," *Publius* 9 (Spring 1979): 77–98, at 91–94.

5. To George Washington, Apr. 16, 1787, *Papers of James Madison*, vol. 9, 384, italics added; *Vices of the Political System of the United States*, ibid., sect. 11, 357. See also Madison to Thomas Jefferson, Oct. 24, 1787, ibid., vol. 10, 214.

6. David Hume, "That Politics May Be Reduced to a Science," *Essays Moral, Political and Literary* (Oxford: Oxford University Press, 1963), 25. This is not simply an apparent echo; see Douglass Adair, *Fame and the Founding Fathers*, ed. Trevor Colbourn (New York: St. Martin's Press, 1974), chap. 4.

7. "Judicial Powers of the National Government," June 20, 1788, *Papers of James Madison*, vol. 11, 163.

8. Ibid., 163.

9. "Observations of the 'Draught of a Constitution for Virginia,'" ca. Oct. 15, 1788, 287. The bracketed word *indigent* is inserted from the editors' notes.

10. Ibid., 287–88.

11. Ibid., 288.

12. On perceptions of factional interests and the use of constitutional formalities to cover factional goals, particularly those organized around economic disparities and class divisions, see Robert J. Morgan, "Madison's Analysis of the Sources of Political Authority," *American Political Science Review* 75 (Sept. 1981): 613–25; cf. Michael Lienesch, "The Constitutional Tradition: History, Political Action, and Progress in American Political Thought, 1787–1793," *Journal of Politics* 42 (Feb. 1980): 2–30, esp. 18–22ff.; Adair, *Fame and the Founding Fathers*, chap. 1.

13. "Property," in the *National Gazette*, Mar. 27, [1792], *Papers of James Madison*, vol. 14, 266 (italics added), 267–68.

14. Ibid., 267. See also the examples in Saul K. Padover, ed., *The Complete Madison* (New York: Harper and Brothers, 1953), 269–75; Marvin Meyers, ed., *The Mind of the Founder: Sources of the Political Thought of James Madison* (Indianapolis: Bobbs-Merrill, 1973), document 16, 243–46. The second sources are reprinted in full in *Papers of James Madison,* vol. 14.

15. *National Gazette,* ca. Jan. 23, 1792, *Papers of James Madison,* vol. 14, 197. Madison's concern that Hamilton's Report on Manufacturers, if adopted, would corrupt the Constitution is evident in numerous letters and essays. See in *Papers of James Madison,* vol. 14: letter to Henry Lee, Jan. 21, 1792; to Edmund Pendleton, Jan. 21, 1792; speech before the House, "Bounty Payments for Cod Fisheries," Feb. 6, 1792; essay in the *National Gazette,* Feb. 18, 1792. See also Neal Riemer, *James Madison: Creating the Constitution* (Washington, D.C.: Congressional Quarterly, 1986), 140ff.; Meyers, *Mind of the Founder,* document 16; the discussion of Madison's and Jefferson's complementary views on equality and economic advantage in J. R. Pole, *The Pursuit of Equality in American History* (Berkeley: University of California Press, 1978), 119–23.

16. On Madison's reactions to Adams administration policies, see Adrienne Koch, *Madison's "Advice to My Country"* (Princeton, N.J.: Princeton University Press, 1966), chap. 3, esp. 119–32; Koch, *Jefferson and Madison: The Great Collaboration* (New York: Oxford University Press, 1950), 184–211. See also letters to ———, 1833, and to Edward Everett, Aug. 20, 1830, exerpted in Meyers, *Mind of the Founder,* documents 21, 40, 41.

17. "The will of the nation being omnipotent for right, is so for wrong also; and the will of the nation being in the majority, the minority must submit to that danger of oppression as an evil infinitely less than the danger to the whole nation from a will independent of it." Letter to Thomas Jefferson, Feb. 17, 1825, in *Letters and Other Writings of James Madison, Published by Order of Congress,* vol. 3 (Philadelphia: J. B. Lippincott, 1867), 483.

18. On the factional view of public authority generally, see Madison's concerns in *Vices,* 354–57.

19. Letter to Edmund Randolph, Apr. 8, 1787, *Papers of James Madison,* vol. 9, 370. See also in *Papers of James Madison,* vol. 9: letters to Thomas Jefferson, Mar. 19, 1787, and to George Washington, Apr. 16, 1787; and, in vol. 10, to Thomas Jefferson, Oct. 24, 1787, esp. 209–14. Madison initially supported popular representation for both houses of Congress. See Forrest McDonald, *Novus Ordo Seclorum* (Lawrence: University Press of Kansas, 1985), 228–40. The debates over whether the states were to be represented in their corporate capacities (in the Senate), or were geographical units of popular representation, carried through the ratification process and of course reemerged in the doctrine of nullification. For some of the problems the issue raised, see J. R. Pole, *Political Representation in England and the Origins of the American Republic* (New York: St. Martin's Press, 1966), 350–67, 374–77, 530–39.

20. Letter to ———, 1833, in Meyers, *Mind of the Founder*, document 40, 530. His earlier remarks to Jefferson on Feb. 17, 1825, are noted in note 17.

21. "Amendments to the Constitution," [June 8, 1789], *Papers of James Madison*, vol. 12, 200.

22. *National Gazette*, ca. Dec. 19, 1791, *Papers of James Madison*, vol. 14, 170. See also his essay in the *National Gazette*, Jan. 18, [1792], 192.

23. "Amendments to the Constitution," [June 8, 1789], 204–5.

24. Madison to Thomas Jefferson, Oct. 17, 1788, *Papers of James Madison*, vol. 11, 298–99.

25. *National Gazette*, ca. Dec. 19, 1791, 170.

26. Alexis de Tocqueville, *Democracy in America*, vol. 1, ed. J. P. Mayer (Garden City, N.Y.: Doubleday, 1969), pt. 2, chap. 7; cf. ibid., vol. 2, pt. 4, chaps. 6–8.

27. *National Gazette*, ca. Dec. 19, 1791, 170. See also his views on how a "consolidation" of public opinion can serve to counter the consolidation of power within the executive in "Consolidation," *National Gazette*, Dec. 3 [1791], *Papers of James Madison*, vol. 14, 138–39. Cf. Tocqueville, *Democracy in America*, vol. 1, pt. 2, chaps. 1–5, 9; vol. 2, pt. 2, chaps. 4–7, pt. 3, chap. 1.

28. Norman Jacobson, "Political Science and Political Education," *American Political Science Review* 57 (Sept. 1963): 561–69, at 562. Cf. C. B. Macpherson, *The Life and Times of Liberal Democracy* (New York: Oxford University Press, 1977), 15, n. 6; Peter Bachrach, *The Theory of Democratic Elitism* (Boston: Little, Brown, 1967), 27.

29. Richard C. Sinopoli, "Liberalism, Republicanism and the Constitution," *Polity* 19 (Spring 1987): 331–52, at 351. For other such views, see, for example, Lienesch, "Constitutional Tradition," 25–29.

CHAPTER 3

The Theory and Practice of Pluralism: Interest Group Liberalism

In the twentieth century, the theory and practice of pluralism emerged as the dominant public philosophy in the United States. The Madisonian model and its largely mechanistic formula for controlling the "factious spirit" outlined in *Federalist 10* served pluralists as the caricature of the founders' theory of constitutionalism, which they believed had proved to be an inadequate framework for understanding political realities. In its place, they proposed pluralism as a contemporary sociological and behavioral improvement.[1] Influenced by the consensus school in American history and adopting the methodology of the behavioral sciences, pluralists emphasized the sociological roles or functions of groups and the behavioral (psychological) constraints on group activities provided by overlapping memberships and "potential" groups. Commentators sought to explain a political system in which "minorities rule" through the processes of interest group accommodation and elite competition, practices supported by an apparently pervasive consensus of support held by a "quiescent" public. They maintained that the multiplicity of groups and the overlapping memberships of individuals that accompanied this pluralism, not the mechanistic Madisonian model, produced interest accommodation and compromise. Much like a "parallelogram of forces," the group process of conflict, compromise, and accommodation and a resultant social consensus were believed to provide the normative or value litmus test for governmental legitimacy and public accountability.[2]

Scholars of public opinion and the electoral process appeared to confirm many of the pluralists' views. They had postulated that a "rational-activist" citizen was at the center of "classical" democratic theories, which "stressed that democracies are maintained by active citizen participation in civic affairs, by a high level of information about public affairs, and by a widespread sense of civic responsibility. These doctrines tell us what a democratic citizen ought to be like if he is to behave according to the requirements of the system."[3] To the surprise of few, the evidence produced by survey research and case study interviews did not support the classical model. In the abstract, citizens supported democratic principles and valued their civic responsibilities, but in concrete cases, there was little consensus for these values. Citizens were found to be nonparticipatory, relatively uninformed and uninterested in political issues, and disinclined to extend democratic values to others with whom they had conflicts (demonstrating, instead, their racial, ethnic, religious, and class intolerance, for example).[4] Far from rational-activist citizens, the citizenry was characterized by its overriding quiescence.

The conclusions that many scholars of the electoral process drew roughly paralleled the pluralist rejection of the Madisonian model in favor of the group process. In *Voting*, Bernard Berelson and colleagues observed that the classical model was simply deficient:

> *Individual voters* today seem unable to satisfy the requirements for a democratic system of government outlined by political theorists. But the *system of democracy* does meet certain requirements for a going political organization. . . . where the classic theory is defective is in its concentration on the *individual citizen*. What are undervalued are certain collective properties that reside in the electorate as a whole and in the political and social system in which it functions.[5]

The sorts of systemic properties these scholars envisioned enabled them to explain political stability, much as the potential group notion permits one to envision group conflicts contained in the parallelogram metaphor. Individual citizens lacked the characteristics believed to be required by the classical theory: "Political apathy seems for most men the more 'natural' state." These apparent deficiencies were compensated, however, by the attributes of political elites: "carriers of the Creed" upheld democratic values and served to maintain political processes more or less within the "rules of the game."[6] Indeed, these latter characteristics were believed to be functional because the classical model's postulates would break down in the face of public intolerance and the citizenry's lack of democratic commitments in times of conflict: "Extreme interest goes with extreme partisanship and might culminate in rigid fanaticism that could destroy democratic processes if generalized throughout the community."[7]

Critics of the public opinion and electoral studies charged that the classical model was derived from caricatures of such theorists as John Stuart Mill, which slighted their stipulations about the prerequisites for and roles of citizen rationality and participation. Civic apathy and quiescence, which electoral scholars viewed to be a "natural" state of affairs for *homo civicus*, were engineered and shaped by elite symbol manipulation in the eyes of the critics. Neither side in the controversy systematically addressed the question of whether the classical democrats were appropriate reference points within the context of Madisonian democracy, partly because each side understood the Madisonian model had little to do with popular participation.[8] One thing was clear for both the public opinion and election scholars and their critics: the implications of behavioral and survey research supported the functional roles of groups and group elites in pluralist theory.[9]

For all practical purposes, pluralists had rediscovered Tocqueville's faith in the "art of association." Tocqueville anticipated that the extension of "equality of conditions" to all Americans would pave the way for majority tyranny, or what Madison had labeled "majority faction."[10] In volume two of *Democracy in America,* however, he observed that the "art of association" tempered equality and counterbalanced some of the tendencies toward the tyranny of faction: "If men are to remain civilized or to become civilized, the art of association must develop and improve among them at the same speed as equality of conditions spreads."[11] Americans might be "born equal," a destabilizing condition from Tocqueville's perspective, but they are also a "nation of joiners," in the terms of twentieth-century commentary on Tocqueville. In his view, the various associations, civic clubs, and interest groups provided individuals with resources they otherwise could not wield as isolated individuals, promoted a healthy democracy by fostering the spirit of "self interest properly understood" to counter the atomistic individualism of excessive egalitarianism, and provided checks on one another and on governmental abuses of power in the name of the majority.[12] In other words, Tocqueville's voluntary associations and interest groups provided a form of *societal* checks and balances, which, for the pluralists, constituted a parallelogram of forces and superseded—even rendered unnecessary—the governmental checks and balances prescribed by Madison in *Federalist 10.*

Tocqueville's emphasis on social pluralism proved to be much more congenial to the twentieth-century pluralists' approach than the institutional theory that they attributed to Madison. Tocqueville stressed the roles of individuals in their natural social settings, groups, rather than in their abstract relationships to the state when he emphasized that voluntary associations and interest groups provided societal checks and balances to limit the power of overbearing majorities or governments acting in the name of majorities. In embracing the group process, however, pluralists all but abandoned the constitutional founders' stress on popular representation, which even Tocqueville had not discounted.[13] Moreover, the pluralist caricature of the Madisonian model ignored the paradoxical aspects of Madison's solution to the problem of faction: how successfully to break and control the effects of faction while simultaneously incorporating factions within the "necessary and ordinary operations of government." By emphasizing the process of interest accommodation, the pluralists transformed what to Madison is problematic at best (the "violence of faction") into a positive good—the "essence of the political process."[14]

For pluralists, the notion of the group or political process was an alternative, and a more realistic one at that, to the mechanisms urged by Madison for attaining "tranquility and stability" and avoiding the "tyranny of majority faction." The process provided an equilibrium standard that served as a functional substitute for the public interest. Glendon Schubert, after denying that the public interest had empirical referents (an argument known in academic jargon as noncognitivism), described the equilibrium alternative: "The job of official decision-makers . . . is to maximize continuity and stability in public policy, or, in other words, to minimize disruption in existing patterns of accommodation among affected interests. The extent to which agitation [by interest groups] continues . . . provides a rough measure of the extent to which adjustment has, in terms of the equilibrium standard, been successful or 'satisfactory.'"[15] These scholars assumed that potential groups—the most encompassing of which is the public itself—would serve to limit excesses by political activists should they begin to contravene the rules of the game (namely, group accommodation). Indeed, even if political elites misjudge these limitations, political resources are so unequally dispersed that no or few elite groups could dominate the process. For these reasons, pluralists could conclude that "the process generates enough agreement on rules and norms so as to permit the system to operate" and that even if potential group interests are widespread and weak at any given moment they "serve to limit in a general way the behavior of the more apparent participants in politics."[16] Consequently, most group interests could be attained and the legitimacy of the process implicitly recognized. Seymour Martin Lipset drew the appropriate conclusion about the political process: "Groups regard a political system as legitimate or illegitimate according to the way in which its values fit with theirs."[17]

Such assertions as Schubert's and Lipset's, that legitimacy depends on the satisfaction of group interests, should be juxtaposed with Madison's efforts to constrain factions through their representation in government. For Madison, legitimate public authority comes about through constitutionally sanctioned popular representation, that is, through the electoral process. There is the risk that such authority might be perceived simply as the factious exercise of power by those whose interests are adversely affected by legislation. Such perceptions, however, are functional, providing additional checks against factional elites. The pluralist emphasis on stability, and on engendering legitimacy through the satisfaction of group demands, downplays the roles expected of citizens and helps justify their acquiescence in elite decision making, primarily decision making of the sort that minimally unsettles or redistributes existing allocations of power, status, and social values. Instead of emphasizing the positive and often conflictual role of popular representation, pluralists stressed the primacy of societal stability derived from group accommodation and a largely indifferent citizenry.

Criticisms of Pluralism: The Deadlock of Democracy

Pluralism has never been lacking critics. The most long-standing body of criticism, the *doctrine of party responsibility,* represents a strand of thought in American politics that stresses electoral and political party reform and is designed to encourage coherent policy leadership and elite accountability to the electorate. The most recent criticisms are made by so-called *neoconservative* scholars and publicists. Some of the neoconservatives contributed to the development of pluralist theory earlier, and their argument for retrenchment stems from perceived failures of pluralism in the aftermath of the civil rights movement and the Johnson administration's Great Society and signals their reactions to political excesses supported by other liberals, egalitarians, and activists from the left. Both party responsibility and neoconservative schools of thought have attracted followings outside the academy: the former among political party activists; the latter among public officials and the media. Both critical positions are inadequate. The former misconstrues the problem of pluralism by placing reform of the electoral process ahead of institutional reform. The latter tends to mistake the symptoms of political pathologies for their causes. These assertions should be justified. Assessments of the doctrine of party responsibility and neoconservatism are appropriate before proceeding to a more significant body of criticism.

Advocates of the doctrine of party responsibility range from such critics of the Madisonian model as James MacGregor Burns, who shares with pluralists similar assumptions about the group nature of American society, to such critics of pluralism as E. E. Schattschneider, who rejects pluralist assumptions on grounds that they weaken the value of Madisonianism.[18] These distinctions are instructive.

Burns argues that the Madisonian model itself is a recipe for the "deadlock of democracy." In his view, the Madisonian system produces a four-party deadlock and undercuts responsible, majoritarian party government. Burns does not ignore the problem of faction, but he believes that it can be ameliorated more adequately in the extended republic's pluralistic society than through institutional checks that produce deadlock. Institutionalized stalemate and media-induced plebiscitary leadership, which promises short-run political fixes for long-term problems, have produced pervasive governmental ineptitude that undercuts the public's trust in its leaders. Burns advocates the doctrine of party responsibility as a solution. Only strong executive leadership—party realignment led by the presidential party in Burns's four-party schema—can rise above political deadlock and restore governmental effectiveness and public confidence.[19]

Rejecting the elitist qualities of Burns's stress on leadership, which relegates citizens to electoral participants and group members, Schattschneider takes a different approach. To him, the majoritarian doctrine of party responsibility represents an institutional means to expand the scope of conflict, that is, to maximize citizen involvement in politics at the expense of interest group dominance—and in lieu of Burnsian heroic leadership.[20] Schattschneider bases his argument for party responsibility squarely on Madisonian arguments—virtually a unique posture among partisans for party responsibility. In an interesting gloss on Madison's famous *Federalist 10* discussion of the inverse relationship between constituency size and factional control, Schattschneider argues that democratic politics in a large arena offers the best means to "socialize conflict." By expanding or socializing the scope of conflict, issues that otherwise might be subjected to "privatization" or control by small, elite groups are brought within the public domain for settlement. Pluralism, however, inverts the Madisonian argument, permitting private associations to control the public's agenda. Majoritarian parties oppose this tendency, bringing to the public agenda the wide range of concerns over which citizens would have no control under the pluralist practice of group accommodation. To win elections and govern, political parties must mobilize around the issue cleavages that enable them to develop electoral majorities. In this way, they may become responsible parties in a very

Madisonian sort of way by extending the sphere and taking in a greater variety of interests, to paraphrase *Federalist 10*.[21]

The major route to party responsibility has been through party and electoral reform, but the pathway is littered with unintended and counterproductive results. Critics of reform—many of the current neoconservatives—assert that "reform is wrecking the U.S. party system" and bemoan the ascendance of "purists" from the new class.[22] The net effect of reform, according to Austin Ranney's survey in *Curing the Mischiefs of Faction*, is that first the program was taken out of the party (through the primary) and then the party was taken out of candidacy selection (through representational and campaign finance reforms). Ranney notes that electoral reform is one of the simpler methods of social engineering, faith in which is a long-standing tradition among American elites.[23] It is also arguably more appealing because it is less controversial than more fundamental reform. Why? The party system evolved from a constitutional setting in which party organizations were required to win local elections (and construct a power base for national elections), not to govern. They have always been *constituent* parties. With party responsibility, the question remains: responsible *to whom?* To the organized or those with access or to the citizen? Electoral reforms that only enhance the leadership standing of party elites will predictably yield unsatisfactory responses to the question.[24] (The assessment of interest group liberalism will justify this assertion.)

The writings of neoconservatives can be characterized as an attempt to develop an alternative ideology for a corrupted liberalism.[25] Pluralism had unintended and counterproductive consequences. Capitalism and productivity have succeeded so well that they risk undercutting the very possessive individualist values that legitimated capitalism and made it viable. Liberal elites have corrupted liberalism by yielding too easily to rising expectations, entitlement claims, equality of "result," overindulgence, and so on. In the end, neoconservatives believe, liberal institutions and values are fragile and easily susceptible to abuse; they require cultivation and legitimating myths by meritocratic opinion leaders and entrepreneurs, whose roles and examples can suggest temperance and restraint for the democracy. Otherwise, liberalism will continue to falter on the neoconservatives' version of governmental deadlock: the governability crisis.[26]

As an antidote to excessive egalitarianism, neoconservatives promote the reestablishment of civic virtue. Civic virtue is a precondition for liberal democracy, both Madison's version and contemporary constitutionalist and participatory versions (discussed in subsequent chapters). Neoconservatives differ from other democratic theorists, however, in the normative import they attach to civic virtue and its role in liberal democracy. For neoconservatives, civic virtue is a property of virtuous opinion leaders, whose limited expectations about the role of government can restrain the expectations of the mass electorate.[27] Madison, among others, did not so unproblematically see the connection between virtuous elites and wise policy or legitimate authority, notwithstanding that neoconservatives frequently mention the "intent of the framers" as justification for their positions. Neoconservatives appear to be preoccupied with the egalitarian symptoms of political pathologies, not their causes. Their civic virtue palliative may be a necessary condition for governance, but, construed simply as a characteristic of virtuous elites, it cannot be generalized as a sufficient condition for democratic government. More plausibly, it constitutes merely a countervailing strategy for "new class" influence—a strategy, as one of their critics asserts, to legitimate the neoconservatives' form of opinion leadership and influence-peddling as members of the new class.[28]

Pluralism as Interest Group Liberalism

Perhaps inadvertently, both pluralists and their party responsibility and neoconservative critics downplay Madison's concern with the important relationship between properly constituted institutions and such political values as public responsibility and civic virtue. Other critics have recognized that the pluralist appeal to stability, which serves as the functional equivalent for somehow attempting to ascertain and strive for a public interest, has conservative overtones. Most notable among them are Grant McConnell and Theodore J. Lowi. They do not accept the Madisonian model caricature but draw a clear distinction between Madison's theory of the relationship between institutions and values and the pluralist theory of interest group representation. The result of their criticism is that pluralist theory has gained its own disparaging caricature: *interest group liberalism.*

McConnell follows Schattschneider's notions of privatizing and socializing conflict and elaborates on Madison's theory of representation in relationship to constituency size and organizational complexity. Briefly, he argues that the pluralist reliance on small, purportedly voluntary associations as the basis for political membership blurs the distinction between public and private and justifies the exercise of private power for public ends. The result amounts to a delegation of public authority to groups that have developed clientele relationships with appropriate administrative and committee organs of government. The important consequences for McConnell are twofold. The pluralist practice of interest representation is an "alternative to the machinery of Congress, legislatures, President, and governors. It is also a reformulation and redistribution of authority."[29] In other words, by granting preference to well-organized interests and by parceling out public authority to them, pluralism abandons the notion of a rule of law based on popular sovereignty and exercised through electoral representation and substitutes the rule of private interests.

Theodore J. Lowi, in *The End of Liberalism,* develops the critical implications of Schattschneider's and McConnell's arguments. In his view, pluralism is nothing more than interest group liberalism. Public officials no longer regulate the effects of faction, as Madison hoped they would. Instead, they parcel out benefits and decision-making authority to organized and well-placed interests. When public authority is delegated to administrative agencies and the interests affected by them, a vacuum of public responsibility is created. The clientele politics of interest group liberalism thus undermines public authority and its legitimacy. Popular representation is largely symbolic since citizens are encouraged to press their claims through interest group bargaining, not through legislative representation. Like McConnell, Lowi concludes that interest group liberalism is far from an improvement on the Madisonian model. It is a virtual abnegation of it, inverting or turning on its head Madison's solutions to the problem of faction.

The remainder of this chapter examines the major liabilities of pluralist theory that have been identified and criticized in Lowi's *The End of Liberalism* and his related writings. Lowi's analysis goes beyond the criticisms of Schattschneider, McConnell, and others. He subjects pluralism to a comprehensive critique under the rubric of interest group liberalism, and, based on this critique and his understanding of constitutionalism, he develops a systematic rather than an ad hoc program for reform. Lowi's analysis of interest group liberalism amounts to perhaps the most systematic and telling critique of pluralism to emerge from the 1960s and 1970s, and many of Lowi's colleagues in the political science discipline have adopted his critical analysis as the definitive assessment of pluralism.[30]

The Sources of Interest Group Liberalism

In *The Governmental Process,* David Truman quotes virtually the entire seventh paragraph of *Federalist 10* on the sources of factional conflict. The paragraph ends with Madison's statement that "the regulation of these various and interfering interests forms the principal task of modern legislation, and involves the spirit of party and faction in the necessary and ordinary operations of the government." Lowi criticizes Truman for failing to stress the negative aspects of Madison's prior definition of faction: an association *"adverse to the right of other citizens, or to the permanent and aggregate interests of the community."* Lowi's criticism implies pluralists like Truman downplay Madison's concern that factions are to be distrusted and that regulating them is the principal task of government. The gist of Lowi's criticism is largely correct, although for other reasons. Truman does not quote the aspect of Madison's definition that Lowi italicizes, but he does recognize the negative aspects of factions and the need to regulate them.[31] Truman and the pluralists, however, interpret Madison's remarks in a manner most congruent with their conception of the group or political process. Where Madison subsequently saw a paradox—how to *regulate* factions *and* to *incorporate* them within governmental deliberations (although *all* factions are dangerous, as Lowi correctly notes)—pluralists see a distinction between "good" factions (that is, legitimate interest groups) and "bad" ones (that is, groups that fail to play by the rules of the accommodation process game).

The pluralists stress the more beneficial roles of factions as interest groups in the political process. For example, Truman infers that Madison "saw the struggles of such groups as the essence of the political process," a process quite similar to the politics of Truman's time. Throughout *The Governmental Process,* Truman discounts Madison's references to the "violence of faction" as allusions to violent groups (for example, the Shaysites). He also indicates that other negative connotations about factions refer to the "evils" of *majority* factions—in keeping with Burns's antimajoritarian view of Madison. In other words, the negativism associated with faction connotes minorities that refuse to play by the rules of the game or majorities—more accurately, partisan leaders, even demagogues—that claim to speak for the public. In Truman's time, the contemporary counterpart to the Shaysites minority might be the Ku Klux Klan or subversives and the counterpart to an Adams administration claiming majority support for the Alien and Sedition Acts might be a Governor Huey Long or Senator Joseph McCarthy.[32] Because the public interest to pluralists is simply an equilibrium standard, reflecting a rough balance in the process of group accommodation, it is *neither legitimate for minorities* to make claims on government without playing by the rules of the game *nor possible for a majority* or its representatives to invoke the public interest on its behalf. On the rare occasions when the rules of the game are bypassed, in the view of pluralists, such claimants would be fair game for "regulation" as "interfering interests," to use Madison's terms.

The political process of interest group liberalism is one of accommodation between competing interest groups. Their struggles are "the essence of the political process," and, like mathematical vectors, they change the outward appearance but not the internal area of the political parallelogram. Tending toward equilibrium and resulting in mutual accommodations and consensus about the rules of the game, the group process signifies that the institutional constraints proposed by Madison are secondary, if not superfluous.[33] In this way, as Lowi observes, interest group liberalism smuggles in Adam Smith's "invisible hand" as the natural ordering assumption under which "natural liberty" unfolds. Or better, as McConnell says, the public interest reappears "in the guise of a belief that the result of the various group forces at work was beneficent."[34] In other words, by moving the center of politics from the public or governmental arena to the natural give-and-take among interests within the social-economic arena, interest group liberalism inverts the Madisonian stipulations about the regulation and control of faction. (Ultimately, one of the major bones of contention raised by McConnell and Lowi is that only the *appearance* of coercion is avoided and that well-organized interests accrue the greatest advantages in the absence of formal institutional constraints.)

The explanatory properties of the interest group liberal approach derive from the invisible hand. Potential groups, dispersed inequalities, and consensus provide the operative framework for political actors and institutions and serve as the safety valves that ensure legitimacy. Dispersed resources, for example, indeed may serve to preclude monopolies of power, but interest group liberals also must demonstrate that individuals or groups lacking resources are not prevented from entering the political process in an active or participatory capacity. This, however, is often done, when attempted at all, only by asserting that the political process is so open-ended that all but the most unreasonable claims can be accommodated. In response to this lacuna, Lowi's *The End of Liberalism* demonstrates how the process responds to organized interests, leaving the unorganized outside the process and without means to have their interests accommodated or met. Moreover, because interest group liberals infer the functions of potential groups not simply from the reactions of "the more apparent participants" (read: elites) to the sorts of norms that potential groups might articulate but principally from the existence of stability or equilibrium, they incorporate a tacit evaluative standard vis-à-vis unorganized groups *or* groups or movements that mobilize in ways contrary to prevailing practices. Recall Lipset's portrayal of the sources of legitimacy: "Groups regard a political system as legitimate or illegitimate according to the way in which its values fit with theirs."[35] In the absence of other criteria—procedural *or* substantive, not simply self-interest perceptions—*inactivity* can be taken as prima facie evidence that groups regard the process as legitimate, hence necessitating no action from elites to meet or anticipate unarticulated claims. At the extreme, political movements that reject the accommodation process can be judged unreasonable or extremist.[36]

The charge that the interest group liberal political process responds to organized interests but not to unorganized ones underscores a crucial and problematic fact of contemporary politics. The consequences of interest group liberalism are more severe, though. Interest group liberalism justifies a vacuum of public responsibility or accountability. *Who* has authority, with *what* consequences, and for *whom* are questions that need never be asked because they are presumed to be covered by the process. Yet when they are asked, Lowi, like others, finds that interest group liberalism does not live up to its pretensions.

The Consequences of Interest Group Liberalism

Lowi's critique of interest group liberalism extends McConnell's themes and is familiar to political scientists. In summary form, the critique involves the following points:[37] (1) interest group liberalism is unrepresentative, elitist, and conservative in its delegations of public authority; (2) it favors organized over unorganized groups and those privileged to be in the right place at the right time; (3) it creates a more subtle and invidious form of coercion through the necessity of group membership and individual conformity to group norms; (4) it does not alleviate problems of injustice (say, poverty) but legitimates the activities of representative members by accommodating them in the bargaining process (for example, the poverty lobby); and (5) in contrast to the regularity and formalism required by democracy, it undermines democratic legitimacy ("A grant to an agency of powers without rules or standards leads to the bargaining, the unanticipated commitments, and the confusions that are the essence of the illegitimate state").[38]

Politics generally and policy-making specifically are determined by a plurality of contending interests. A choice among conflicting claims must be made, and government power must be authoritatively used to uphold the decision. Modern politics in particular is permeated by complexity and unresolved human demands and injustices. These create universally shared expectations that government "do something" (for example, "put an end to poverty"). In the first case of mediating between contending interests, distributive choices must be made; in the other, where moral decisions are required to allocate how much justice to whom, redistributive choices.[39] In each, however, there are winners and losers. It follows that "government is coercion; it is the performance of collective necessities." Coercion without legitimacy, however, is nothing other than "raw, brute force." There must therefore be standards for its actions that transcend the claims of particular interests and elevate such mundane things as "regularity, predictability, and consistency" above discretion, accommodation, and other virtues of interest group liberalism.[40]

The theorists and practitioners of interest group liberalism believe that they promote a political process that acts as a neutral umpire for competing groups and a public administration that is objective and value free. In fact, theirs is an attempt to avoid the crux of politics. Interest group liberalism seeks to make everyone a winner—or at least to avoid losers—by accommodating conflict (through logrolling, for instance) and thereby rendering the need for coercion secondary, if not irrelevant. In a pluralistic society composed of interest associations with voluntary memberships, power need not appear as power. It can be exercised by parceling out or delegating sovereignty to the affected interests. Delegation of authority has many apparent advantages. Most important, it minimizes the state's visibility when authority or legitimate coercion is exercised by agents—delegates—of the state. Accommodations reached between affected interests may produce no definitive winners but also no obvious losers: nobody is out anything in the process. The Madisonian necessary evil—factions, organized around the freedoms of members, curtailing the freedoms of others—is transformed into a greater good, since group conflicts and accommodations represent the "essence of the political process." Moreover, the transformation can be rationalized in the name of democracy. Delegation, decentralization, and "participatory" politics and programs rely on voluntary acquiescence of the affected interests, and such agreement, construed as consent, stands in lieu of coercion and is taken to be preeminently a democratic criterion.

Delegation of authority in programs without standards entails more than misrepresentation or a lack of representation of the unorganized. It relegates responsibility to personal leadership and thereby leads to "discretionary justice." Leaders (interest representatives) define their responsibilities without reference to a broader context of, say, the purposes of the program. They define them—and quite understandably so—as obligations to serve their clientele. Clientele politics—or the politics of personal leadership in lieu of governance—allows for discretion and inconsistency. It creates false expectations, as it did, for example, in the War on Poverty, a program that was expected to end poverty but merely co-opted the leadership of those interested in ending poverty and legitimated their lobby. Clientele politics is the predictable natural politics of co-optation that emerges when the boundaries and limits of the policy arena are left open-ended or without standards: "When the goals of government action are not provided for as a matter of policy . . . the institutions of government are likely to be misused regardless of the composition of the elites."[41] Lowi has extended this theme in his analysis of the personalized, plebiscitary presidency.[42] Leaders are human, and their humanity understandably leads them to disregard a broader conception of the public interest when their constituents' interests and their own status are at stake. Indeed, in the end they want solace, not intellectual (or constitutional) consistency; they cannot elevate themselves above the eternal problems of hate and fear without external prods; they will always be inclined to accept the biblical dictum that "the poor ye always have with you," because it is not directly in their interest to alleviate human suffering. What is needed, Lowi asserts, is "an antidote for leadership."[43]

The Rule of Law Antidote

"If men were angels," these problems would be moot, and democratic government could be sustained by responsible or virtuous elites. But, to continue paraphrasing Madison, experience teaches the necessity of auxiliary precautions. The alternative to interest group liberalism and the antidote for its pathological consequences, according to Lowi, is to restore the rule of law, or democratic constitutionalism.[44] The case for the rule of law—he calls it *juridical democracy*—is far more compelling than the panacea of party responsibility and the jeremiadic pleas of neoconservatives for virtuous elites to restrain the *demos*. Neither is a sufficient antidote for the consequences of interest group liberalism.

The doctrine of party responsibility has gained acceptance with some liberal elites and has inspired numerous reforms, which, however, have been marked by controversy.[45] On balance, party and electoral reforms appear to have been counterproductive to date, but not simply because they yield the results charged by their neoconservative critics, who eschew egalitarian politics and the unanticipated consequences of pluralism. Issues of party and electoral reform invariably tap people's partisan interests, and criteria for reform are unavoidably influenced by these interests. This liability contrasts sharply with the central assumption underlying Lowi's rule of law alternative: the public interest is better served when people "know they are going to be judged and sanctioned by standards over which they have no control."[46] The doctrine of party responsibility is simply a case of putting the cart of political mobilization before the horse of public deliberation, granted that getting the horse to move may prove to be more difficult than shifting the cart's position. To put the cart before the horse is to pursue electoral reform before the appropriate incentive system for political elites is in place.

As for the neoconservatives, many of the interest group liberal critics would not disagree with their contention that civic virtue has educative and legitimating roles to play with respect to public authority. But not many of the critics—certainly not Lowi—would accept the neoconservative corollary that elite commitment to the inculcation of civic virtue is the sufficient condition for attaining it, following the necessary condition of deflating mass expectations. For example, many of Lowi's complaints about the false expectations and cooptation generated under interest group liberalism are echoed in the now classic study, *Implementation,* by Jeffrey L. Pressman and Aaron Wildavsky. These authors, however, draw substantially different conclusions from such problems than does Lowi. Where Lowi infers that interest group liberalism requires reform because it corrupts the Constitution's rule of law, Pressman and Wildavsky infer that excessive expectations are unrealistic in a system originally designed simply to be inefficient and unresponsive. This stance leads Wildavsky in his other writings to rail against rising expectations that undercut the state's ability to govern and sustain the basic conditions for a capitalist economy.[47]

Neoconservative arguments that the loss of legitimacy is attributable to citizen demands and declining elite authority confuse cause with effect. For Lowi, as for Madison earlier, the problem of legitimacy is primarily institutional. Both adhere to the proposition that institutional practices can shape interests and values. Both also adhere to the proposition's normative corollary that these values and their roles should be evaluated in the light of institutional practices, not that institutional functions (or pathologies) are products of interest claims. Human action takes place in a context provided by formal institutions and institutional practices. People can be expected to act as citizens when they are judged in terms of sanctions they cannot control, as noted previously. Interest claims (values) cannot be eliminated, but they can be constrained if the institutional context and its standards for behavior are well known and clearly defined. This sounds almost Burkean, but the parallel should not be pushed too far. Interest group demands and false expectations—problems neoconservatives, for instance, characterize as alien values and the overindulgence manifested in the democratic distemper—*do not cause* institutional breakdown and ideological bankruptcy; they *follow from* these.[48] Pathological values are symptomatic of pathological institutional practices, not the other way around.

The case for juridical democracy provides a well-articulated argument about the costs incurred when rule of law principles are devalued. In the next chapter, its theoretical grounding and its status as a proposal for reform are evaluated. Juridical democracy requires an assessment of what constitutes a just distribution of political (and other) resources and then a reevaluation and restructuring of the institutional incentives that motivate public actors. Not surprisingly, to change institutional practices and priorities is an unlikely option, since existing incentives under interest group liberalism militate against change. This suggests that a strategy for juridical democratic reform faces obstacles similar to those confronted by partisans of party responsibility and neoconservatives. It requires a change in public values to sustain its recommended changes in institutional practices. Juridical democracy, however, proves to be on strong theoretical ground, and the significance of its rule of law principles cannot be discounted. In the concluding chapters, the case for reviving real representation incorporates pertinent rule of law standards in conjunction with guidelines developed from theories of functional representation and the workplace democracy variant of participatory democracy.

NOTES

An earlier version of sections three and four of this chapter appeared in "Interest Group Liberalism and Juridical Democracy" in *American Politics Quarterly* 6 (Apr. 1978). © 1978 Sage Publications, Inc.; used by permission of the publisher.

1. See Robert A. Dahl, *A Preface to Democratic Theory* (Chicago: University of Chicago Press, 1956), chaps. 1, 3–5 (esp. 18–22, 30–32, 134–35). Pluralism is not monolithic. For example, during the 1960s there were

disputes over differences between pluralists (mainly political scientists) and functionalists (mainly sociologists) and over the meaning of *process* (used metaphorically or as constitutive of system or functionalism). Pluralism, with its emphasis on process and equilibrium, is a form of functionalism (thus the citations to Lipset and others under the pluralist rubric). See John D. Astin, "Easton I and Easton II," *Western Political Quarterly* 25 (Dec. 1972): 726–37; Paul F. Kress, "Self, System, and Significance: Reflections on Professor Easton's Political Science," *Ethics* 77 (Oct. 1966): 1–13. The discussion in chapter 3 is illustrative and representative, not comprehensive or exhaustive.

2. Perhaps the outstanding example of the genre is David B. Truman, *The Governmental Process* (New York: Alfred A. Knopf, 1951), who develops the concepts of overlapping memberships and potential groups (see esp. 4–5ff., 50–51ff., 114, 448ff., 501ff.). On minority rule and quiescence, see, respectively, Dahl, *Preface to Democratic Theory*, 132; Murray Edelman, *The Symbolic Uses of Politics* (Urbana: University of Illinois Press, 1964). The notion of a parallelogram of forces is usually attributed to Earl Latham, *The Group Basis of Politics* (Ithaca, N.Y.: Cornell University Press, 1952), 27, 35–38, 49.

3. Gabriel A. Almond and Sidney Verba, *The Civic Culture* (Princeton, N.J.: Princeton University Press, 1963), 9; see also 186–207. "Classical" in this context referred to Jefferson or John Stuart Mill or (sometimes) Rousseau—"populist" as opposed to "Madisonian" democracy (the Madisonian model purportedly having little to do with popular participation).

4. A substantial literature expressed these findings. Some of the classics are Angus Campbell, Philip E. Converse, Warren E. Miller, and Donald E. Stokes, *The American Voter* (New York: John Wiley, 1960); Philip E. Converse, "The Nature of Belief Systems in Mass Publics," in *Ideology and Discontent*, ed. David E. Apter (New York: Free Press, 1964), 206–61; James W. Prothro and Charles M. Grigg, "Fundamental Principles of Democracy: Bases of Agreement and Disagreement," *Journal of Politics* 22 (May 1960): 276–94. Others are cited in notes 6, 7, and 9.

5. Bernard R. Berelson, Paul F. Lazarsfeld, and William N. McPhee, *Voting* (Chicago: University of Chicago Press, 1954), 312.

6. The quotations are from Herbert McClosky, "Consensus and Ideology in American Politics," in *Empirical Democratic Theory*, ed. Charles F. Cnudde and Deane E. Neubauer (Chicago: Markham, 1969), 268–302, at 286–87 (reprinted from *American Political Science Review* 58 [June 1964]: 361–82). See also Berelson et al., *Voting*, 312–23.

7. Berelson et al., *Voting*, 314–15. On these liabilities in democratic citizens generally, see Seymour Martin Lipset, *Political Man* (Garden City, N.Y.: Doubleday, 1963), chaps. 3–4, 6–8.

8. Whether quiescence is a human characteristic or engineered by more or less elitist politics was controversial when the electoral studies gained currency. See Jack L. Walker, "A Critique of the Elitist Theory of Democracy,"

American Political Science Review 60 (June 1966): 285–95; Christian Bay, "Politics and Pseudopolitics: A Critical Evaluation of Some Behavioral Literature," *American Political Science Review* 59 (Mar. 1965): 39–51. For a critical view of such conclusions as McClosky's, see Isaac D. Balbus, "The Concept of Interest in Pluralist and Marxian Analysis," *Politics and Society* 1 (Summer 1971): 151–77, at 165. Cf. Lester M. Salamon and Stephen Van Evera, "Fear, Apathy, and Discrimination: A Test of Three Explanations of Political Participation," *American Political Science Review* 67 (Dec. 1973): 1288–1306.

9. Robert A. Dahl, *Who Governs?* (New Haven, Conn.: Yale University Press, 1961), 223–28 on *homo civicus* and 314–24; Lipset, *Political Man,* 31–45, 64–79, 227–29; Giovanni Sartori, *Democratic Theory* (New York: Frederick A. Praeger, 1965), 88–89.

10. Alexis de Tocqueville, *Democracy in America,* vol. 1, ed. J. P. Mayer (Garden City, N.Y.: Doubleday, 1969), pt. 2, chap. 7.

11. Ibid., vol. 2, pt. 2, chap. 5, 517; see Tocqueville's preface to vol. 2, 417–18.

12. The quote about self-interest rightly understood is from ibid., vol. 2, pt. 2, chap. 8, 526–27.

13. "Often to a European a public official stands for force; to an American he stands for right. It is therefore fair to say that a man never obeys another man, but justice, or the law." Ibid., vol. 2, pt. 1, chap. 5, 95. Cf. ibid., vol. 1, pt. 2, chap. 10, 395–99, to the claims of Madison cited in chapter 2, and to Jefferson, letter to John Taylor, May 28, 1816, exerpted in Saul K. Padover, ed., *Thomas Jefferson on Democracy* (New York: New American Library, 1939), 39–42, and letter to John Adams, Oct. 28, 1813, in Merrill D. Peterson, ed., *The Portable Thomas Jefferson* (New York: Viking Press, 1975), 537–38.

14. Truman, *Governmental Process,* 5.

15. Glendon Schubert, "Is There a Public Interest Theory?" in *The Public Interest,* NOMOS V, ed. Carl J. Friedrich (New York: Atherton Press, 1962), 162–76, at 169–70. Similar positions on the nonexistence or subjectivity of the public interest notion are in Frank J. Sorauf, "The Conceptual Muddle," ibid., 183–90; Martin Meyerson and Edward C. Banfield, *Politics, Planning, and the Public Interest* (New York: Free Press of Glencoe, 1955), 285–329, esp. 322–29; Truman, *Governmental Process,* 50–52.

16. Respective quotations from Dahl, *Who Governs?* 316; Truman, *Governmental Process,* 114. The potential group (or "hidden hand") explanation has wide appeal. In addition to previous Truman references, see Dahl, *Who Governs?* 312–25; Latham, *Group Basis of Politics,* 29–33; Truman, *Governmental Process,* 138, 159, 448–49, 486–87, 506–7, 511–16, 523–24; Berelson et al., *Voting,* 305–23; Robert E. Lane, "The Politics of Consensus in an Age of Affluence," *American Political Science Review* 59 (Dec. 1965): 874–95.

17. Lipset, *Political Man,* 64.

18. This paragraph glosses over a large literature representing a long-standing point of view. For a partial survey, see Austin Ranney, *Curing the Mischiefs of Faction* (Berkeley: University of California Press, 1975).

19. James MacGregor Burns, *The Deadlock of Democracy* (Englewood Cliffs, N.J.: Prentice-Hall, 1963), chaps. 9–11, 14 (esp. 275–79); Burns, *The Power to Lead: The Crisis of the American Presidency* (New York: Simon and Schuster, 1984).

20. See E. E. Schattschneider, *The Semisovereign People* (New York: Holt, Rinehart and Winston, 1960). Schattschneider was the principal author for the American Political Science Association's Report of the Committee on Political Parties, "Toward a More Responsible Two-Party System," *American Political Science Review* 44, supplement (Sept. 1950). In general, critics of party responsibility oppose its majoritarian and mass participatory requirements. See Evron M. Kirkpatrick, "Toward a More Responsible Two-Party System: Political Science, Policy Science, or Pseudo-Science?" *American Political Science Review* 65 (Dec. 1971): 965–90.

21. Schattschneider, *Semisovereign People,* 5–18, chaps. 2, 4.

22. Everett Carl Ladd, Jr., " 'Reform' Is Wrecking the U.S. Party System," *Fortune,* Nov. 1977, 177–85; Jeanne Kirkpatrick, *The New Presidential Elite* (New York: Russell Sage Foundation, Twentieth Century Fund, 1976), esp. chaps. 3, 8; Nelson W. Polsby and Aaron Wildavsky, *Presidential Elections,* 6th ed. (New York: Charles Scribner's Sons, 1984).

23. Ranney, *Curing the Mischiefs,* chap. 6.

24. "Constituent" parties provide constituent benefits largely through distributive policies. See Theodore J. Lowi, "Party, Policy, and Constitution in America," in *The American Party Systems,* ed. William Nesbit Chambers and Walter Dean Burnham (New York: Oxford University Press, 1967), 236–76.

25. For general assessments, see Peter Steinfels, *The Neoconservatives* (New York: Simon and Schuster, 1979); Michael Walzer, "Nervous Liberals," *New York Review of Books,* Oct. 11, 1979, 5–9; Lawrence B. Joseph, "Democratic Revisionism Revisited," *American Journal of Political Science* 25 (Feb. 1981), 160–87.

26. See Irving Kristol, *Two Cheers for Capitalism* (New York: Basic Books, 1978), esp. chaps. 6, 23, and Epilogue; Daniel Bell, *The Cultural Contradictions of Capitalism* (New York: Basic Books, 1978), esp. 61–80; Samuel P. Huntington, "The United States," in *The Crisis of Democracy,* ed. Michel J. Crozier, Samuel P. Huntington, and Joji Watanuki (New York: New York University Press, 1975), 59–118.

27. See for example, Kristol, *Two Cheers,* chap. 7 and Epilogue.

28. Lewis Coser, "Intellectuals on Tap," *Dissent* 25 (Summer 1978): 281–83.

29. Grant McConnell, *Private Power and American Democracy* (New York: Alfred A. Knopf, 1966), 164; see also, 91–118, 157–65, 336–68.

30. Lowi's standing among political scientists is noted in Walter B. Roett-

ger, "Strata and Stability: Reputations of American Political Scientists," *PS* 11 (Winter 1978): 6–12; John S. Robey, "Reputations vs Citations: Who Are the Top Scholars in Political Science?" *PS* 15 (Spring 1982): 199–200.

31. Theodore J. Lowi, *The End of Liberalism*, 1st ed. (New York: W. W. Norton, 1969), 296–97; Truman, *Governmental Process*, 4–5. The Madison quotations are from these works as they appear therein.

32. Truman, *Governmental Process*, 5; see 4–8, 520–24.

33. Ibid., 5; cf. Dahl, *Preface to Democratic Theory*, 19–22, 30–32, 134–35.

34. Lowi, *End of Liberalism*, 1st ed., 71; McConnell, *Private Power*, 160.

35. See Lipset, *Political Man*, 64–70, 227–29, quoted from 64. The reference to the "more apparent participants" is from Truman, *Governmental Process*, 114.

36. This is a theme pursued by Lipset and others concerned with the "ungovernability" of democracies (see chapter 5). See, for example, Seymour Martin Lipset and Earl Raab, *The Politics of Unreason* (New York: Harper and Row, 1970). For a critical view of inferring group satisfaction from inactivity, see Michael Parenti, "Power and Pluralism: A View from the Bottom," *Journal of Politics* 32 (Aug. 1970): 501–30; cf. Salamon and Van Evera, "Fear, Apathy, and Discrimination." The now classic argument for understanding that the absence of elite decision making is an exertion of power is Peter Bachrach and Morton Baratz, "The Two Faces of Power," *American Political Science Review* 56 (Dec. 1962): 947–52.

37. For a further discussion and indictment of these points, see Lowi, *End of Liberalism*, 1st ed., chaps. 2–3, 5, 10; Lowi, *The Politics of Disorder* (New York: W. W. Norton, 1971), chaps. 1–3, 6; Lowi, Foreward to Harold F. Gosnell, *Machine Politics Chicago Model*, 2d ed. (Chicago: University of Chicago Press, 1968), viii–xiii; Lowi and Benjamin Ginsberg, *Poliscide* (New York: Macmillan, 1976), passim, esp. 287–89, 292–95.

38. Lowi, *End of Liberalism*, 1st ed., 313.

39. Ibid., 281–82.

40. Lowi, *Politics of Disorder*, 55–61, 177–85 (quotations at 181); *End of Liberalism*, 1st ed., 57–58, 76–77, 85, 131ff., 154–55, 186–88.

41. Lowi and Ginsberg, *Poliscide*, 16–17, 287–95 (quotation at 288). See also Lowi, *Politics of Disorder*, 175–85. On the War on Poverty, see Lowi, *End of Liberalism*, 1st ed., chap. 8; the theme there is supported in Norman Furniss and Timothy Tilton, *The Case for the Welfare State* (Bloomington: Indiana University Press, 1977).

42. Theodore J. Lowi, *The Personal President* (Ithaca, N.Y.: Cornell University Press, 1985).

43. Lowi, *Politics of Disorder*, 185 (see 170–85); *End of Liberalism*, 1st ed., 194–99.

44. Lowi, *End of Liberalism*, 1st ed., 296ff.; Lowi and Ginsberg, *Poliscide*, 291; Lowi, *Politics of Disorder*, 175–85; Lowi, "A Reply to Mansfield," *Public Policy* 19 (Winter 1971): 207–11.

45. Between the 1968 and 1980 national conventions, the Democratic party instituted several reforms from which it backpeddled, beginning with the 1984 convention. See Robert E. DiClerico and Eric M. Uslaner, *Few Are Chosen* (New York: McGraw-Hill, 1984), 8–34.

46. Lowi, "Reply to Mansfield," 210.

47. Jeffrey L. Pressman and Aaron Wildavsky, *Implementation*, 3d ed. (Berkeley: University of California Press, 1984). Cf. Sanford Weiner and Aaron Wildavsky, "The Prophylactic Presidency," in *The Third Century*, ed. Seymour Martin Lipset (Chicago: University of Chicago Press, 1979), 133–52.

48. On alien values and the democratic distemper as, among other things, causes of political disorder, see, respectively, Kristol, *Two Cheers;* Huntington, "The United States."

CHAPTER 4

Interest Group Liberalism
and the Rule of Law

Juridical democracy is Theodore Lowi's antidote for the pathological consequences of interest group liberalism. It is a reaffirmation of the founders' commitment to constitutionalism, with the following qualifications. First, it is taken for granted that the positive state and its nationalized policies in the modern industrialized economy have displaced the minimal state of Madison's time. Second, these changes require a more overt emphasis on majority rule, equality, and citizenship than is traditionally attributed to the Madisonian model—a qualification that is arguably not out of line with Madison's actual position, discussed in chapter 2. When Lowi first proposed juridical democracy, some commentators believed it was an overly formal and unrealistic theory of public institutions that depended ultimately on the role of the judiciary. Lowi does urge the judiciary to restore the long-disregarded *Schechter* rule, and this reinforces the tendency to overemphasize the *juridical* side of the label (the "rule of law operating in institutions"). The *democratic* side of the juridical democracy label, however, should be given equal or greater attention ("majority rule democracy" in which the state, through legislative representation, addresses "the citizen in us").[1]

With respect to the juridical component of Lowi's proposal, his arguments for reinvigorating the rule of law require that three standards be upheld: (1) the articulation of public purpose (a policy) in statutory law by the legislative body; (2) legislative specification of implementation and enforcement criteria within the statute; and (3) statutory language enabling the law to be generalized to anyone affected by the policy. Law that specifies such criteria restricts the range of discretion for administrative officials. It therefore lessens the extent to which a delegation of rule-making authority is also a delegation of legislative authority—the authority to specify public ends and criteria for action. Juridical democracy thus delineates legislative-administrative responsibilities. It is designed to revive the separation of powers in its traditional form.[2]

The standards address the substantive elements of juridical democracy—precisely those features most visibly downplayed by interest group liberalism. The *democratic* component addresses the procedural requirements for juridical democracy. Specifically, it addresses *how* juridical democracy can be realized. Legislative action must be based on popular representation, not clientele or functional representation. A corollary, which is integral to the substantive standards as well, requires that legislation address and affect the lives of citizens. These requirements imply the existence of publicly shared values that support the articulation of the rule of law standards by public officials. Lowi has been criticized for failing to pay sufficient attention to the democratic requirements for juridical democracy, criticisms discussed in the next section. He does appear to be preoccupied with the rule of law in his proposal. In fairness, however, the prominence he gives to the rule of law clearly seems to be based on the proposition that the institutional practices of interest group liberalism are in need of reform, not the democratic capabilities of citizens.

The case for juridical democracy is not self-contained. It emerges from a series of separate but related arguments. A brief overview of its specific requirements illustrates how the arguments are interconnected.

First, *juridical democracy requires legislative deliberation about public purposes*. Legislative deliberation may include, but it is not limited to, a discussion of the interests at stake in rule formulation and rule application. Law carries the moral force of legitimacy if it is defensible on principle—that is, in terms of a public interest that can affect *anyone*—not on grounds of particularistic interest accommodation affecting *someone*.

Second, *juridical democracy requires that public purpose be articulated in the form of a generalizable rule (a law)*. Bargaining, accommodation, and mutual adjustment are essential and always will be, but *one bargains on the rule itself*—on public purpose and on standards for enforcement—*not on whether, or how, to apply the rule*, depending on calculations of costs and benefits to the individuals affected (winners and losers). This latter kind of bargaining obscures the public purpose behind the rule.

Third, *rule application should directly affect (control) the conduct of citizens*. Rules that directly regulate conduct invite consistency and continuity in realizing public purposes. By contrast, interest group liberalism tends to regulate the environment of conduct, not conduct itself. It invites discretion on a case-by-case basis in policy implementation and thus not only avoids but also erodes and loses sight of the original purpose of the policy.

Fourth, because open deliberation on public purposes establishes generalizable rules that directly regulate individual conduct, *juridical democracy can mobilize citizens as citizens, not as private actors.* Restoring the rule of law thereby can contribute to the resurrection of *civic virtue.* Under juridical democracy, citizens would "act" vicariously through their legislative representatives. Citizens would be constituent actors in the process of formulating the purposes and rules that affect them directly. Discretionary policies, however, invite citizens to think as private individuals and to act as constituents of private interests, protecting their domains against public encroachment.

Fifth, *juridical democracy produces egalitarian and "fair" (equitable) public policy.* Public deliberation that mobilizes constituents performs a public education function. Citizens are reminded that they are tied to one another by reciprocal relationships. They therefore have a stake in demanding egalitarian and equitable policies from their legislative representatives, policies that are generalizable to *anyone,* not limited to *someone.*[3] By contrast, under interest group liberalism, citizens are encouraged to view public policy as action serving or affecting vested interests and hence to demand dispensations from legislators according the principle of "each according to his claim."[4]

Each of the preceding is a necessary condition for juridical democracy. None alone is sufficient, but together, they produce juridical democracy. Does the case for juridical democracy sustain the values of liberal democracy, and does it serve as a plausible program for state reform? The discussion in the next three sections provides an affirmative response to the first question. As a proposal for reform, however, juridical democracy faces serious obstacles. These are discussed in the last section with reference to Congress, the key institution for juridical democracy.

Juridical Democracy and the Liberal Tradition

Initial assessments of Lowi's argument for juridical democracy in the first edition of *The End of Liberalism* were critical. Harvey C. Mansfield, Jr., charges Lowi with failing to recognize that liberal democracy must have virtuous elites to filter out extreme and unwise values and that their roles must be disguised to avoid envy, conflict, and leveling. Juridical democracy emphasizes the effect of virtue rather than virtue itself (something Mansfield also attributed to pluralism), and Mansfield fears that it might "substitute for moderation" a "moralist formalism, which could be compared to majority tyranny without the majority." Juridical democracy also does not sit well with critics who assess liberalism from the left. William E. Connolly locates Lowi squarely within the "liberal consensus" and its welfare state. He concludes that "Lowi's prescriptions require a citizenry imbued with civic virtue" but that "the civic virtue required . . . is most likely to emerge when the state already supports the public interest."[5]

Lowi responded to Mansfield's charges, and his response applies also to Connolly's criticism. Lowi argues that two criteria guide the policy analysis in *The End of Liberalism*, criteria requiring that state action sustain and reinforce civic virtue: "First, is the state, through a given statute, directing itself to the citizen in us? Second, is the state dealing with the citizen in us in terms that we can fully understand prior to taking private action?"[6]

Under the first criterion, juridical democracy should ensure that an individual can interact with others and with the government on the basis of one's "individual rights and obligations as a citizen." For citizens, individual commitments are not commitments made in isolation from one's peers but are reciprocal commitments vis-à-vis rules defining rights and obligations; therefore, "the primary obligation of a government is the relatively negative one of protecting civil liberties."[7] Taken by itself, the first criterion may provide only empty formalism. Virtually any legislation can specify citizen rights and obligations in the form of generalizable rules and constraints, but it can simultaneously allow organized groups and administrative agencies to bargain over legislative intent and application of the rules, thus producing an empty and "moralistic formalism," as Mansfield fears. In Lowi's view, however, juridical democracy can avoid this because his two criteria must be considered together rather than separately. Juridical democracy should limit bargaining and accommodation "to those points in the system where decisions on rules can be made or reformed"—the legislative arena, in which the rules are formulated and their costs and benefits debated, rather than agency-clientele arenas, in which the content and application of rules are negotiated.[8]

In clarifying his criteria, Lowi believes he demonstrates that juridical democracy can sustain the values of the liberal tradition. His two criteria provide the basis for citizens to understand their rights and responsibilities because they act, albeit vicariously, through public representation. Most individuals, of course, may be totally unaware of a particular legislative debate. Lowi's point, however, is that legislative deliberation at least provides citizens a forum for participation through their elected representatives. On the other hand, interest group liberalism makes this forum virtually insignificant and instead invites interest group accommodation within the agency-clientele arenas that have been delegated legislative authority. Juridical democracy enables any citizen to act; interest group liberalism allows participation only for interests that happen to have organizational resources and agency access.

Lowi's case is not compelling. For example, in the first edition of *The End of Liberalism,* he avers that "the juridical approach does not dictate a particular definition of justice, of virtue, or of the good life. . . . The juridical principle can convert a consumer economy into a just society without altering in any way the virtue of consumption or the freedom to consume."[9] Without further qualification, however, juridical democracy could as easily convert a just society into a consumer society. The case for juridical democracy in the first edition of *The End of Liberalism* therefore does not preclude it from being reduced to debates about rules governing civil liberties while allowing inequalities in political resources to make public representation little more than a goal—a symbolic one at that. Connolly pointedly states the problem: "Nothing in Lowi's argument ensures more effective leverage for oppressed and unorganized minorities. . . . For since the capitalist system . . . is incompatible with significant reductions in economic inequality, the welfare state must redress these distributive outcomes only at the margin."[10]

Implicit in Connolly's criticism is the broader charge that Lowi's appeals to the liberal tradition, justice, equity, and the like are weak. Demonstrating the compatibility of juridical democracy and these values requires more than formalizing the notions of citizen and law. Citizens might be equal before the law, but Lowi needs to show that lawmaking itself does not simply institutionalize and legitimate advantages that strategically located groups secure under interest group liberalism.[11] Short of doing so, Lowi can be charged with failing to consider the extent to which the premises and values underlying liberalism itself are faulty or no longer applicable. For example, C. B. Macpherson, in his criticism of the "possessive individualist" variant of liberalism (within which he includes Madison and the constitutional founders as antecedents of pluralists), argues that possessive individualism, or "the linkage of market society with liberal democratic ends," must be broken.[12]

Criticisms such as Connolly's, and by implication Macpherson's, carry weight against the case for juridical democracy as it is presented in the first edition of *The End of Liberalism.* These criticisms, and his conclusion that interest group liberalism had been institutionalized in the so-called Second Republic, afforded Lowi the opportunity to strengthen his case for juridical democracy. This he offered in the second edition of *The End of Liberalism,* including guidelines for understanding how juridical democracy sustains liberal democratic values. With this revision, however, Lowi does not overtly challenge the desirability of possessive individualist values and incentives as Macpherson does. Instead, he reaffirms the argument that properly constituted institutional practices can shape and mold public values, overcoming their dysfunctional manifestations encouraged under interest group liberalism.

Neo-laissez-faire: Reducing the Scope of Government

Interest group liberalism has always worked to the advantage of the organized, and it is now, Lowi contends, fully institutionalized as the "Second Republic of the United States." This Second Republic is characterized as a state of permanent receivership. By *permanent receivership,* Lowi means a state that systematically socializes risk (as opposed to socializing the means of production or distribution), on the grounds that "any institution large enough to be a significant factor in the community may have its stability underwritten. It is a system of policies that sets a general floor under risk, either by attempting to eliminate risk or to reduce or share the costs of failure."[13] In theory at least, pluralism is analogous to the economic market. Entrepreneurial interest groups invest in the political marketplace (the group process). Some gain through their investments (favorable policies, increased membership, and the like); some lose. But interest group liberalism is a corrupted pluralism—or, to continue the analogy, it is an imperfect market with oligopolistic tendencies. It preserves the gains of the advantaged and effectively closes the market to newcomers. Risks, which established organizations would otherwise take in the ideal pluralist market, are underwritten by their governmental clientele in the Second Republic. Unable to distinguish institutions that warrant conserving from those that are inequitable, inefficient, or costly to maintain—business or otherwise—receivership policies guarantee political (and economic) survival to organizations, regardless of merit. Traditional liberal values of individual freedom and equal opportunity and the accountability of public officials are consequently further eroded.

As an antidote to receivership policies, Lowi proposes neo-laissez-faire, which is to be accompanied by a general "deflation" of the scope of government and a strengthening of those governmental regulatory powers that do not serve merely to protect interests from competition. *Neo-laissez-faire* is a strategy or policy that might facilitate arriving at juridical democracy; in this respect, it is similar to the *Schechter* rule's attempt to invalidate overly broad delegations of legislative authority.[14] The proposal to reduce governmental responsibilities under neo-laissez-faire anticipated the deregulatory moves and pricing mechanisms of the 1980s. It constitutes a reduction in the scope of government insofar as that scope is largely a function of the state of permanent receivership, working to the advantage of the organized and well-placed. It differs substantially, however, from national policies beginning with the 1981 Economic Recovery and Tax Act (ERTA) to cut back social service entitlements while sustaining national security "entitlements" or to further the parceling out of public authority under the rubric of "privatization."

Such strategies as neo-laissez-faire would seem to have no bearing on the problem of unequal political resources and the criticism that juridical democracy would simply institutionalize and legitimate the advantages of strategically located groups. One might understandably ask of Lowi, why not socialism instead of neo-laissez-faire? Lowi, however, disavows a socialist alternative for the United States as "pure political rhetoric" or "creative fantasy." His rejection of socialism is not an attack on socialism per se. It is a virtual corollary of the rationale behind the neo-laissez-faire proposal. The capacity of any government to influence its economy and society is limited, particularly when they are as large and complex as those of the United States. Neo-laissez-faire is proposed within the twin contexts of a largely capitalist system of resource allocation *and* a largely capitalist belief system (ideology). Under these circumstances, it is simply unrealistic, if not dangerous, to assume a smooth transition to socialism without acknowledging that there would be an "interim sacrifice of civil liberties."[15]

The preference for neo-laissez-faire over socialism may appear to be weakly grounded since the preceding remarks emphasize mainly the liabilities of developing a socialist alternative to the prevailing economic system and its ideology. Moreover, because neo-laissez-faire takes possessive individualist values for granted, Lowi's position may appear to be susceptible to the criticism implicit in Connolly's argument and articulated by Macpherson, as noted previously. This reaction would be inappropriate, however, for two reasons.

Lowi's advocacy of neo-laissez-faire does not incorporate, or necessitate, claims supporting the *desirability* of possessive individualist values and incentives, as Macpherson or Connolly might charge. Nor does it lend support to *criticisms* of positions that oppose the sorts of excessive societal demands that presumably are inherent tendencies of possessive individualism—namely, neoconservative criticisms that rising expectations, demand overload, or equality of result are in and of themselves negative values and the products of special interest demands (egalitarian and new class). These are secondary, even misleading, issues. The status of possessive individualism—positive or negative—is a function of institutional practices. The primary issue is how government governs, how its rules affect citizens. A capitalist economy and its ideology may benefit from constitutional provisions that rely on neo-laissez-faire—or from interest group liberal perversions—but the constitutional provisions that allow advantages to the well-organized also guarantee civil liberties.[16] Even Connolly, one of Lowi's critics, acknowledges virtually the same point in a different context: "constitutionalism always has two sides. . . . to reject the negative side . . . is to affirm, and not just temporarily, an ideal of socialism that is *intrinsically* authoritarian."[17] The burden of proof for juridical democracy is to link *constitutionalism,* which may benefit the organized and well-placed while sustaining civil liberties, with *democratic representation.*

Public Representation and Civic Virtue

In the second edition of *The End of Liberalism,* Lowi asserts that the two components of his proposal—the juridical and the democratic—are interdependent or mutually reinforcing:

> Taken by itself, the juridical principle appears to be comfortable with, say, segregation as well as integration laws, as long as the laws possess legal integrity. But within the context of democracy, especially if one lived by the juridical principle, it would simply not be possible to support segregation in any form, because a democracy cannot abide two systems of law, two criteria for the provision of governmental services—in brief, unequal protection of the laws. On a host of issues, therefore, juridical democracy has very clear and profound substantive implications; it is not merely a procedural matter.[18]

This statement suggests two propositions about the advantages of juridical democracy: (1) juridical democracy sustains a form of public policy-making that is egalitarian and just ("fair"); and (2) juridical democracy resurrects civic virtue within the citizenry, both as an important legitimating and stabilizing support for the regime and as an end of the polity. The first proposition is explicit in the quoted assertion; the second is a corollary of the first.

The first proposition rests on the premise that citizens must be political equals in a liberal democracy. Democratic law therefore either produces egalitarian and just public policy or is undemocratic and hence unlawful. The proposition is not simply analytic, however; juridical democracy is not democratic by definition. When Lowi says that "in our government, it is not necessary to define justice, because there is something about liberalism that prevents us from raising the question of justice at all," he is thinking of the notion of natural liberty in the liberal tradition in which each individual is the best judge of his or her own interest.[19] In this context, a liberal democratic regime may not, indeed cannot, define justice in some substantive sense, but it can, and must, define it in procedural terms that will have substantive implications ("justice as fairness"): the rules (law) within which politically equal citizens may act freely.

The extent to which juridical democracy sustains democratic values obviously will be more difficult to ascertain in some cases than in others. In certain situations, juridical democracy might produce policies designed to rectify past discrimination; in others, it might generate policies allowing for the competitiveness that equality of opportunity implies. In the first instance, counterclaims of reverse discrimination will predictability emerge; in the second, charges of maintaining privilege will be leveled. One of the substantive implications of juridical democracy for these types of controversies, however, is that various economic and social advantages resulting from public policy should become more equitably distributed. Why? Criteria for testing the position are explicit, not assumed to be met by the bargaining, logrolling and co-optation that characterize interest group liberalism.

The first proposition is tested by asking in each case *who* has authority, with *what* consequences, for *whom?* Interest group liberalism is discretionary and arbitrary, formulated by and for the interests of the organized against the unorganized. Nothing in juridical democracy precludes policies that, on the merits of individual cases, favor the organized. Neo-laissez-faire clearly has more positive implications (economic and organizational) for those with capital holdings than for those without. But it precludes the fact of being organized and strategically advantaged in policy-making as a sufficient criterion for lawfulness. It "speaks to the powerless as well as the powerful [who often] would be immobilized if they had to articulate what they were going to do before they did it."[20]

The second proposition, civic virtue, follows if, and only if, the first is operative. Lowi does not use the term *civic virtue*. The second proposition does not incorporate a particularly ennobling portrayal of civic virtue, but it is civic virtue nonetheless. Lawmaking under juridical democracy involves the language of criteria for planning and implementation—costs and benefits, not goals and aspirations—and citizens can assess the criteria as these affect them. Juridical democracy provides incentives for elected lawmakers to be responsible partisans, to advocate positions in which they have a stake as representatives because the consequences of their actions are known to their constituents. Lawmaking and its costs and benefits involve a process of "consent-building prior to taking authoritative action in law." Lawmaking, in effect, goes public.[21] Civic virtue arises with the public debate and citizen action (through legislative representation) that lawmaking invites. Legislators, let alone citizens, do not begin with civic virtue, nor do they end up talking about it. Civic virtue is not a set of specific values self-consciously held, particularly in a liberal society that does not define justice and allows "natural liberty" to operate. Civic virtue can emerge out of public discourse when lawmaking goes public, when citizens act vicariously through elected representatives. Civic virtue may *not* arise out of this process—particularly if practitioners and beneficiaries of interest group liberalism continue to prevail and conduct business as usual—*but it cannot arise without this process.*

Civic virtue has two functions that are mutually reinforcing: education and legitimation. Public debate and action force individuals to come to terms with the reciprocal relationships they share as citizens; the development of civic virtue thereby promotes civic education. In turn, civic virtue reinforces the likelihood, under juridical democracy, that equitable public policies will be formulated, thus strengthening public perceptions of regime legitimacy. Civic virtue is undermined by delegating authority—and with delegated authority, the function of public debate—to those who happen to be organized or happen to have gained access to policymakers based on their strategic advantages. When there is no public debate, there is no chance for civic virtue and hence no chance to acknowledge that citizenship is a reciprocal relationship, not a discrete property of an isolated individual.

The second proposition is diametrically opposed to interest group liberalism. Citizens may well be imbued with possessive individualist

values, but under juridical democracy they are also afforded the opportunity to recognize their public roles and reciprocal responsibilities. Under interest group liberalism, however, they only have incentives to pursue values believed vouchsafed by their private interest
associations and, hence, policy stances that are indeed inegalitarian
and "protective" of their domains. In his indictment of interest group
liberalism, Lowi thus asserts that its receivership policies "provide no
civic education whatsoever because they do not provide any opportunities at all for discourse about the priorities or moralities in back
of public choice."[22] As long as public policy responds to and reinforces the priorities of the organized, civic virtue has little chance of
being resurrected, let alone being reinforced. Instead, one would expect a quiescent citizen body and elite cynicism and paternalism. Under these circumstances, political elites have all the incentives necessary to sustain the politics of interest group liberalism.

Congress, the Rule of Law, and Reelection

All public policy is redistributive. It allocates resources—that is, income, in the broadest sense. If someone gains, someone else must lose
because resources are finite. While it is conventional to classify policies as distributive, redistributive, and regulatory or according to
some other schema, such as the distribution of costs and benefits, the
simple point that policy redistributes should be kept in mind. Lester
Thurow underscores the point with respect to so-called regulatory
legislation: "whatever the overt objective, the implicit objective is always to alter the distribution of income and this is almost always the
real reason for the existence of any regulation." The advantage of
calling something regulatory when it is redistributive is obvious:
"Voters will not put up with large direct subsidies, but large indirect
subsidies can be hidden from the voter if rules and regulations are
used."[23]

Juridical democracy squarely confronts the redistributive character
of public policy. At a minimum, it makes the issues at stake a matter
of public record. (Agricultural price supports are subsidies, not market stabilizers; affirmative action addresses economic injustice, not
simply prejudice.) The reason for its lack of appeal among those who
establish the public agenda is straightforward. Juridical democracy
asks beneficiaries of interest group liberalism to redistribute their political "income" to others. This the beneficiaries are not about to do.
One specific example may suffice to support this conclusion. It is the
central example for juridical democracy, the case of Congress.

Lowi provides numerous examples of the advantages of juridical democracy, and he offers several proposals for reform. Some proposals are found in each edition of *The End of Liberalism:* restoring the *Schechter* rule and establishing tenure of statutes acts (sunset laws, several of which have been established in states). Some early proposals were omitted in the second edition: establishing the ombudsman-cum-senior civil service and strengthening the role of the states (a victim of revenue-sharing abuses).[24] Several new proposals or modifications are introduced in the second edition of the book. Constitutional justification of presidential vetoes is recommended in lieu of policy justifications. Policy changes per se (namely, tightening nondiscretionary fiscal policy) are no longer discrete proposals. In the second edition of *The End of Liberalism,* they are incorporated under the neo-laissez-faire rubric and placed in the context of Lowi's most significant change in emphasis: *institutional* reform, most notably the reform of Congress.[25]

President Harry Truman may have believed that "the buck stops here," but for juridical democracy the buck stops with Congress. Congress, however, is notorious for passing the buck—and quite literally so in the form of the pork barrel. The intent of pork barrel policies is straightforward: to benefit constituents and to provide a base for reelection. Today, the notion of the pork barrel may be stretched a bit to include receivership policies (which, being "off budget," impose no visible tax cost but gain enormous credit amongst the beneficiaries) and congressional casework.

Delegation of legislative authority has enhanced the importance of congressional casework. Incumbents can facilitate federal programs within districts and assist constituents in coping with regulatory problems. They gain from the problems they create or the lawmaking they abdicate since, as Morris Fiorina argues, "vanishing marginals" (or fewer competitive districts) are increasingly explained by this form of the pork barrel as opposed to party-linked benefits and "safe district" reapportionment. Perhaps this is not surprising (and it certainly should not be to advocates of party responsibility). Congress is structured to be the pork barrel institution par excellence.[26] A call for abolishing or even restricting the pork barrel by codifying standards for the application of law to specific cases and by instituting sunset laws, as Lowi recommends, is counterproductive in view of the incentive system within which members of Congress operate. It asks incumbents to replace their basic, short-term instincts for reelection with a longer view, which may mean their electoral defeat in the short term.

As a *theoretical* alternative to interest group liberalism—an ideal-type normative framework—juridical democracy is on solid ground, though. Its juridical *and* democratic requirements reaffirm liberal democracy's basic values and underlying premises—such values as citizenship, equality, and civic virtue—which are obscured by interest group liberalism, and together they provide a framework for political scientists to assess political practice. Delegation, accommodation, and discretion are salient features of interest group liberalism, and juridical democracy would not eliminate them; they are aspects of governing a modern, industrialized and nationalized polity. There is, however, an important difference between the delegation of legislative authority and the delegation of rule-making authority that is constrained by prior legislative deliberation. By imposing standards under which delegated rule-making authority is to function, juridical democracy shrinks the gap between liberal democratic theory and interest group liberal practice. Juridical democracy would tend to centralize points of access within the national elective bodies, making access for the organized and privileged more difficult to obtain. The claims of vested interests must be made in the context of publicly articulated rules, principles, and values developed on the democratic or legislative deliberation side of juridical democracy. The stakes, and the fact that the current losers also have a stake in the action, become much clearer in juridical democracy than they do under interest group liberalism. What is at stake is measured in terms of the state's interest, as the democratic representative of its citizenry, not in terms of the interests of the organized and well-placed.

NOTES

An earlier version of this chapter appeared as "Juridical Democracy and Democratic Values" in *Polity* 16 (Spring 1984). Used by permission of the publisher.

1. Theodore J. Lowi, "A Reply to Mansfield," *Public Policy* 19 (Winter 1971): 207–11, at 208.

2. For a somewhat different but complementary version, see Richard F. Bensel, "Creating the Statutory State: The Implications of a Rule of Law Standard in American Politics," *American Political Science Review* 74 (Sept. 1980): 734–44. For a different and more critical view of rule of law, see Lyle Downing and Robert B. Thigpen, "A Liberal Dilemma: The Application of Unger's Critique of Formalism to Lowi's Concept of Juridical Democracy," *Journal of Politics* 44 (Feb. 1982): 230–46. The interpretation of juridical democracy developed here is criticized in Donald R. Brand, *Corporatism and*

the Rule of Law (Ithaca, N.Y.: Cornell University Press, 1988), which takes a more "Hamiltonian" than "Madisonian" approach to constitutionalism and raises issues similar to those of Mansfield (see note 5). Other significant criticisms are taken up in the next section of this chapter.

3. Logically this follows from the first condition. For a cogent defense of the public interest concept along these lines, see Theodore M. Benditt, "The Public Interest," *Philosophy and Public Affairs* 2 (Spring 1973): 291–311, esp. 306–11.

4. Theodore J. Lowi, *The End of Liberalism*, 2d ed. (New York: W. W. Norton, 1979), 297.

5. Harvey C. Mansfield, Jr., *The Spirit of Liberalism* (Cambridge, Mass.: Harvard University Press, 1978), 50; see also 69, 71 (Mansfield's critique was originally published as "Disguised Liberalism," *Public Policy* 18 [Fall 1970]: 605–28). William E. Connolly, *The Public Interest* (Washington, D.C.: American Political Science Association, 1977), 45–46, 50–51; see also Connolly, "Liberalism under Pressure," *Polity* 2 (Spring 1970): 357–67.

6. Lowi, "A Reply to Mansfield," 208.

7. Theodore J. Lowi, *The Politics of Disorder* (New York: W. W. Norton, 1971), 61, 177.

8. Theodore J. Lowi, *The End of Liberalism*, 1st ed. (New York: W. W. Norton, 1969), 155; also 304–5, 312.

9. Lowi, *End of Liberalism*, 1st ed., 312.

10. Connolly, *The Public Interest*, 50.

11. Congress can generalize in statutory language and still pursue interest group liberal objectives, witness the rider proposed by Senator Charles Mathias to the tax bill to enable Chris-Craft Industries to purchase the *Washington Star*: "The rider does not actually mention The Star or Chris-Craft by name. It would give a 50 percent tax credit on losses to any failing newspaper in the District of Columbia with a circulation of 200,000 or more. The Star is the only paper fitting such a definition." See *Boston Globe*, July 31, 1981. Similarly H.R. 5274 was written to restrict anticompetitive mergers, but it was intended to prevent the Mobil Oil acquisition of Marathon Oil. See Otis Pike, "The House Was Out to Stick It to Mobil," *Ann Arbor News*, Jan. 10, 1982. Numerous other instances of interest group liberal legislating have occurred since. For example, the 1986 tax reform bill produced innumerable transition rules in its wake, many of which were incorporated as "technical corrections" in 1988.

12. C. B. Macpherson, *The Life and Times of Liberal Democracy* (New York: Oxford University Press, 1977), 22.

13. Lowi, *End of Liberalism*, 2d ed., chap. 10, at 280. See also Lowi, "Towards a Politics of Economics: The State of Permanent Receivership," in *Stress and Contradiction in Modern Capitalism*, ed. Leon N. Lindberg, Robert Alford, Colin Crouch, and Clause Offe (Lexington, Mass.: D. C. Heath, 1975), 115–24; Alan Stone, "Planning, Public Policy, and Capitalism," in

Nationalizing Government, ed. Lowi and Stone (Beverly Hills, Calif.: Sage Publications, 1978), 427–42.

14. See, for example, *End of Liberalism,* 2d ed., 93–107, 291–94, 300–309. With a general deflation of government's scope, one would not expect a twentieth-century national legislature to return to the ad hoc role of the nineteenth-century Congress (concerned primarily with "distributive" legislation) in which Congress itemized horse blankets for the army and specified river and harbor project designs in statutes. See, for example, the fate of congressional attempts to develop specific methods for reducing air pollution through "agency forcing" in Bruce A. Ackerman and William T. Hassler, *Clean Coal/Dirty Air* (New Haven, Conn.: Yale University Press, 1981), a study that relies on criteria different from Lowi's but supports the main point here (but see their *Schechter*-like "principle of textual priority," 108–9ff.).

15. Lowi, *End of Liberalism,* 2d ed., 294; see also 289–94.

16. Ibid., 294, 298–99; cf. 125–26; and *End of Liberalism,* 1st ed., 155–56.

17. William E. Connolly, "Freedom under Socialism," *Political Theory 5* (Nov. 1977): 461–72, at 471.

18. Lowi, *End of Liberalism,* 2d ed., 299. The possibility that juridical democracy could not choose between segregation and integration was raised in an assessment of the first edition of Lowi's book. See Robert C. Grady, "Interest-Group Liberalism and Juridical Democracy," *American Politics Quarterly 6* (Apr. 1978): 213–36, at 232.

19. Lowi, *End of Liberalism,* 2d ed., 296. Many of the points in the remainder of this section complement and even parallel the assessment of Madison's views about civic virtue developed in chapter 2.

20. Lowi, *End of Liberalism,* 2d ed., 298–99.

21. The quotation about consent-building is from Lowi, *End of Liberalism,* 1st ed., 293. Many of the points that follow are similar to those raised by George Armstrong Kelly in delineating the conditions of the civic and the civil, particularly his "Civil II." See his "Who Needs a Theory of Citizenship?" *Daedalus* 108 (Fall 1979): 21–36.

22. Lowi, *End of Liberalism,* 2d ed., 291.

23. Lester C. Thurow, *The Zero-Sum Society* (New York: Basic Books, 1980), 123, 145.

24. Lowi, "Europeanization of America?" in *Nationalizing Government,* ed. Lowi and Stone, 20–22.

25. For the various proposals, see Lowi, *End of Liberalism,* 2d ed., 124–26, 292–94, 299–310. Some related options are suggested by Douglas Yates, *Bureaucratic Democracy* (Cambridge, Mass.: Harvard University Press, 1982), 50–58, from a perspective at odds with Lowi's.

26. Morris P. Fiorina, *Congress: Keystone of the Washington Establishment* (New Haven, Conn.: Yale University Press, 1977), chaps. 5, 7, 9, esp.

chap. 5. See also Marcus E. Ethridge III, "Legislative-Administrative Interaction as 'Intrusive Access,' " *Journal of Politics* 43 (May 1981): 473–92, at 474–81; Richard F. Fenno, Jr., *Home Style: House Members in Their Districts* (Boston: Little, Brown, 1978); David R. Mayhew, *Congress: The Electoral Connection* (New Haven, Conn.: Yale University Press, 1974), 49–77. The point about the design of Congress as a pork barrel institution is based on Willmoore Kendall, "The Two Majorities," *Midwest Journal of Political Science* 4 (Nov. 1960): 317–45.

CHAPTER 5

The Socialization of Risk
and the Appeal of Corporatism

After the New Deal, the ground rules for the regulated but competitive economy went virtually unquestioned for several decades. Up through the early stages of the Great Society, conflicts about who pays, who benefits, and who represents whom as the government undertook its regulatory activities were muted because certain public interest expectations about economic affluence, social welfare, and equity were met. The pluralist theory of bargaining and accommodation among interest groups and government agencies in formulating public policy helped explain the public consensus that legitimated the role of the state. The basis for consensus, however, dissolved in the last two decades. The U.S. economic leadership of the world has waned. Declining and emerging industries have scrambled for various governmental supports. Citizens have increasingly become disaffected because of unemployment, inflation, and taxes. Such problems as these have become divisive issues. Many people now doubt that it is possible for the nation to achieve both economic growth and social equity.

Scholarly criticisms of pluralism coincided with the collapse of the post–New Deal consensus. Pluralist theory has been discredited as nothing more than interest group liberalism. Very few scholars or public figures have heeded the call to promote the public interest by restoring the rule of law to its proper place in the governmental process,[1] but many of them have addressed the challenges to government's role in maintaining the conditions for market competition and social well-being. Beginning in the 1980s, so-called neoliberals responded first to the nation's economic problems and then to Reagan administration appeals to "unleash free enterprise" by proposing that government should be responsible for industrial policy. They contend that the U.S. economy can neither compete internationally nor provide an adequate standard of living domestically without a national industrial policy. The neoliberals range from people like Robert B. Reich, who urges a systematic national industrial policy guided by democratic planning, through Felix Rohatyn, who advocates a resurrection of the Reconstruction Finance Corporation, to Lester C. Thurow, who proposes a mix of policies to encourage investment in new technologies and to mitigate the effects of declining industries.[2]

A plausible interpretation of the neoliberal proposals is that they offer no more fundamental change than putting interest group liberalism in elaborate dress.[3] Plausible, but not particularly enlightening. Industrial policy exceeds the limits of interest group liberalism's bankruptcy of public authority. It requires the state to be an authoritative participant in, and guarantor of, specific types of investment and productivity decisions for specific firms or sectors of the economy. This has evoked criticism from both the right and the left. Neoconservatives argue that proposals to expand the roles of the positive state are counterproductive. They contend that the performance of the economy has become controversial because the industrialized democracies have undertaken too many economic and social functions. Group demands for governmentally provided benefits and excessive public expectations risk "overloading" the political process and exceeding government's inherently limited ability to allocate resources. These have interfered with the proper functioning of the state, reduced its authority, and undermined consensus.[4] Critics from the left believe that the breakdown in consensus is attributable to the inherent failures of capitalism, or "corporate" capitalism. Their solutions are for more, not less, democracy in the forms of public controls over corporations, economic or industrial democracy, and increased decision-making responsibilities for workers concerning questions of capital outlays, work processes, productivity, and the like.[5]

The industrial policy neoliberals reject these sorts of contentions. They blame neither excessive popular demands nor inherent deficiencies of capitalism for inadequate social and economic policies and the collapse of the post–New Deal consensus. In fact, they believe that democracy and capitalism are not necessarily antagonistic and can be made compatible. The nation's problems, they argue, are due to an avoidance of hard choices by public officials and business leaders. In place of the regulatory state, the neoliberals propose a general framework for a managed capitalist economy that goes beyond the consensual ground rules for the regulated but competitive economy.[6] In general, they are troubled by the awkward relationship between democratic aspirations for popular control over public policy in a society in which business is, to them, disproportionately influential. They also are troubled about how this relationship between public and private power affects equity or distributive justice.

Here the central concern is with the extent to which the idea of an industrial policy framework for a managed economy is compatible with basic values and criteria for liberal democracy. Specific policy issues and the debates among industrial policy protagonists are secondary. The case for industrial policy poses two requirements for the liberal democratic state.

First, the framework for industrial policy provides for a managed capitalist economy in which the state assumes major responsibility for ensuring the conditions that will facilitate capital accumulation by the private sector. That is, industrial policies require the *socialization of risk* for what otherwise are presumed to be private sector investments designed to enhance productivity and thus capital accumulation.

Second, successful development of an industrial policy framework and implementation of appropriate policies require the *representation of functional interests* within policy-making arenas, a requirement that is most adequately described by the term *corporatism*. This policy-making arrangement is supposed to enable risk to be socialized in ways that are consistent with ideals of equity and distributive justice.

Both requirements are problematic for traditional liberal democratic thought. The socialization of risk is assessed in this chapter; functional representation and corporatism, in the next.

The Socialization of Risk

Broadly construed, *socialization of risk* refers to governmental assumption of responsibility for conditions that permit the development or continuation of firms, sectors, or markets and responsibility for ensuring the success of decisions and policies that traditionally have been viewed as private sector functions in an otherwise entrepreneurial society. The key referents are (1) *governmental*—or public—*assumption of responsibility* and (2) activities *traditionally believed to be* private sector.

The socialization of risk is undertaken when specific types of policies are developed to attain more or less specific objectives. Typically, these involve governmental efforts to underwrite failing businesses (for example, Lockheed and Chrysler loan guarantees), to provide incentives and protection for fledgling industries, and to insure against default, loss, or liability for activities as diverse as student loans, crop failures, nuclear generation of electricity, and so on.[7] The socialization of risk, however, also involves a category of activities that is more diffuse than the preceding one, which targets identifiable firms, sectors, and policy arenas. This includes the provision of certain basic conditions that are requisite if business is to do business: infrastructure (roads, communication, transportation), finance (stable banking system and money supply, international trade agreements), and natural resources (leasing oil and timber lands, water supplies), for example. In a pure or ideal-type laissez-faire world, these would constitute part of the risk taken by entrepreneurs. In the modern mixed economy, however, these are not construed as governmental supports for business or investor risks. Instead, they are euphemistically considered "services," part of what government provides in the "public interest." These so-called services are taken for granted in a capitalist economy since they are ordinarily contrasted with the policies of states that socialize the means of production or other prerequisites to production, such as utilities and transportation.

Notwithstanding their apparent differences, the two general categories of socializing risk are related. The normal requirement that local governments provide the infrastructural conduits for commerce (roads and sewers, for example) removes a theoretical constraint on businesses. It also enables them to bargain with local jurisdictions over cost sharing when they make location decisions, in effect creating tax abatement competition between jurisdictions to attract firms. Likewise, a stable banking system and money supply reduce investor risks, and deposit insurance inaugurated during the New Deal constituted not an abrupt change but a corollary of government's responsibility to provide stable conditions under which investors could do business. In summary, the contemporary focus on the socialization of risk by public officials and business leaders is not *whether* to do it—that was resolved by early twentieth-century progressives and the New Deal—but *how* to utilize it. Industrial policy advocates have, they believe, the appropriate approach.

Not surprisingly, the socialization of risk has pejorative connotations for some scholars. In his criticism of interest group liberalism, Theodore Lowi argues that risk socialization has become so pervasive that the United States is now a "state of permanent receivership." In economic parlance, government puts firms in receivership by underwriting their solvency until creditors are secured or reorganization restores efficiency. With "permanent" receivership, it attempts to secure major institutions or sectors whose performance impacts the larger society before they collapse—the savings and loan bailout from

1989 onward and the earlier Lockheed, New York City, Chrysler, and steel industry bailouts simply represent the extreme cases.[8] This brings to mind neo-Marxist arguments that the state's function under "advanced capitalism" is to provide the conditions for capital accumulation after capitalism has exhausted its market system capabilities.[9] Permanent receivership, however, is an outgrowth of the politics of interest group liberalism, not an aspect of the logic of capitalism. Capitalists may be the *primary* beneficiaries, since business and corporate interests are best established and best organized to be the recipients of policies that anticipate and forestall failure. The critique of interest group liberalism, however, underscores advantages accruing to any and all established and organized groups. Interest group liberalism cannot distinguish institutions that warrant conserving from those that are inequitable or inefficient—business or otherwise.[10] Two conclusions follow. The state's pretensions to democratic legitimacy are eroded; government "buys" its legitimacy by indiscriminantly socializing risk for the highest bidders. Moreover, capitalism loses its moral capital; the entrepreneurial spirit is entrepreneurial no more.

Neoliberal proponents of industrial policy, however, argue that the socialization of risk can be used constructively and without the usual negative connotations. In their view, policymakers have employed double standards with respect to economic productivity and equity. They have rescued large firms and permitted individually owned businesses to decline, thereby undercutting the risk of failure, which is capitalism's prime motivator, and handicapping small owners for no justifiable reason.[11] Their criticisms parallel Lowi's to some extent, but they do not conclude that socializing risk entails some form of permanent receivership. They propose to rectify the dilemma of imposing double standards with a series of political-economic changes that make criteria for productivity and equity interdependent.[12]

In a theoretical sense, the socialization of risk can benefit everyone in the long term. For this to occur, the responsibilities for risk-socializing policies must be community, or public, responsibilities. Public officials, in conjunction with the firms targeted for aid, set the guidelines and implementation procedures for policy. Citizens must be adequately represented in this process to assure that provisions for both productivity and equity are incorporated in the policy. This requirement suggests that it must be a "rational-comprehensive" process designed for long-term planning. Otherwise, it might provide only productivity incentives in response to ad hoc problems, and, in the absence of adequate public representation, it may exclude those interests lacking necessary resources to lobby for assistance or omit public equity considerations. Politics operates in the short term, though, if for no other reason because today's decisions affect tomorrow's calculations.[13] In the short term, two basic points stand out: (1) citizens are the ultimate risk takers under policies that socialize risk; (2) businesses and other actors immediately associated with them (for example, unions) are generally the immediate beneficiaries. The likelihood of formulating risk-socializing policies in a manner that enhances popular control (let alone distributive justice) at the expense of disproportionate business influence is therefore remote.

This overview of the neoliberal concern to make productivity and equity interdependent is cursory but suggestive. In a sense, the goal is an adaptation of the neo-Marxist analysis of the capitalist state's "accumulation" and "legitimation" functions. This analysis holds that the capitalist state attempts to balance two contradictory functions. As an agent of the capitalist class, it must sustain capital accumulation. Simultaneously, it must maintain legitimacy before a public electorate by appearing to pursue the public interest and to give priority to the demands of citizens over those of special interests.[14] Industrial policy, however, is an attempt to resolve the contradiction. Its advocates argue that the liberal democratic state can provide the context for capital accumulation *in return for* its legitimacy by linking economic growth (capital accumulation) to equity or redistributional goals (legitimacy).[15] Nonetheless, the most persistent critics of industrial policy are from the left. They claim either that specific proposals are counterproductive panaceas, which lead, for example, to "deindustrialization," or that they belie commitments, which, in disproportionately benefiting corporate interests, are conservative, if not undemocratic. To the critics, one does not gain state-promoted capital accumulation without a cost, namely, equity and democratic representation and accountability.[16]

The Growth-Equity Equation

Reich and Thurow have concluded that traditional electoral and representational institutions are inadequate to the requirements of a complex, modern economy. The "zero-sum society" is similar to the world of interest group liberalism. Policymakers, as noted, rely on double standards for economic productivity and equity. As a result, policy options are trapped in a quagmire of zero-sum conflicts. A comprehensive approach to industrial policy, they argue, can correct these deficiencies. The United States cannot return to the productivity level of yesteryear—a level that was artificially inflated anyway by various international advantages and domestic protections (for example, deflated domestic energy prices). It can, however, establish internationally competitive productivity levels. They further argue that this can be accomplished while meeting domestic societal demands by moving toward a more acceptable range of equity, which itself is essential to worker productivity.

These industrial policy advocates give traditional democratic values prominence, but as a means to alleviate zero-sum conflicts and engender economic growth, not as ends. Reich thus asserts that "social justice is not incompatible with economic growth, but essential to it." "A collective willingness to endure major economic change," he maintains, "can come about only when citizens trust that the burdens and the benefits of such change will be shared equitably."[17] Thurow echoes the point: "a more equitable society is not in conflict with a more productive society—quite the contrary. . . . When sacrifices are needed in a democratic society, equity is the key."[18] Current economic policies, however, discourage facing up to equity or redistributive issues and therefore exacerbate the problem of attaining appropriate levels of growth. Their failures are traceable in large part to the ideological predispositions of business and policy elites, who tend to assume that equity flows from productivity, if they consider equity at all.[19]

The failure of policymakers to address equity and growth is nowhere better exemplified than in the 1981 Economic Recovery and Tax Act (ERTA). The presumption of growth helped justify tax slashes and accelerated depreciation to spur reinvestment, while blinding elites to the interrelationship between growth and equity.[20] The promise of economic growth has been a surrogate for addressing distributive justice, since it is widely believed that equity will flow from abundance. In a no-growth or low-growth economy, however, failure to address equity comes home to roost in the form of, among other things, increased state welfare expenditures that further attenuate economic recovery. Growth does not create equity; it simply provides more leeway for equity decisions in a world of insatiable wants. ("Economic growth for everyone cannot solve the problem because the demands are not for more but for parity.")[21] One does not increase female income beyond 59 percent of male income without decreasing male income proportionately. On average, gains may exceed losses (more likely where redistribution occurs in the context of growth), but starting or ending in the net loss column is real to the individuals who constitute the average. Policies that neglect this relationship between growth and equity only intensify the zero-sum character of an interest group liberal society. Nonetheless, sustaining economic growth (increasing productivity) is essential to establishing equity, however defined. The problem is to develop policies that allow for real growth in which the equity demands of former losers (women and minorities) and the gains of former winners (white males) can be accommodated or reconciled.[22]

Capitalism, for Thurow and Reich, has value as an allocation device, not as an ideology, though their writings are filled with examples of capitalist ideology informing, poorly, allocation decisions and market uses. They call for a series of policies designed to utilize the market allocation system while tapping into the incentive system that informs the behavior of business and policy elites. Thurow's proposals for the *productivity* side of the growth-equity equation include the establishment of a national investment committee, governmental funding for recapitalization and process research and development, investment guarantees to encourage moves from "sunset" to "sunrise" industries, a socialized sector of employment, and a government-funded safety net for individuals. Many of these parallel and complement Reich's proposals to utilize job vouchers, regional training programs, and investment incentives to upgrade the workforce and to replace mass production techniques with "flexible system" production.[23]

The Thurow-Reich proposals place the burden of risk squarely on the government. The goals of their proposals are straightforward. In Thurow's case, for example, the policies do designate obvious beneficiaries, and that is precisely the point. They are not hidden. The beneficiaries of the policies are articulated in terms of the public purposes behind the policies (productivity and equity), not hidden behind a sentiment that amounts to a generality (maintaining or unleashing free enterprise or invoking capitalist ideology as a smoke screen). The policies involve constraints or sanctions—they come with strings attached—to achieve the public ends. In Thurow's view, the adoption of the proposals would avoid the double standard of rescuing one interest at the expense of another or, as critics aver, of attempting to salvage major political interests simply because they control extensive capital investments, established labor pools, and the like.[24]

How plausible or viable the proposals are in the context of prevailing economic wisdom—the ideology and incentives of policy elites—is another matter. For example, Thurow recognizes that his proposals threaten vested interests and, in the case of the socialized employment program, require a restructuring of the economy. His call, in 1980, for responsible political parties acknowledged that the major problem is political but also that his analysis failed to deal adequately with the roles and values of interest groups, particularly business, in policy-making. By 1985, Thurow echoed Reich in calling for business leaders to recognize the value of giving workers greater responsibilities in more participatory workplaces.[25]

The Privileged Position of Business

The theoretical argument for justifying the socialization of risk—ultimately for resolving the "contradiction" between capital accumulation and political legitimacy—is best made by Charles E. Lindblom in *Politics and Markets*. Lindblom delineates the basic constraints that state and market interrelationships place on policy choices in a liberal democracy. Policymakers have a limited range of options that essentially require them to calculate trade-offs between economic needs and political values in making their decisions. Economic requirements normally take priority because policymakers accept the conventional wisdom that businesses require two preconditions, or "privileges," to do business: "those that directly assure profitability and those that give the corporation autonomy to pursue profits with little constraint." Lindblom recommends a combination of financial inducements to businesses to enhance their productivity and profitability in exchange for a measure of government control over them—in effect, a reduction in business autonomy by paying businesses to "waive some of their privileges."[26] Hereafter, his recommendation is termed the *pay-to-waive* strategy.

The pay-to-waive strategy is based on Lindblom's argument about the "privileged position of business." Business privilege derives from a dual system of public authority, which, he claims, characterizes liberal democracies. The institutions, practices, and traditions of liberal democratic governments ("polyarchies," in Lindblom's parlance) constitute one form of public authority. The activities of business and the role of the market constitute the other. In effect, public authority is "shared" by business, but the sharing is highly unequal. Business competes with government and political institutions and attempts to dominate democratic politics and its interest groups, parties, and elections. The competition tends "to restrict polyarchal rules and procedures to no more than a part of government and politics, and to challenge them even there."[27] The political agenda, in other words, is a function of the scope of conflict (to recall E. E. Schattschneider's useful phrase), and the prominence of business, and of political leaders' acquiescence to business, limits rather than expands the agenda. (Furthermore, with a limited agenda, citizens learn to acquiesce to business needs, internalizing business values as their own.)[28] The result of these phenomena is that business influence and success are greater than the influences and successes of other political institutions and practices within liberal democracies. Disproportionately greater: to gain approval for their policies, public officials must make concessions to business.[29]

In view of business privilege, two obvious questions stand out regarding the pay-to-waive strategy. Why would business leaders have any incentives to waive any privileges and accede to any measure of popular control? If they did, what would they get in return?

It is commonplace that American business claims to be averse to government regulations. Research on the attitudes and values of business leaders indicates that they have a generalized psychological disposition against regulations, an aversion built around the presumed virtues of the free enterprise system. This disposition enables them as a matter of course to oppose regulations that appear to contravene their activities, even if such regulations may promise greater gains for them in the future. As David Vogel puts it, "They do not understand that the American capitalist system requires a large degree of state intervention for its very survival; they only want to support those policies and agencies that directly benefit their firm or industry." At the same time, business people take for granted that the state should encourage productivity and its precondition, profitability.[30]

Business people can rationalize these contradictory attitudes about regulatory constraints and state-supported productivity because, in their minds, the free enterprise system is natural and integral to a free society. They thus predict, and often produce, dire consequences both in the aftermath of regulations and in the absence of favorable dispensations. If, for example, they believe that tax relief is necessary to spur investment, they often decide to defer new investments until taxes are reduced or tax abatements are granted.[31] Or, they accept or even support such favorable regulations or dispensations as protections and subsidies for sunset industries, since these are rationalized as exceptional cases.[32] They also accept regulations that effectively reallocate responsibility and blame from the firm to the state—regulations governing labor relations, unemployment compensation, employee drug use, health-related absenteeism, civil rights, affirmative action, and so on.[33]

How, then, is business to be induced or paid to waive any of its privileges? What incentives must government provide, and what can be gained in return? Several of the industrial policy advocates criticize business attitudes and practices, claiming that business managers look to the short term (the annual report to stockholders as the measure of managerial success) rather than to the long-term productive status of their firms and industries. Their recommendations, they believe, would provide incentives for business to take the longer view.[34] What is at stake, however, are not simply the terms and conditions of productivity. At stake are businesses' prerogatives or privileges in seeking these terms: "what is precious [to business leaders] about the American system is not so much its superior performance but rather the relative autonomy that its managers enjoy. . . . the real relevant meaning of freedom for the American bourgeoise is the ability of those who own or control economic resources to allocate or appropriate them as they see fit—without interference from either labor unions or governmental officials."[35] The main thing business leaders value is managerial autonomy, not simply greater productivity and profitability. Industrial policy proposals designed to improve economic productivity by socializing reinvestment risks are simply unrealistic if, in return for the benefits to business, public policy appears to constrain managerial autonomy.

Lindblom suggests two interrelated approaches that help illustrate how such proposals as Reich's and Thurow's could be adopted by public officials and reconciled with business privilege.[36] First, he proposes a "planner sovereignty" approach. Government could regulate demand, and thus indirectly production, by purchasing products. By regulating demand, such an approach would provide a general framework for implementing a version of Thurow's proposed shift from sunset to sunrise industries.[37] Second, he proposes a straightforward strategy to socialize risk. The market delegates to businesses decisions about resource allocation—decisions about reinvestment, diversification, technological innovation, organization of the work force, plant location, and so on. These decisions shape the economy's industrial structure and its abilities to save, invest, and consume; they therefore effectively constrain demand-side market controls (whether consumer or government purchases).[38] Resource allocation decisions, however, always incur risk, which business managers want to reduce. Policies that shift the costs of risk from individual firms to the state can reduce potential corporate costs.[39] Further, they can provide governmental sanction for various public interest objectives that concern Reich and Thurow, such as environmental quality, energy conservation, unemployment levels, and employee retraining, which involve factors that are external to the firm. Lindblom thus provides a framework of trade-offs—incentives for business and gains for public concerns.

There are practical limitations to the two approachs. The first offers inducements but with no real trade-offs in terms of government controls, and it does not directly address the issue of managerial autonomy or corporate discretion. The second is limited because, when risk is socialized, the prerequisites of businesses limit the trade-offs to those things with which business leaders are willing to part. Since their needs are practically all-encompassing (they need "income and wealth, deference, prestige, influence, power, and authority, among others"), their inclination to negotiate meaningful trade-offs is virtually nil. The point, however, can be generalized to both approaches. Public officials need to maintain conditions necessary for adequate business performance because business performs functions that officials "regard as indispensable."[40] Policymakers may attempt to utilize the wide range of incentives that motivate business people, but at the same time they are constrained by them and by the general dispositions of business managers to maintain and enhance their autonomy in a free enterprise system. For their part, business leaders may claim that only exceptional circumstances require supportive public policies, but they consistently ask for and receive appropriate inducements and incentives from public officials. In short, public officials and business elites have shared and reciprocal interests in maintaining an "acceptable" level of economic performance without constraining business activity.

A Rationale for Corporatism

The framework for industrial policy aims to attain the interdependent goals of productivity and equity. It relies on the reciprocal incentives of business and government elites to develop policies that socialize risk for their mutual benefit. The pay-to-waive strategy provides the sort of explicit rationale needed to justify incorporating major business interests within the policy process. Presumably, the policy framework and its outcomes would help resolve the contradiction between the state's need to sustain capital accumulation and growth for business and its need to maintain its legitimacy before the public. It raises a different sort of contradiction for liberal democracy, however, because its mutually beneficial exchanges between the state and business are the type that are central to *corporatist* explanations of the policy process. Thurow, Reich, and Lindblom understandably do not acknowledge this. Thurow and Reich write for popular audiences; the industrial policy debate is polemical, and proposals are often designed for specific constituencies. Thurow specifically disclaims any corporatist overtones, but his discussion of tripartite bargaining that puts an end to adversarial conflicts between businesses and public officials characterizes a policy process that parallels most accounts of corporatism.[41]

Regardless of their sentiments against government intrusion in a free enterprise system, business leaders are adept at rationalizing supportive governmental sanctions and subsidies. Moreover, public officials, recognizing the need to maintain adequate business performance, give their support. One manifestation of this relationship is the so-called political business cycle, in which public officials attempt to avoid blame at election time for poor economic performance (or receive credit for good performance).[42] State inducements to business in the context of electoral expectations can cut two ways, however. By adapting to popular expectations, public officials may pursue economic expansionist policies that simultaneously benefit business, and its need for an environment of growth, and constrain the autonomy of business elites, whose investment and marketing strategies must be undertaken in the context of policies keyed to electoral returns. Nonetheless, benefits overshadow constraints for the following reasons.

From the perspectives of business elites, there are two strong incentives to seek corporatist policy-making arrangements. First, corporatist policy-making tends to be insulated from electoral pressure, particularly for the larger organizations and their associated actors interacting with the bureaucracy. Second, business people's rhetoric may be opposed to government intrusion, but, to maintain the prerogatives of their free enterprise system, they find the constraints of policy elites, who understand the needs of business, less threatening than those the public would demand, particularly at times when popular distrust of business increases.[43] For example, business people surveyed about possible scenarios for business-government relationships had marked preferences for a libertarian scenario but also strong preferences for a corporatist alternative. Interestingly enough, more government policymakers than business people preferred the libertarian scenario; fewer policymakers than business people favored the corporatist one.[44] Thurow underscores the relevance of these incentives (insulation from adverse publicity) in a somewhat different context. He points out the hidden benefits of indirect subsidies that parade as regulatory market stabilizers: "no Congress would ever pass a law simply giving large farmers several hundred thousand dollars apiece. The same Congress will, however, pass price support legislation that does exactly the same thing. . . . this is one of the reasons why direct subsidies should be used rather than indirect subsidies. If we would not support them overtly, probably we should not support them covertly."[45]

These two incentives, especially the first, are reciprocated by policy elites. Public officials conceivably could utilize the political business cycle to pursue a classic divide-and-conquer strategy among various sectors of the economy, but they do not consistently do so. The advantages of a corporatist form of policy-making often outweigh such a strategy. Corporatism effectively reduces the scope of the electoral agenda. It tends to reduce pressures on elected officials to solve economic problems when these are transformed into technical problems to be dealt with by experts. It also frees administrative elites (the bureaucracy) from their putative responsibilities for adhering to legislative guidelines and exercising public authority when their functions are transferred to the sectors or organizations responsible for performance.[46] Nevertheless, administrative officials may have somewhat more autonomy than do their elective counterparts, who must compete on an electoral playing field in which the scope of conflict or the public agenda tends to be dominated by business values. (Few candidates for office would openly campaign on a pro-recession platform to slow inflationary growth.) Ironic as it seems, it is possible that the state's bureaucracy may have greater freedom to constrain business advocacy of state promotionalism and corporatistlike policy-making arrangements than elected officials do.[47] This possibility, however, represents an extreme and highly conjectural case. More plausible is the point that the shared interests of business people and public officials, both elective and administrative, can justify a more or less corporatist framework for the policy-making process.

To conclude that these implications of the industrial policy framework are problematic for traditional liberal democratic theory is an understatement. Corporatism is a policy framework for organizational elites. As such, it could be construed simply as a variation on the interest group liberal motif of interest accommodation—an improvement at that, since the relevant actors would be known as a matter of public record. Above all else, corporatism is justified on the basis of functional interest representation, on the basis that individual interests are best served through their functional organizations, not through their political participation, and that organizational elites are best situated to speak for these interests. Not even interest group liberalism purports to supersede popular constituencies with functional ones, since it justifies group access and accommodation partly on the grounds of citizens' overlapping memberships in ever-changing groups.

NOTES

An earlier version of this chapter appeared as "Reindustrialization, Liberal Democracy and Corporatist Representation" in *Political Science Quarterly* 101 (Fall 1986). Used by permission of the publisher.

1. Paul E. Peterson, Barry G. Rabe, and Kenneth H. Wong, *When Federalism Works* (Washington, D.C.: Brookings Institution, 1986), 132, report a few efforts to incorporate juridical-type guidelines. Bruce A. Ackerman and William T. Hassler, *Clean Coal/Dirty Air* (New Haven, Conn.: Yale University Press, 1981), provide a case study of one such effort that in fact proved to be counterproductive.

2. Robert B. Reich, *The Next American Frontier* (New York: New York Times Books, 1983); Felix Rohatyn, "The Coming Emergency and What Can Be Done about It," *New York Review of Books,* Dec. 4, 1980, 20–26, and "Reconstructing America," *New York Review of Books,* Mar. 5, 1981, 16–20 (these and other essays are reprinted in Rohatyn, *The Twenty-Year Century* [New York: Random House, 1984]); Lester C. Thurow, *The Zero-Sum Society* (New York: Basic Books, 1980) and *The Zero-Sum Solution* (New York: Simon and Schuster, 1985). On their neoliberalism, see Randall Rothenberg, *The Neoliberals* (New York: Simon and Schuster, 1985); David Osborne, *Laboratories of Democracy* (Cambridge, Mass.: Harvard Business School Press, 1988). Several of the neoliberals were active in 1984, 1988, and 1992 Democratic presidential campaign efforts. The 1988 effort was disparaged as "leveraged liberalism" by the *Wall Street Journal,* June 23, 1988.

3. William E. Hudson, "The Feasibility of a Comprehensive U.S. Industrial Policy," *Political Science Quarterly* 100 (Fall 1985): 461–78, at 468–72.

4. Samuel Brittan, "The Economic Contradictions of Democracy," *British Journal of Political Science* 5 (Apr. 1975): 129–59, at 130; Samuel P. Huntington, "The United States," in *The Crisis of Democracy,* ed. Michel Crozier, Samuel P. Huntington, and Joji Watanuki (New York: New York University Press, 1975), 59–118, at 106–15. See the discussion in chapter 3 herein.

5. Samuel Bowles, David M. Gordon, and Thomas E. Weisskopf, *Beyond the Waste Land* (Garden City, N.Y.: Anchor Books, 1984); Martin Carnoy and Derek Shearer, *Economic Democracy: The Challenge of the 1980s* (Armonk, N.Y.: M. E. Sharpe, 1980). Some of these issues are addressed in chapter 7 herein.

6. In certain respects the controversy is similar to one during Roosevelt's first New Deal, but that one was set aside (or at least its significance ob-

scured) by the second New Deal's shift from a "concert of interests" to the regulated but competitive economy. For an overview, see Arthur M. Schlesinger, Jr., *The Coming of the New Deal* (Boston, Mass.: Houghton Mifflin, 1959) and *The Politics of Upheaval* (Boston, Mass.: Houghton Mifflin, 1960).

7. For a comprehensive but critical survey, see Yair Aharoni, *The No-Risk Society* (Chatham, N.J.: Chatham House Publishers, 1981).

8. See the brief discussion in chapter 4.

9. On the neo-Marxist analysis of the state's accumulation and legitimation functions, see Ralph Miliband, *Marxism and Politics* (New York: Oxford University Press, 1977), chap. 4; James O'Connor, *The Corporations and the State* (New York: Harper and Row, 1974), chap. 6; Claus Offe, "The Theory of the Capitalist State and the Problem of Policy Formation," in *Stress and Contradiction in Modern Capitalism,* ed. Leon N. Lindberg, Robert Alford, Colin Crouch, and Clause Offe (Lexington, Mass.: D. C. Heath, 1975), 125–44.

10. This contrasts also with neoconservative criticisms that socializing risk supports new class and economically disadvantaged interests rather than traditional community and business interests. See Sanford Weiner and Aaron Wildavsky, "The Prophylactic Presidency," in *The Third Century,* ed. Seymour Martin Lipset (Chicago: University of Chicago Press, 1979), 133–52, esp. 144–52; James R. Bennett and Thomas J. DiLorenzo, *Underground Government: The Off-Budget Sector* (Washington, D.C.: Cato Institute, 1983).

11. Thurow, *Zero-Sum Society,* 19–24, 76–82, 203–11; Reich, *American Frontier,* 176–200.

12. See Robert B. Reich, Lester C. Thurow, Gus Tyler, and Michael Harrington, "'A Path for America': Three Comments on Michael Harrington's Article and His Reply," *Dissent* 30 (Winter 1983): 25–32; Lester C. Thurow, *What Kind of Industrial Policy?* (Washington, D.C.: Democracy Project Reports, No. 2, Jan. 13, 1982), 5–12.

13. Charles E. Lindblom, "The Science of 'Muddling Through,'" *Public Administration Review* 19 (Spring 1959): 79–88, is the classic essay distinguishing rational-comprehensive policy-making from the "incrementalist" version. Some scholars view it as a defense of the interest group liberal process of accommodation, but cf. Lindblom's *The Intelligence of Democracy* (New York: The Free Press, 1965).

14. See note 9. Admittedly, the point here overgeneralizes since it collapses the distinction between *instrumental* and *structural* Marxism.

15. Cf. Douglas A. Chalmers, "Corporatism and Comparative Politics," in *New Directions in Comparative Politics,* ed. Howard J. Wiarda (Boulder, Colo.: Westview Press, 1985), 56–79, at 62ff.

16. Barry Bluestone and Bennett Harrison, *The Deindustrialization of America* (New York: Basic Books, 1982); Bowles, Gordon, and Weisskopf, *Beyond the Waste Land,* esp. 208–25, cf. 321–22, 383; Alan Wolfe, *Amer-*

ica's Impasse (Boston: South End Press, 1981); theme sections of *Working Papers* 7 (Nov.–Dec. 1980) and *democracy* 1 (July 1981). Rohatyn is most frequently charged with promoting business conservatism and, by one critic, authoritarian planning. See Maurice Zeitlin, "Democratic Disinvestment," *democracy* 2 (Apr. 1982): 69–80.

17. Reich, *American Frontier*, 20, 200. See also Rohatyn, "Reconstructing America," 16–20.

18. Thurow, *Zero-Sum Solution*, 382.

19. Leonard Silk and David Vogel, *Ethics and Profits* (New York: Simon and Schuster, 1976), chaps. 7–8, esp. 189–97, 232–39, cf. 136–51; David Vogel, "The Inadequacy of Contemporary Opposition to Business," *Daedalus* 109 (Summer 1980): 47–58.

20. Lester C. Thurow, "Getting Serious about Tax Reform," *Atlantic Monthly*, Mar. 1981, 68–72; Robert B. Reich, "Beyond Reaganomics: How the Rage for Supply-Side Riches Is Impoverishing Our Politics," *New Republic*, Nov. 18, 1981, 19–25, expanded as chap. 8, in Reich, *American Frontier*.

21. Thurow, *Zero-Sum Society*, 190.

22. See ibid., 16–24, 178–89, 194–208; *Zero-Sum Solution*, 21ff., 60–66, chaps. 3, 5, 12. See also Reich's concerns with dislocation and retraining and investments in human capital in *American Frontier*, 208–23, 239–46, 256–75. Cf. Fred Hirsch and John H. Goldthorpe, eds., *The Political Economy of Inflation* (Cambridge, Mass.: Harvard University Press, 1978), esp. chap. 2; Hirsch, *Social Limits to Growth* (Cambridge, Mass.: Harvard University Press, 1976), 9–12, 117–22, 173–90. By 1991, women's wages had increased to 78 percent of men's, and annual earnings to 68 percent, but men's wages declined, according to a Labor Department report. See Mary Kane, "Women Narrowing Wage Gap," *Ann Arbor News*, Sept. 26, 1991.

23. See Thurow, *Zero-Sum Society*, 78–102, 145–53, 167–211; Thurow, *Zero-Sum Solution*, chap. 9. See citations to Reich, *American Frontier*, in the preceding note, esp. 239–46, and his arguments for flexible system production, 127–39.

24. In effect, Thurow proposes to make systematic the ad hoc policies criticized in Theodore J. Lowi, *The End of Liberalism*, 2d ed. (New York: W. W. Norton, 1979), 271–94, and Reich, *American Frontier*, 176–86. For debate over Thurow's position, see Barry Bluestone, Harley Shaiken, and Lester Thurow, "Roundtable: Reindustrialization and Jobs," *Working Papers* 7 (Nov.–Dec. 1980): 47–59.

25. Thurow, *Zero-Sum Society*, 203–7, 212–14; Thurow, *Zero-Sum Solution*, chap. 6; Reich, *American Frontier*, chaps. 11–12.

26. Charles E. Lindblom, *Politics and Markets* (New York: Basic Books, 1977), 345–51, at 349–50. For examples and their problems, see 98–103, 147–48, 152–57, 174–75.

27. Ibid., 190. On the dual system of authority and business privilege, see

chaps. 10–14. Strictly speaking, polyarchy is not a form of government or a type of political system. *Polyarchy* refers to the essential rules, practices, and traditions that constrain struggles for political authority, establish basic rights and expectations, and inform the roles and behavior of political actors and institutions (elected officials, parties, interest groups). Practically speaking, polyarchies and liberal or constitutional democracies are synonymous. See, more particularly, ibid., chaps. 10, 12.

28. Lindblom calls this process of indoctrination *circularity.* See ibid., chaps. 15–16.

29. Charles E. Lindblom, "Why Government Must Cater to Business," *Business and Society Review,* no. 27 (Fall 1978), 5–6 and n. 15.

30. David Vogel, "Why Businessmen Distrust Their State: The Political Consciousness of American Corporate Executives," *British Journal of Political Science* 8 (Jan. 1978): 45–78, at 69. This disposition is not monolithic, however. See James O'Toole, "What's Ahead for the Business-Government Relationship," *Harvard Business Review* 57 (Mar.–Apr. 1979): 94–105. The rest of this section draws on Vogel's essay; Silk and Vogel, *Ethics and Profits,* 162–77, 193–217; Edward S. Herman, *Corporate Control, Corporate Power* (New York: Cambridge University Press, 1981), chap. 5; Thurow, *Zero-Sum Society,* chap. 6.

31. Lindblom, *Politics and Markets,* 173–75, 180–85.

32. Vogel, "Why Businessmen Distrust," 67–69. See also Herman, *Corporate Control,* 251–301.

33. See the insightful comments on affirmative action by Barbara R. Bergmann, "An Affirmative Look at Hiring Quotas," *New York Times,* Jan. 10, 1982. On business interests in the antismoking campaign, see Alexander Cockburn, "The Great American Smoke Screen," *Wall Street Journal,* June 16, 1988. On business advantages under the new regulation, see Herman, *Corporate Control,* 182–84.

34. Reich, *American Frontier,* 140–72; Felix G. Rohatyn, "Time for a Change," *New York Review of Books,* Aug. 18, 1983, 46–49.

35. Vogel, "Why Businessmen Distrust," 54. For supportive arguments, see Bowles, Gordon, and Weisskopf, *Beyond the Waste Land,* 62–121, 158–60, 163–70, 252–58.

36. Lindblom, *Politics and Markets,* 98–103, 147–48, 152–57. The approaches are discussed in greater detail in Robert C. Grady, "Reindustrialization, Liberal Democracy, and Corporatist Representation," *Political Science Quarterly* 101 (Fall 1986): 415–32, at 425–27.

37. The relationships between the Department of Defense and the defense industry seem to provide examples of planner sovereignty, examples Lindblom would not recommend. It is unclear, to say the least, if DOD purchases affect production or if the promise of new products affect purchase orders. See James M. Fallows, *National Defense* (New York: Random House, 1981).

38. Lindblom dismisses the view that corporate managers have developed a sense of "social responsibility" that guides their delegated responsibilities;

whatever their values, they exercise discretion. See *Politics and Markets,* 155–56. For a survey of problems associated with corporate responsibility, see Herman, *Corporate Control,* chap. 7.

39. Lindblom assumes that government is no more error-prone in efficiency pricing than business is. See *Politics and Markets,* 156–57.

40. Ibid., 174–75.

41. Thurow, *Zero-Sum Solution,* chap. 9, esp. 290–91. In all likelihood, Thurow conflates "liberal" and "state" corporatism, a distinction made in the next chapter. See also, Rohatyn, *Twenty-Year Century,* esp. chaps. 1, 7.

42. Edward R. Tufte, *Political Control of the Economy* (Princeton, N.J.: Princeton University Press, 1978). For an overview of this topic, see Kristen R. Monroe, "Political Manipulation of the Economy: A Closer Look at Political Business Cycles," *Presidential Studies Quarterly* 13 (Winter 1983): 37–49.

43. On the first point, see Lester M. Salamon and John J. Siegfried, "Economic Power and Political Influence: The Impact of Industry Structure on Public Policy," *American Political Science Review* 71 (Sept. 1977): 1026–43; David R. Cameron, "The Expansion of the Public Economy: A Comparative Analysis," *American Political Science Review* 72 (Dec. 1978): 1243–61. On the second, see Silk and Vogel, *Ethics and Profits;* Vogel, "Inadequacy of Contemporary Opposition to Business," and Thurow, *Zero-Sum Solution,* 285–89ff., on business leaders wanting to have it both ways: government aids without government constraints. See also Seymour Martin Lipset and William Schneider, *The Confidence Gap,* rev. ed. (Baltimore: Johns Hopkins University Press, 1987), esp. chaps. 8–9.

44. O'Toole, "What's Ahead for the Business-Government Relationship." These kinds of preferences are reiterated in Chris Welles, "The 'Competitiveness' Craze: A New Name, an Old Idea," *Business Week,* Jan. 19, 1987, 31.

45. Thurow, *Zero-Sum Society,* 145; see also his points at 21–22, 122–23, 203–11. Thurow might now acknowledge that Congress will pass out enormous sums in direct subsidies because of the explosion in farm support expenditures in the 1980s. See Jonathan Rauch, "The Great Farm Gamble," *National Journal* 29 (Mar. 1986): 759–62.

46. On the limits of a divide-and-conquer strategy, see Eric A. Nordlinger, *On the Autonomy of the Democratic State* (Cambridge, Mass.: Harvard University Press, 1981), 138–39; Frank Hearn, "The Corporatist Mood in the United States," *Telos* 56 (Summer 1983): 41–57.

47. See Nordlinger, *Autonomy of the Democratic State,* 144–202, esp. 157–74, for suggestions. See also Wolfgang Streeck and Philippe C. Schmitter, eds., *Private Interest Government: Beyond Market and State* (Beverly Hills, Calif.: Sage Publications, 1985), 19–20.

CHAPTER 6

Corporatism and Liberal Principles

In many of the advanced industrialized nations, elites prefer that policy be initiated and implemented in an interactive process between the state and its major functional organizations. Theorists of corporatism claim that it can explain the policy process under such circumstances, whereas pluralism, or its interest group liberal perversion, is inadequate. Interactive policy-making is a product of architectonic design—at least theoretically. Exchanges between economic and policy elites are designed and undertaken for mutual benefit; they are not simply by-products of countervailing powers or accommodations and compromises between contending interests.[1]

Corporatism may be preferable to pluralism as an explanatory theory of the policy process, but is it an improvement over the elitism and undemocratic aspects of interest group liberalism? Superficially it is not, although corporatists are not unanimous in answering such a question. Corporatism long carried conceptual baggage associated with European statism and Latin American authoritarianism, but it is no longer burdened with such connotations. Scholars now distinguish between "state" or "authoritarian" corporatism and "liberal," "societal," or "neocorporatism." The first involves an imposed form of control over key sectors that primarily aims to benefit organs of the state; the second, a form of state-sanctioned (and often but not necessarily state-induced) functional representation in which organizational leaders serve as interest intermediaries between individuals, the organization, and the state, reciprocally benefiting all three sets of actors.[2] The second notion of corporatism is applied to comparatively weak states, that is, states with a tradition of constraints on their power typical of liberal democracies. Because there are no pure corporatist states, some scholars prefer the term "quasi-corporatism" for assessing real-world cases.[3] Quasi-corporatism also seems to be preferable to liberal corporatism, which, when juxtaposed with state or authoritarian corporatism, suggests that functional representation in a liberal democracy is not as problematic as it is. Hereafter, *corporatism* and *quasi-corporatism* are used in reference to what corporatist scholars label *liberal, societal,* or *neocorporatism.*

Notwithstanding the appeal of today's version of corporatism over the statist or authoritarian varieties, elite governance of interest group membership is always a central aspect of corporatism. It is a form of political management involving decision making between public and private sector elites and the "top-down" ability of elites to represent *and* constrain the interests of individuals in their jurisdictions. Corporatists take for granted the proposition that individuals' social and economic needs and values are shaped by their membership in associations that hold their primary allegiance. To be sure, individuals have a variety of interests, and their votes in political elections may reflect these interests (whether "private" or "civic"). Ultimately, however, the importance of their interests is measured by the collective priorities of the organization and is subordinated to them. Organizational representatives negotiate with public officials and conclude policy agreements for which they also may have enforcement responsibilities. Social and economic problems, which otherwise are subject to electoral mandates, can be "depoliticized" and transformed into technical problems to be dealt with by experts. In return for corporate representation, increased "governability" and stability can be provided through the abilities of functional interest representatives to control member demands, and the "unruliness" and instability of popular representation may thereby be ameliorated. The net effect is to reduce the electoral agenda and help insulate public officials, both elected and administrative, and private interest elites from popular constraints. Corporatism thus deflates the significance of traditional forms of influence on politics by citizens qua citizens.[4]

It does not follow that maintenance of the status quo is the norm. Certain types of interest organizations have a greater degree of autonomy and independence from government control than others do. In bargaining with so-called peak associations of capital and labor, governments must make concessions to them in return for their political cooperation. In Europe, organized labor has been a major beneficiary because tripartite bargaining "opens up a range of issues to working-class demands which go way beyond the limited, institutionally segregated economistic demands of collective bargaining under liberal capitalism" in contemporary pluralist states.[5] But it does not further follow that incurring representative responsibilities and reaping benefits of mutual cooperation serve as incentives to democratize functional organizations and the process of corporatist decision making. The principal objective is the mobilization of group members and resources in support of public policy rather than the expansion of political representation and influence through functional interest interaction and accommodation.[6] For this reason, corporatism may be viewed as a variation on the neo-Marxist theme that the state acts to ensure the conditions for capital accumulation and for its own legitimacy, often with only token gains for such other interests as labor.[7]

Clearly, corporatism has explanatory advantages over pluralism. Critics charge that pluralists fail to acknowledge the significance of reciprocal incentives of government and interest group elites to accommodate themselves at the expense of public accountability. At best, however, pluralism can be criticized for its inconsistency or confusion; at worst, in its interest group liberal reincarnation, it can be criticized for being elitist by default. Pluralist theory is not elitist by design, though. Pluralists do not claim that politics is a process of conflict mediation and resolution between functionally differentiated interests, a process that necessitates decision rules and decision-making organizations designed to differentiate between functional (and thus hierarchical) needs. Corporatists do make this claim. In this and other respects, corporatism is at odds with certain fundamental norms of constitutional or liberal democratic theory. Economic and political elites attempt to minimize the role of legislatures in delineating the authority and actions of functional bodies, to reduce public constraints on their actions, and to exercise authority for, and over, their constituents. This chapter examines the problematic relationship between corporatism and liberal theory after considering, in the next section, whether corporatism is viable in the United States.

Corporatism in the United States

Critics of pluralism considered corporatism a label for interest group liberal politics. They demurred from using it, notwithstanding abundant evidence that quasi-corporatist forms of policy-making are the norm for major areas of public policy (namely, industrial and regulatory policies; utility, transportation, and agricultural policies; labor relations, and professional association "licensing" practices).[8] The industrial policy debate, however, has brought the issue of corporatism in the United States back to center stage, at least for its intellectual protagonists. Corporatist theoreticians are enamored of European experiences with corporatism, as are the industrial policy advocates, who cite tripartite framework agreements and the social contract device as models for U.S. policymakers. They pay scant attention to the conditions that made pluralism the dominant public philosophy and interest group liberalism palatable, though.

Notwithstanding corporatism's appeal, there are some fairly predictable criticisms of using it to explain the policy process in the United States and to develop an industrial policy framework. The United States is one of the weakest of traditionally weak liberal democratic states because of its fragmentation through federalism and the separation of powers. The prevailing values of its political culture are antagonistic to corporatist practices. The national government's jurisdictions are simply too large and diversified.[9] These sorts of criticisms focus primarily on the context of the national state and a presumably monolithic political culture that supports it. They are understandable but misleading or mistaken on three grounds.

First, a corporatist state is not monolithic; it is corporatist or pluralist by degrees and varies from one policy arena (or sector) to another. The criticisms, however, presume that the state is either corporatist or not and that what many corporatist scholars label quasi- or predominantly corporatist forms of plural bargaining and interest intermediation are simply advanced or efficiently organized forms of pluralism.[10] Up to a point, this assessment seems appropriate. Many characteristics of economic and policy elites and their reciprocal incentives for seeking the advantages of corporatist policy-making, which were examined in the preceding chapter, have familiar contours. They describe phenomena with a long-standing history in the literature critical of pluralism. Well-known arguments by Theodore Lowi, Grant McConnell, and others regarding the delegation of legislative authority and the role of private governments demonstrate that, in practice, American liberals have accommodated themselves to functional representation as though it were merely a theoretical inconvenience.

Consider, however, some implications of a simon-pure approach to delineating corporatism and pluralism. This sort of position would require one to conclude that the pluralist critics McConnell and Lowi simply misunderstood American politics or misinterpreted such seminal pluralist scholars as Earl Latham and David Truman. Political reality is variable, and the theoretical frameworks designed to explain politics are more fruitfully envisioned as points along a continuum. One corporatist scholar suggests a continuum ranging from discipline or control (authoritarian corporatism), through variations of corporatism and pluralism involving representation and coordination, to "contestation" (representation without exerting control over or compromising group interests). Others suggest variability across continua ranging from strong corporatism, through moderate (or medium) and weak corporatism, to pluralism or structured pluralism.[11] These suggestions understandably downplay variability within the pluralist dimensions. A modified continuum that taps variations within pluralism is the following:

| State | Liberal | Interest Group | "Classic" |
| Corporatism | Corporatism | Liberalism | Pluralism |

As pluralist practices shift from purely voluntary interest groups operating with the state as neutral umpire to well-organized interests that rely on, among other things, state regulatory policies to gain advantages, they begin to shift on the continuum toward the characteristics of interest group liberal practices. In some cases, the tendency results in quasi-corporatist practices of the sort noted earlier; in others, it simply results in interest group liberalism. Further along the continuum is liberal corporatism (or simply corporatism in the language used here), then state (or authoritarian) corporatism. In summary, if the variability of politics is assumed and the purist criticisms discounted, variations on pluralism and corporatism can be anticipated for differing policy arenas and at various subsystem levels within a national state.

Second, criticisms that the political values of the United States are unreceptive to corporatist practices presuppose a predominantly libertarian interpretation of political culture. The nation's political culture is much more complex than that, though. It is made up of a mosaic of values and assumptions that confront individuals with ongoing conflicts. Such individualist values as equal opportunity and individual initiative often cannot easily be reconciled with the organizational requirements of political and economic processes that rely on these values as incentives for action but produce inequalities and dependency. These conflicts result from long-standing commitments to individualist values and organizational or "public" goods—commitments that may be irreconcilable in any precise philosophical sense but are present nonetheless.[12]

Throughout American history, possessive individualist values have rationalized various forms of government promotions for business interests, frequently under the guise of promoting individual opportunities and choices. Appeals to individualism have helped justify such governmentally sanctioned and supported efforts as Hamilton's economic policy proposals, winning the West with railroad land grants and subsidies, assisting agricultural development through the land grant colleges, and developing interstate highway and air passenger transportation systems based on national defense priorities (and, in the case of the latter, on aircraft originally developed for military use). Some writers have relied on elite or class domination theories of history to explain the persistent connection between individualist ideals and the public's support for organizational objectives.[13] In assuming capitalist hegemony over the political culture, however, they make the obverse error of those who deny the political culture is receptive to corporatism. Other writers stress the complex and sometimes contradictory facets of the political culture and how these can help sustain the sorts of policy-making processes and outcomes that are characteristic of corporatism. Charles Lindblom's distinction between "grand" and "secondary" issues exemplifies this sort of analysis.

Grand issues concern the proper distribution of economic resources and power. These are frequently subordinated to secondary issues: questions about improper governmental interference with the market and the responsibility of government, not business, for the economic and social well-being of citizens. The distinction is one of several that Lindblom makes in analyzing the pervasiveness of popular preferences for the private sector, even when its activities are sustained by government acceding to business demands for privileges.[14] Better yet is Louis Hartz's imaginative use of the Horatio Alger myth and the law of Whig compensation to illustrate how individualist ideals were reconciled with Hamiltonian capitalism (in Hartz's parlance, state *promotionalism* of business interests) when it superseded Jeffersonian democracy. The Alger myth of individual initiative and self-help enabled individuals to rationalize state promotionalism because they believed it supported those who earned their advantages and did not affect those who lacked initiative. Whig economic elitism, discredited as a vestige of aristocracy by the Jeffersonians, thus was compensated with the emergence of capitalism.[15] Elite theorist critics of pluralism might refer to the analysis of Lindblom, Hartz, and others as examples of collusion between the state and capitalists. Whatever one's ideological bent, their analysis portrays the emergent characteristics of corporatistlike arrangements that have been encouraged by supportive public values.[16]

Third, there is some validity to the criticism that the United States is too large and its constituencies too diversified to promote and sustain a corporatist system.[17] Factors of scale and diversity underlie corporatist scholars' recognition that a state is corporatist by degrees and that the extent of its corporatist practices varies from one policy arena (or sector) to another. (As Lester Thurow notes, only critics of industrial policies, not their proponents, assume a monolithic, centralized framework.)[18] In fact, much of the focus in the corporatist literature is on the national level. This is understandable. The more visible industrial policy advocates hope to encourage coordination of the national economy and a reduction in the level of dysfunctional subsystem conflicts and fragmented, ad hoc policies. Some policy arenas seem to presuppose national centralization—for example, trade policy and assistance with sunset and sunrise industries—but the national officials' support for industrial policies tends to decline after the initial, highly general proposals are transformed into specific plans that risk alienating established constituencies.[19] Other policy arenas, however, are compatible with decentralization—for example, infrastructural investment (transportation, communication, physical resources) and economic development activities (investment banking, job training, tax abatements, and loan guarantees). With these, state and local jurisdictions overcome some of the objections to national level corporatism (scale, diversity, and so forth).[20]

State officials often have more clearly defined policy needs and economic constituencies than their national counterparts have, and they are able to support fairly well-defined industrial policy proposals. For example, the Rhode Island "Greenhouse Compact" proposed several specific programs for industrial and economic development through incentives, governmental supports, and minimal constraints on business management autonomy. The compact emerged from tripartite negotiations between business, labor, and public officials, along with representatives of the banking community and outside consultants— compared with national politics, a relatively narrow range of constituents. Nevertheless, it failed ratification by a 4−1 margin in a popular referendum. Interestingly, the compact failed partly because of the required referendum, which undercut the advantages of its insulation from politics during the elite negotiations, where its terms were agreed upon.[21]

Several factors make corporatist arrangements palatable at the state level while they remain unpalatable at the national level. State and local versions of corporatism are encouraged by federal programs designed to support urban and infrastructural redevelopment and by fiscal austerity that has inspired local jurisdictions to promote the development of taxing and policy authorities. The latter are relatively insulated from politics and organized around the "viewpoints of banking and business participants."[22] Moreover, state and local government activities frequently have an almost mercantilistic quality in the context of the national economy. State governments held hostage to "capital flight" (corporate disinvestment and relocation across state lines) are compelled to develop protectionist or imperialistic economic policies—protectionist policies characterized Michigan's collaboration with General Motors and the United Automobile Workers to develop the Poletown Cadillac plant, and imperialist policies were manifest in competitive state bidding for the GM Saturn plant in Tennessee and the Toyota plant in Kentucky.[23] These problems may exacerbate national problems that national industrial policies are designed to ameliorate, but they reinforce state and local incentives to undertake corporatist forms of policy organization.

The constraints placed on states and their incentives for developing corporatist strategies to attain economic objectives suggest that the U.S. system of federalism provides a supportive framework for corporatism at the subnational level. The states are vulnerable to changes in the national economy and frequently are dependent on providing satisfactory inducements to corporations that otherwise have the capacity to leave one geographic jurisdiction for another. Quasi-corporatist policy arrangements provide a means for satisfying various constituents in the states while adjusting to corporate needs.[24] While the research on corporatist practices in the federal system is piecemeal and developed from examples and case studies, the situation of the small democracies of Western Europe (Scandanavia, the Benelux nations, Austria, and Switzerland), which are constrained by the broader European economy, provides an analogous model for the roles of state governments. These nations have been more supportive of corporatist arrangements than their larger European counterparts have because they have proved to be more vulnerable to changes in the international economy.[25] By analogy, the mercantilistic and protectionist roles of state governments are predicated on the interstate mobility of corporations in the national economy. Intrastate constituents hope to realize a reduction in economic dislocation and the promise of economic development, in return for the provision of various incentives required by businesses (infrastructural improvements, tax abatements, land acquisition, educational and training packages for the workforce, and the like).[26]

Reconciling Corporatism with Liberal Democracy

In the 1970s, when students of comparative politics helped revive the notion of corporatism by freeing it from statist and authoritarian connotations, they promoted it as an alternative to both pluralist and

Marxist explanatory frameworks.[27] Subsequently, several scholars accepted the compatibility of corporatism with liberal democracy or discounted the significance of its differences with pluralism.[28] Most of the leading theorists of corporatism, however, acknowledge that its relation to democracy is problematic. Compatibility is contingent on the level or extent of corporatist organizational development, the nature of internal conflicts and external relations with other states, governmental structures and administrative organization, and so forth.[29]

Philippe Schmitter, one of the more prolific corporatists, opines that corporatism may subordinate the individualist and egalitarian norms of traditional liberal democracy to a form of "vicarious" democracy. In vicarious democracy, mass politics and the voluntary associations of pluralism become the domain of largely symbolic rituals, displaced by a "science of organization" in which the "reasonable, well-staffed and recognized association" of fairly well-developed corporatist regimes becomes "the basic unit of democracy."[30] In Schmitter's scenario, governments may indeed become accountable and responsive, but not necessarily to the voluntary associations that members join to advance their most salient interests. Instead, governments may become more accountable and responsive to the organizations that have become best organized and most strategically located, through skill or luck, to advance ends promoted by their technical elites and professional staffs. Schmitter's concerns are not merely speculative. Since the 1970s, interest group research has noted the increased importance of entrepreneurial organizations, often developed around single or narrow issues, which rely more heavily on technical experts than on constituency size and pressure politics. Many of these organizations promote policy agendas that are independent of the broad spectrum of interests actually preoccupying their members, and they represent primarily the organization leadership when the membership is largely formal and inactive.[31]

Schmitter has faith, however, that vicarious democracy will prove to be only a temporary stage in the development of corporatist-based democracy. He believes that in the long run the traditional liberal adage, "each person is the best judge of his or her own interests," will be vindicated as governments and organizational elites respond to the "real" interests of individual citizens. When corporatist regimes respond to these "really felt" interests, they will shape and modify the practices and objectives of organizations to accommodate citizens, both members of organizations and others previously excluded, and to incorporate these individuals within participatory constituency units.[32] However hopeful he may be, Schmitter is not overly optimistic in attributing democratic progress to corporatism, since it is easily corrupted by conservative or statist elites, but even more caution is appropriate. Corporatism may permit greater political equality between functional organizations that are *recognized* as actors in the policy process than do the informal arrangements of pluralism, but it tends to institutionalize inequalities between the organized and recognized and the informal and unrecognized, or between the "more equally competent and privileged class, sectoral and professional interests and [the] less equally competent and organized ones." The result is "a sort of corporatism for the functionally privileged. . . . [and] a sort of residual pluralism for the distributionally disadvantaged and the culturally underprivileged." [33]

Schmitter's caveat is familiar to students of pluralism. Lowi has disparaged interest group liberalism as a form of "socialism for the organized, capitalism for the unorganized." The seminal pluralist, David Truman, discounted functional representation in a similar if less extreme manner. Referring to the earlier guild socialist proposals to institutionalize representation along occupational lines, he made the obvious point that occupational groups are not the sole claimants on functional representation and that "even in so restricted an arrangement the distribution of seats would have to be relatively arbitrary." Truman further averred that "if this difficulty were surmounted, the resulting scheme would freeze the patterns of access and confine them to groups recognized in the apportionment," favoring "organized interest groups against the unorganized." [34] Critics of pluralism argued, of course, that the problems Truman anticipated were latent in pluralist theory and became manifest when pluralism evolved, or degenerated, into interest group liberalism.

Corporatism involves significant grants of public authority to the organizations and interests that participate in the policy process; they literally are authorized to act on behalf of their membership and to implement the policy outcomes within the organizations. The problem facing advocates of corporatism is that their proffered theory would appear to exacerbate the sorts of tendencies the critics ascribe to pluralism and interest group liberalism. Precisely how is the power of the private association, and its claims on constituency representation, to be justified? In the absence of any explicit justification for the public authority of private interests, the corporatists' assumption that adequate representation and accountability can be secured in policymaking arrangements between governments and major interest organizations is problematic and begs the question. Furthermore, the burden for corporatist theorists is not merely to demonstrate why extant organizations should be represented and play authoritative roles in policy-making. For a variety of reasons having to do with expertise, efficiency, economic stability, and the like, this case can plausibly be made. The burden also is to demonstrate why other interests should be excluded (or, why they should also be incorporated).

Liberal theory can accommodate delegations of authority to functional interests, but such delegations must be carefully and explicitly circumscribed. At least two principles should govern the delegation. The delegation should be granted to secure public ends, and public ends should be established by the elected legislative body. (These points are further developed in chapter 9.) Past practices do not provide grounds for optimism, however. Legislative bodies are not ordinarily adept at articulating clear and precise standards to govern their delegations of authority, as the critics of interest group liberalism show. Moreover, the net effect of unconstrained delegations of authority to agencies and interest organizations is to sanction the claims of private interests to exercise public authority. In the United States, the familiar litany of criticisms about the inadequacies of interest group liberalism underscores the problem facing corporatists.

Many functional bodies have been authorized through delegations of legislative authority involving deliberations that are minimal or imprecise about the ways and means to attain public ends. The legitimacy of their decisions has been measured by the extent to which they accommodate the groups represented, not by their correspondence to public objectives established in legislative deliberations. For example, state public utility and federal trade regulatory policies were initially authorized in legislative programs providing for functional bodies that would effect the public interest as it was promulgated by legislative action. The history of practices by these bodies, however, has been to shield their roles from legislative review and to make decisions that accommodate affected interests, not to meet the public interest criteria.[35] Independent regulatory agencies' practice of undertaking their legislative and juridical roles (rule-making and case-by-case adjudication) in conjunction with private interests claiming to represent relevant constituencies spawned a large body of literature about the agency-capture or clientele-capture thesis.[36] In addition, agricultural commodity supports—for example, the tobacco subsidy—have consistently been governed by functional interests. The fact that their policies are regularly reviewed and sanctioned by Congress can be cited to support claims that this practice approximates the guidelines for delegating authority based on legislative deliberations that establish public interest criteria. But the practice is one of the few exceptions to general practices typified by utility and trade regulatory policies, and how closely it approximates the criteria is controversial.[37]

Typically, justifications invoking the public interest are based on the assumption that the development of appropriate policies will satisfy functional needs and thereby political (or economic) system needs. Advocates of industrial policies have promoted corporatist decision-making forums of government, business, and labor representatives to enhance business productivity and socioeconomic equity. They believe that systemic requirements of consensus and stability can be attained through economic growth (business and state or local needs) and through equity (needs of workers and citizens of state governments). Their implicit presupposition appears to be that legislative deliberation should play the relatively limited roles of identifying relevant functional interests and authorizing them to develop public interest policies in the context of tripartite bargaining dominated by business and labor, that is, apart from legislative guidelines. The authorization of relevant functional interests is believed to be sufficient sanction for corporatist decision making. Joint action by these interests, they hope, should produce the sorts of appropriate policies that the unilateral actions of interest groups cannot (lobbying Congress for subsidies, for example). In effect, advocates of industrial policies tend to confound liberal democratic *outcomes*—equity, welfare, economic growth, and political stability—and liberal democratic *procedures*, or, worse, they tend to give priority to the outcomes under which the procedures are subsumed.[38]

It seems overly optimistic to claim that legislative bodies can revitalize their deliberative roles and avoid these pitfalls when they delegate their responsibilities to corporatist forums. Legislators require incentives to undertake reform, and, as the hurdles facing juridical democracy attest, currently prevailing incentives derive from functional interests, not popular constituencies. There is an alternative: revitalize popular representation through functional jurisdictions, on the grounds that functional units have displaced traditional democratic constituencies. Efforts to develop participatory democracy in the workplace are cases in point. Results of such contemporary reforms are decidedly mixed, as will be seen in the next chapter. Were these to succeed in a significant way, however, they might provide legislative bodies with incentives to respond to popular interests, albeit through functional constituencies, rather than to elite interests.

NOTES

1. Colin Crouch, "The State, Capital and Liberal Democracy," in *State and Economy in Contemporary Capitalism*, ed. Crouch (New York: St. Martin's Press, 1979), 13–54; Leo Panitch, "The Development of Corporatism in Liberal Democracies," *Comparative Political Studies* 10 (Apr. 1977): 61–90; Philippe C. Schmitter, "Modes of Interest Intermediation and Models of Societal Change in Western Europe," *Comparative Political Studies* 10 (Apr. 1977): 7–38; Philippe C. Schmitter and Gerhard Lehmbruch, eds., *Trends toward Corporatist Intermediation* (Beverly Hills, Calif.: Sage Publications, 1979); Wolfgang Streeck and Philippe C. Schmitter, eds., *Private Interest Government: Beyond Market and State* (Beverly Hills, Calif.: Sage Publications, 1985).

2. Panitch, "Development of Corporatism"; Schmitter, "Modes of Interest Intermediation." The essay generally credited with the rehabilitation of corporatism to intellectual (and ideological) respectability is Schmitter's "Still the Century of Corporatism?" in *The New Corporatism*, ed. Fredrick B. Pike and Thomas Stritch (Notre Dame, Ind.: University of Notre Dame Press, 1974), 85–131.

3. Panitch, "Development of Corporatism."

4. Charles W. Anderson, "Political Design and the Representation of Interests," *Comparative Political Studies* 10 (Apr. 1977): 127–52, at 136–40, 143–44; Leo Panitch, *Social Democracy and Industrial Militancy* (New York: Cambridge University Press, 1976), 246–50; Panitch, "Development of Corporatism," 67–68, 74–82; Philippe C. Schmitter, "Interest Intermediation and Regime Governability in Contemporary Western Europe and North America," in *Organizing Interests in Western Europe*, ed. Suzanne Berger (New York: Cambridge University Press, 1981), 285–327; Schmitter, "Democratic Theory and Neo-Corporatist Practice" (Florence, Italy: European University Institute, Working Paper No. 74, 1983); Andrew Shonfield, *Modern Capitalism* (New York: Oxford University Press, 1965), chaps. 8, 10, and part 4. See also the related discussion in the concluding section of chapter 5 herein.

5. Crouch, "State, Capital and Liberal Democracy," 23; see also 16–24.

6. Colin Crouch, "Pluralism and the New Corporatism: A Rejoinder," *Political Studies* 31 (Sept. 1983): 452–60; Panitch, "Development of Corporatism"; Schmitter, "Modes of Interest Intermediation."

7. Panitch, "Development of Corporatism," 65–66, 74–82. See also his observations concerning the role of Labour and the TUC in constraining union members to accede to business needs under the guise of the national interest (an incomes policy) in *Social Democracy and Industrial Militancy*, 246–50.

8. Theodore J. Lowi, *The End of Liberalism*, 2d ed. (New York: W. W. Norton, 1979); Grant McConnell, *Private Power and American Democracy* (New York: Alfred A. Knopf, 1966). Lowi concluded that corporatism would be an adequate description but that it had inappropriate connotations for a

society whose public values still reflected traditional liberalism, not European statism (50). An exception is the analysis of the "corporativist" roots of interest group liberalism in R. Jeffrey Lustig, *Corporate Liberalism* (Berkeley: University of California Press, 1982); see also Donald R. Brand, *Corporatism and the Rule of Law* (Ithaca, N.Y.: Cornell University Press, 1988).

9. See Graham K. Wilson, *Interest Groups in the United States* (Oxford: Clarendon Press, 1981), esp. 132–37ff., and "Why Is There No Corporatism in the United States," in *Patterns of Corporatist Policy-Making,* ed. Gerhard Lehmbruch and Philippe C. Schmitter (Beverly Hills, Calif.: Sage Publications, 1982), 219–36; Robert H. Salisbury, "Why No Corporatism in America?" in *Trends Toward Corporatist Intermediation,* ed. Schmitter and Lehmbruch, 213–30; Raymond H. Seidelman, "Pluralist Heaven's Dissenting Angels: Corporatism in the American Political Economy," in *The Political Economy of Public Policy,* ed. Alan Stone and Edward J. Harpham (Beverly Hills, Calif: Sage Publications, 1982), 49–70, at 60–69.

10. Claims that interest group liberalism and quasi-corporatism are largely indistinct are made by Ross M. Martin, "Pluralism and the New Corporatism," *Political Studies* 31 (Mar. 1983): 86–102; Frank L. Wilson, "French Interest Group Politics: Pluralist or Neocorporatist?" *American Political Science Review* 77 (Dec. 1983): 895–910. Arguments that attempt to set apart corporatism from the interest group liberal view of pluralism are in Crouch, "Pluralism and the New Corporatism"; John T. S. Keeler, "Situating France on the Pluralism-Corporatism Continuum," *Comparative Politics* 17 (Jan. 1985): 229–49. Along the latter lines, see Gabriel A. Almond, "Corporatism, Pluralism, and Professional Memory," *World Politics* 35 (Jan. 1983): 245–60; Gerhard Lehmbruch, "Concertation and the Structure of Corporatist Networks," in *Order and Conflict in Contemporary Capitalism,* ed. John H. Goldthorpe (Oxford: Clarendon Press, 1984), 60–80; Crouch, "State, Capital and Liberal Democracy."

11. Crouch, "Pluralism and the New Corporatism"; Keeler, "Situating France"; Lehmbruch, "Concertation and the Structure of Corporatist Networks."

12. See the dilemmas of "Wayne Bauer" in Robert N. Bellah, Richard Madsen, William M. Sullivan, Ann Swidler, and Steven M. Tipton, *Habits of the Heart* (New York: Harper and Row, 1985), 17–20, 190–91, 203–7, 214–18.

13. Cf. Douglas F. Dowd, *The Twisted Dream,* 2d ed. (Cambridge, Mass.: Winthrop Publishers, 1977); Edward S. Greenberg, *Capitalism and the American Ideal* (Armonk, N.Y.: M. E. Sharpe, 1985).

14. See the discussion of business privilege in chapter 5, and the citation there in note 28. Lindblom has been criticized for attributing power to economic organizations without providing appropriate operational indicators to demonstrate how the mere presence of corporate organization influences or controls consumer or citizen behavior. See James Q. Wilson, "Democracy and the Corporation," *Wall Street Journal,* Jan. 11, 1978; Aaron Wildavsky, "Changing Forward Versus Changing Back," *Yale Law Journal* 88 (Nov.

1978): 223–27. However, the concerns that Lindblom addresses—or should be understood to address—are the roles and consequences of values and normative priorities that have evolved over time, not the relationships between discrete political actors.

15. Louis Hartz, *The Liberal Tradition in America* (New York: Harcourt, Brace and World, 1955), 96–113, 134–42, 225–27, 251–52.

16. See Lustig, *Corporate Liberalism;* Stephen Skowronek, *Building a New American State* (New York: Cambridge University Press, 1982).

17. See the citations in note 9.

18. Lester C. Thurow, *The Zero-Sum Solution* (New York: Simon and Schuster, 1985), chap. 9.

19. See Ross K. Baker, "The Bittersweet Courtship of Congressional Democrats and Industrial Policy," 12–18, 32–34, and W. Thomas Kephart and Roger H. Davidson, "Congress Explores Industrial Policy: A Case of Agenda Setting and Policy Incubation," papers presented at the Midwest Political Science Association annual meetings, Chicago, Ill., 1986.

20. The arenas are from Mel Dubnick and Lynne Holt, "Industrial Policy and the States," *Publius* 15 (Winter 1985): 113–29. See also Michael E. Bell and Paul S. Lande, eds., *Dimensions of Industrial Policy* (Lexington, Mass.: Lexington Books, 1982); Susan E. Clarke, "Urban America, Inc.: Corporatist Convergence of Power in American Cities?" in *Local Economies in Transition,* ed. Edward M. Bergman (Durham, N.C.: Duke University Press, 1986), 37–58.

21. William E. Hudson, Mark S. Hyde, and John J. Carroll, "State Level Perspectives on Industrial Policy: The Views of Legislators and Bureaucrats," paper presented at the Northeastern Political Science Association annual meetings, Philadelphia, Pa., 1985; Hudson, Hyde, and Carroll, "Corporatist Policy Making and State Economic Development," *Polity* 19 (Spring 1987): 402–18.

22. Annmarie Hauck Walsh, *The Public's Business* (Cambridge, Mass.: MIT Press, 1978), 6. On fiscal restraint and the concomitant growth of public-private cooperative enterprises, see Joseph H. Ohren, "Changing Budgeting: Are We More or Less Democratic?" paper presented at the American Political Science Association annual meetings, Atlanta, Ga., 1989. On federal programs that support corporatist policies, see Clarke, "Urban America, Inc.," esp. 42–58.

23. On capital flight, see Gar Alperovitz and Jeff Faux, *Rebuilding America* (New York: Pantheon Books, 1984), 143–47; Barry Bluestone and Bennett Harrison, *The Deindustrialization of America* (New York: Basic Books, 1982). A study of efforts to locate a Mazda facility in the old Ford location at Flat Rock, Michigan, attempts to downplay the state competition noted here. See Lynn W. Bachelor, "Flat Rock, Michigan, Trades a Ford for a Mazda: State Policy and the Evaluation of Plant Location Incentives," in *The Politics of Industrial Recruitment,* ed. Ernest J. Yanarella and William C. Green (New York: Greenwood Press, 1990), 87–102. However careful Michigan and Mazda officials were to avoid a bidding war with other states,

their actions were informed by the costs (losses) of Ford's disinvestment and the advantages of a skilled workforce and a contiguous network of suppliers in comparison with other locations.

24. Clarke, "Urban America, Inc.," 42–43; David Wilmoth, "Regional Economic Policy and the New Corporatism," in *Sunbelt Snowbelt: Urban Development and Regional Restructuring,* ed. Larry Sawers and William K. Tabb (New York: Oxford University Press, 1984), 235–58. Cf. Paul E. Peterson, *City Limits* (Chicago: University of Chicago Press, 1981), chaps. 2–3.

25. See Peter Katzenstein, *Corporatism and Change* (Ithaca, N.Y.: Cornell University Press, 1984).

26. For useful surveys of the constraints typically placed on states and reviews of six automobile plant location decisions, see the essays in *The Politics of Industrial Recruitment,* ed. Yanarella and Green.

27. See note 2.

28. Martin, "Pluralism and the New Corporatism"; Wilson, "French Interest Group Politics."

29. Schmitter, "Democratic Theory and Neo-Corporatist Practice," 26–30; see also Katzenstein, *Corporatism and Change.*

30. Schmitter, "Democratic Theory and Neo-Corporatist Practice," 53–54.

31. See Jack L. Walker, "The Origin and Maintenance of Interest Groups in America," *American Political Science Review* 77 (June 1983): 390–406; Hugh Heclo, "Issue Networks and the Executive Establishment," in *The New American Political System,* ed. Anthony King (Washington, D.C.: American Enterprise Institute, 1978), 87–124.

32. Schmitter, "Democratic Theory and Neo-Corporatist Practice," 55–56.

33. Ibid., 45–46, italics deleted. See the telling commentary in Norberto Bobbio, *The Future of Democracy,* trans. Roger Griffin, ed. Richard Bellamy (Minneapolis: University of Minnesota Press, 1987), chap. 2, esp. 49–52.

34. Lowi, *End of Liberalism,* 2d ed.; David B. Truman, *The Governmental Process* (New York: Alfred A. Knopf, 1951), 525–26.

35. James Q. Wilson, "The Politics of Regulation," in *The Politics of Regulation,* ed. Wilson (New York: Basic Books, 1980), 357–94; Alan Stone, *Economic Regulation and the Public Interest* (Ithaca, N.Y.: Cornell University Press, 1977). A seminal study that reviews prior research and practice is Avery Leiserson, *Administrative Regulation* (Chicago: University of Chicago Press, 1942).

36. For the locus classicus on agency capture, see Marver Bernstein, *Regulating Business by Independent Commission* (Princeton, N.J.: Princeton University Press, 1955). For a dissent, see Paul J. Quirk, *Industry Influence in Federal Regulatory Agencies* (Princeton, N.J.: Princeton University Press, 1981). For a critical overview of the life cycle and capture theories, see Alan Stone, *Regulation and Its Alternatives* (Washington, D.C.: Congressional Quarterly Press, 1982), 228–31.

37. William P. Browne, *Private Interests, Public Policy, and American Agriculture* (Lawrence: University Press of Kansas, 1988); A. Lee Fritschler, *Smoking and Politics,* 3d ed. (Englewood Cliffs, N.J.: Prentice-Hall, 1983). Commodity supports are clearly "distributive" or "client" policies, to use the Lowi-Wilson parlance, but they often parade as regulatory policies, as do utility and trade regulations, while having significant "distributive" aspects.

38. This is clearer with Thurow than with Reich. Reich's sympathies lie close to the participatory values of economic or workplace democracy, although his conceptions of politics and citizenship are shaped by corporate, not political, values and are guided by desired policy outcomes (for example, equity), not procedural democracy. See Robert B. Reich, *The Next American Frontier* (New York: New York Times Books, 1983), 246–54, 280–82. Cf. Lester C. Thurow, *The Zero-Sum Society* (New York: Basic Books, 1980), 203–7, 212–14, and *The Zero-Sum Solution* (New York: Simon and Schuster), chap. 6.

CHAPTER 7

Workplace Democracy and Possessive Individualism

In the 1960s and 1970s, various forms of participatory democracy were proposed as alternatives to existing political practices. At the time, they were often dismissed as impractical ideals; however, concerns in the 1980s with economic dislocations, the perceived lack of corporate and political accountability, and the industrial policy debate inspired participatory theorists to renew their calls for reform. In doing so, they refined participatory theory and emphasized either economic democracy (or industrial democracy) or workplace democracy to alleviate economic problems and restore democratic legitimacy to the political process. The theories of economic and workplace democracy are distinct, although some writers incorporate the latter within the broader framework of the former, and others disagree over how they should be differentiated and the adequacy of either one as a program for change.[1]

Economic democracy requires a radical transformation of the political economy under which public controls and public ownership would be extended into the traditional private sector domain of ownership and control of investment and capitalization decisions.[2] The earlier discussion of corporate autonomy, the incentives motivating business elites, and the ways in which the public rationalizes the roles of business and the discretion of business elites suggest the enormous hurdles confronting the advocates of economic democracy. Workplace democracy initially appears to be more feasible than economic democracy since it has more narrowly defined objectives. Advocates of workplace democracy seek to revitalize civic participation and accountable representation by developing democracy in the workplace. They believe democratic workplaces can provide the basis for expanding democratic participation in the larger political system. They further believe the process of democratization can be extended to the state without *necessarily* requiring the more radical transformation of economic values and practices required by economic democracy.

This chapter assesses the practical problems of workplace democracy and also the sorts of hurdles that a predominantly liberal, pluralist political system poses for it. The principal emphasis is on the problem of developing democracy in workplaces, not on the broader issues of expanding democratic participation to the political system and democratizing the state; the latter is addressed in the following chapter. The major claim here is that theories of workplace democracy must accommodate pluralist practices and self-interested incentives and turn them to advantage in advancing the ideals of participatory theory. Specifically, efforts to democratize workplaces can be successful to the extent that they recognize, and can be reconciled with, the more or less pluralist practices and capitalist values that characterize American politics. Liberalism's possessive individualist values and incentives can be instrumental to the attainment of participatory ideals, not hindrances as is usually supposed. In fact, other modes of attaining participatory ideals—the so-called direct democracy and socialist alternatives associated, respectively, with movement politics and economic democracy—may be counterproductive in a possessive individualist culture that, as Louis Hartz observed, typically resists changes that appeal to values outside the liberal consensus.[3]

To assess the strengths and weaknesses of workplace democracy, it is appropriate first to spell out the underlying assumptions and objectives of the theory. Advocates of workplace democracy have a twofold set of objectives. They attempt to provide both the normative justifications and the explanatory or instrumental grounds to further the attainment of democracy, first, in the workplace and, second, in the state. Meaningful democratic participation in the workplace should modify corporate priorities and thus the values represented in elite decision making, and it should serve the educational function of inculcating democratic values in the "citizens" of the workplace. The educative function of democratic workplace participation should then be transferred to the political system or polity. Workers who learn they can control their destinies in the workplace will renew their civic consciousness with which they can constrain public officials and help shape public policies through elections and popular representation.[4] Theorists of workplace democracy frequently intertwine these two objectives in their arguments. They are conceptually distinct, however. The second objective, the assumption that the experience of democracy in the workplace will encourage democratic participation in the larger political system, is beyond the scope of this chapter, although it will be necessary to include it occasionally in the discussion. Emphasis is given principally to the first objective of workplace democracy, the democratization of the organization and its citizens.

Unlike pluralism, which has served as political science's paradigm for several decades, and the corporatist industrial policy framework, which has attracted a large elite following and is operative in state and local jurisdictions, participatory democracy has existed outside the mainstream of the discipline and public debate. Like the constitutionalist or juridical democratic alternative to interest group liberalism, which has been promoted by Theodore Lowi and a few other kindred critics, the contemporary participatory democracy paradigm has been framed by three prominent theorists: Peter Bachrach, Carole Pateman, and C. B. Macpherson. The assumptions and prescriptions in their writings merit brief examination before turning to the specific issues raised by workplace democracy.

Bachrach has argued that political scientists should expand their conceptions of the political, which pluralists limit chiefly to electoral and interest group politics, to include workplace communities. By doing so, they can assess the extent to which democratic empowerment exists and can be expanded "to inculcate among people . . . a justifiable feeling that they have the power to participate in decisions which affect themselves and the common life of the community, especially the immediate community in which they work and spend most of their waking hours and energy."[5] Pateman echoes an implication of Bachrach's recommendation in arguing that political efficacy is a function of meaningful political participation. She concludes that "only if the individual has the opportunity directly to participate in decision making and choose representatives in the alternative areas [workplaces, schools, and so on] . . . can [one] hope to have any real control over the course of his life or the development of the environment in which he lives."[6] Both Bachrach and Pateman acknowledge the criticisms that most individuals have little interest in national politics, but they counsel political scientists to assume at least, in the absence of actual evidence about the effects of participation, that participatory experiences would enable citizens to better assess the performance of their national representatives and the impact of national policies on their own lives.[7]

Like Bachrach and Pateman, Macpherson argues that efficacy is a function of participation and that democratic workplace values can be generalized to the political system: "Those who have proved their competence in one kind of participation, and gained confidence there that they can be effective, will be less put off by the forces which have

kept them politically apathetic, more able to reason at a greater political distance from results, and more able to see the importance of
decisions at several removes from their most immediate concerns."
Participatory workplaces thereby can contribute to the attainment of
liberal democratic ends ("the equal right of every man and woman to
the full development and use of his or her capabilities") in ways that
an otherwise formalized and meaningless citizenship cannot.[8] Somewhat more explicitly than the others, he also recognizes that the beneficial effects of a participatory workplace should be linked with the traditional electoral and representational vehicles of liberal democracy:
"We cannot do without elected politicians. We must rely, though we
need not rely exclusively, on indirect democracy. The problem is to
make the elected politicians responsible."[9]

In the 1960s and 1970s, there existed relatively few experiments in
workplace democracy and thus little evidence to support these propositions about participatory democracy. A virtual growth industry on
workplace democracy has since emerged, though. A substantial number of new proposals, motivated in most instances by perceived failures of existing economic arrangements, have developed variations on
the Bachrach-Pateman-Macpherson themes.[10] Further, although some
of the proposals are ideological or polemical, their feasibility has been
supported by research that analyzes the increasing number of experiments with workplace democracy.[11] The remaining sections of this
chapter provide a critical assessment of this growing body of evidence.

Workplace Democracy: Practical Considerations

Four general approaches are utilized to enhance worker participation, ranging from management-initiated to worker-initiated: (1) "hu-
manization of work" reforms, (2) "quality of work life" activities
(QWL), (3) worker-owned enterprises, and (4) worker-owned and
controlled, or "self-managed," enterprises.[12] The first two constitute
reforms of the old "scientific management" approach to corporate
organization and are initiated by management, the first representing
management-induced changes in work processes, the second, changes
in work processes developed through worker-management consultation.[13] The third can provide partial worker ownership initiated by
management (through employee stock ownership plans, or ESOPs),
complete worker ownership initiated by workers (as members of pro-
ducer cooperatives, by utilizing ESOPs to assume control, as in the
case of Weirton Steel, or a combination of the two), or a mixture of
worker-management ownership initiated by either management or

workers (for example, through open-market stock purchases). Only the fourth approach constitutes more than a reform of traditional managerial discretion, providing both employee ownership and employee control (or "self-management"), although cooperatives and stock buyouts dominated by workers can approximate the degree of control of self-managed enterprises. A fifth approach does not always require workplace participation. It involves community- or local government–financed buyouts or control (through tax and zoning policies and economic development incentives). This can incorporate either worker participation, worker control, or both. It also can be based on traditional managerial approaches.[14]

Although evidence of successful initiatives to enhance popular, local, or worker control of community and workplace decisions exists, it is unclear whether increased worker participation has the desired results in the long run. Numerous constraints limit the development of democratic practices in the workplace. These include such basic problems as workers' being co-opted by managerial values and market requirements' limiting the scope of democratic decision making in firms. Many of these problems are practical and context specific, subject to bargaining and negotiations in specific economic jurisdictions—the roles of management and labor, for example. Other problems of a different order of magnitude and complexity also confront workplace democracy. For example, there is the readily apparent and circular problem of inculcating democratic values in workers, whose civic lives reinforce self-interest and nonparticipation, without first attaining participatory democracy in the polity. This problem exemplifies constraints associated with the economic market, and its supporting ideological framework, and with the role of the state. The first sorts of constraints are addressed in this section; the latter, in the balance of this chapter.

First, values shared by the workers themselves affect the long-term success of employee-initiated efforts in a variety of ways. A corporate culture of adversarial labor-management relationships that preceded an employee-initiated participatory endeavor may pervade or undermine the effort.[15] Employee "deskilling" under existing work processes and the prevalence of consumer or "privacy" values can inculcate apathy about workplace responsibility and participation.[16] Worker-managed or worker-owned firms may practice or develop corporate self-interest vis-à-vis market forces and thus force individual workers to choose between participatory values and employment security (usually the latter). Worker-owners, who hire outside management, often defer to managerial expertise and discretion.[17]

Second, such arrangements as quality circles, shop-floor commit-tees, and "human relations" management encourage participation, but they are usually designed to attain managerial objectives of greater productivity, decreased absenteeism, and the like, not to produce "democratic" corporate citizens. In other words, participatory envi-ronments constructed to attain managerial objectives tend to co-opt workers to accept managerial goals and thus tend to be paternalistic instruments of benign management.[18] There is some evidence, how-ever, that the *effects* of these activities, regardless of their objectives, support increased demands for further participation and for even a degree of decision-making authority over investment and production decisions.[19] Both unionized and nonunion employees may be articu-lating the need for ground-up rather than top-down decision making with these demands.[20] Moreover, as workplace participation experi-ments increase, public acceptance of them also appears to increase. Two-thirds of the respondents in one survey prefer work in firms owned and managed by employees.[21]

Third, employee-initiated forms of workplace participation are fre-quently short-term successes but develop longer-term problems. The long-term success, for example, of buyouts and cooperatives as going economic enterprises often depends on the availability of capital and the related ability of the enterprise to modernize or become more technologically efficient. Yet these enterprises are often undercapital-ized, a function of investor risk aversion, laws of property that facili-tate governance in a traditional corporation but limit access to and control over capital by cooperative ventures, unanticipated or unreal-istically estimated recapitalization costs to modernize (primarily in plants that corporations planned to shut down), and the like.[22] Under these circumstances, economic and market requirements tend to take precedence over and constrain the ability of worker-managers or worker-owners to develop viable democratic mechanisms. In other words, many of these limitations on employee-initiated efforts to de-mocratize workplaces are rooted in values and in long-standing legal and institutional practices about ownership and the market.

To recapitulate, the evidence is mixed at best on a variety of prac-tical considerations that affect workplace democracy. On the one hand, a modification of corporate priorities and the democratic edu-cation of workplace citizens—the first objective for workplace demo-crats—may be partially attainable in some settings. On the other hand, co-optation under management-initiated participatory schemes and the longer-term effects of, among other things, market restric-tions and risk averse investors tend to undercut this objective. Given prevailing socioeconomic values and political practices, these constraints are also understandable. If employee participation ultimately is to affect the goals and options of the corporation as advocates of workplace democracy aver, the context of decisions in a participatory workplace must be established jointly by employers and employees, not imposed by business leaders. *Effective* joint decision making, not merely ritualistic or symbolic codetermination or quality circle efforts, would seem to require a reduction in the scale of the workplace and its organization *and* some degree of voluntary membership for employees as well as employers. The workplace of the modern corporation is neither small nor voluntary, however. Ultimately, the scope of employee decision making depends on the economic growth objectives of the corporation. Both industrial policy and economic democracy advocates recognize that "capital flight" (the shifting of production facilities from one political jurisdiction to another) and "capital strike" (disinvestment or the failure to reinvest) further limit freedom of mobility for workers.[23] Problems of organizational scale and involuntary membership thus are not primarily practical problems subject to bargaining within firms, as many of the other constraints discussed earlier are.[24] These problems require an assessment of the constraints existing in the relationship between the workplace and the market and its supportive possessive individualist political culture.

Political Culture and the Market

Although workplace democracy does not require the radical transformation of capitalism that economic democracy does, the preceding constraints suggest that some form of public, quasi-public, or cooperative control over capital is necessary. Such control could be designed to avoid employee co-optation by management-initiated participatory activities and to provide incentives for employees to learn, or relearn, the values of responsible citizenship, corporate or political. The values of a capitalist economy, however, militate against the socialization of capital, not only by governments but also by worker cooperatives. Overcoming resistance to cooperative control over capital, not to mention public control, may appear more or less realistic in the context of European politics, but the likelihood of this occurring in the United States seems remote. Compared with European corporations (many under government mandates requiring labor representation), U.S. corporations have resisted even worker representation on their boards of directors, a measure far less threatening to corporate autonomy than any form of capital socialization would be.[25] This underscores their "privileged position," to recall Charles Lindblom's assessment (see chapter 5). Clearly, therefore, advocates of workplace democracy must account for the roles played by the market and capitalist values in the political culture.

Macpherson would go further than simply accounting for these factors with strategies that, say, accommodate workplace democracy to capitalism. He asserts that "the linkage of market society with liberal-democratic ends" can and should be broken. By *market society* he means a society permeated by the possessive individualist values and incentives so well essayed in his early work. Macpherson urges the break because he cannot envision an adequate theory of workplace democracy based on possessive individualist values. His assertion is feasible, he believes, because the market is no longer a necessary condition to alleviate scarcity: "we have now reached a technological level of productivity which makes possible a good life for everybody without depending on capitalist incentives."[26] Some advocates of economic democracy agree. They believe, with Macpherson, that a democratic economy would entail decentralized production responding to local needs, a reduced workweek, less economic pressure to move from a community in search of work, and the like. It would thereby enable individuals to develop their capabilities as persons and community members: "Communities would . . . acquire much more focused definition in people's lives," and, they conjecture, "a boom may be anticipated in sports, cooking, dieting, block parties, local politics, and the pursuit of self-understanding."[27]

These are very contentious propositions and conjectures. Other recent proposals for economic democracy are inspired instead by evidence of economic decline or scarcity. Assessments are mixed, however, about whether the growth and development of workplace democracy, let alone the conditions for economic democracy, are fostered by a healthy economy that satisfies subsistence needs or by a declining economy of scarcity. One view is that economic growth provides incentives for management—and unions—to "share the wealth," not only economically through higher wages and profit sharing or ESOPs but also through cooperative decision making. Another view is that economic decline and a general "economic crisis" atmosphere increase the political militancy of workers, the influence of movements for reform, and the like.[28] In the light of available evidence, the dismissal of possessive individualism seems too facile.

The optimistic scenario of Macpherson and others who rely on enhanced economic well-being and improvements in technology and productivity may encourage participatory theorists to minimize the importance of assessing the actual impact of the market on achieving workplace democracy. These writers assume the development of democratic workplace values and the transformation of community values take place in the context of an economic and political system that is optimally supportive of democratic values. When this context is not present, however, when it is instead dominated by possessive individualist and interest group liberal values, constraints imposed by economic market requirements may tend to override democratic values inculcated in more or less democratic workplaces.[29] The significance of the workplace, or any other constituent organization (communities, neighborhoods, clubs), will vary in importance as circumstances, wants, and human needs change. A reduction in the workweek to, say, thirty hours would surely reduce the significance of the workplace *qua* workplace. All other things being equal (namely, a possessive individualist political culture), workers with increased free time would likely pursue different personal, not shared, interests, thus engendering a multiplicity of diverse recreational interests and undertaking "private" and "consumer" pursuits, not "public" or "civic" ones.

Macpherson also discounts the roles of possessive individualist values in a market society because, he believes, they have lost their moral basis. State intervention justified on "public interest" and "economic justice" claims has largely displaced the independent market by allocating rewards through welfare policies and subsidies. Specifically, Macpherson argues that the link between the market and democracy can be broken for four reasons: (1) the growth of the welfare state based on popular movements, unions, and parties; (2) the decline of market competition, displaced by monopolistic and oligopolistic practices that "control markets instead of being controlled by them"; (3) government intervention in the form of the welfare state; and (4) the fear that the preceding might lead to a "corporatist or plebiscitarian state."[30] It is not at all clear, however, that claims on behalf of economic justice for the welfare state have eroded possessive individualist values. To the contrary, it is just as plausible to argue that the American version of the positive or "social security" state relies on and reinforces these values through a pluralist process of bargaining over entitlements. This argument is persuasively supported by the analysis of Norman Furniss and Timothy Tilton, who review the unsystematic mix of welfare policies, each constrained by popular and elite values favoring self-help over need, and by the analysis of Theodore Lowi, who decries the conservatism of the Great Society programs, which, developed under the auspices of interest group liberalism, favored entrenched interests at the expense of the unorganized.[31]

The lesson, derived from these conflicting views about the relation-

ship between the state of the economy and the opportunities for reform, is that the economic market and the possessive individualist
values of a market society play independent or intervening roles relative to the participatory workplace. In a study of the Puget Sound
plywood cooperatives, Edward Greenberg underscores the importance of accounting for the market and its values: "the findings seem
to suggest . . . that the *market* is a more powerful educative tool than
is the cooperative experience itself. Or to put it differently, so long as
the economic well-being of enterprise members depends upon success
in the marketplace, whether it be based on ownership of shares, or on
profit sharing, bonuses, or other such devices, behavior appropriate
to that success will be encouraged even within self-managed enterprises."[32] Greenberg's remarks point to the roles that possessive individualist or ownership values and incentives play in participatory
workplace ventures. Greenberg does not deny that participatory experiences in the workplace influence political participation outside the
firm; in fact, they exert a positive influence. But he finds that individuals are attracted to the cooperatives in the first place for "pecuniary
and not political motives," "commitment[s] to the pursuit of personal
self-interest" associated with "possessive individualism or competitive individualism." A variation on his interpretation is the proposition that cooperative membership is chosen by workers who would
prefer to have individually owned businesses but settle for cooperative membership as a second best alternative to employment by a
corporation.[33]

Behavior attuned to the market is rooted in possessive individualist
values; these values cannot simply be dismissed on the optimistic
grounds that progress in technology and productivity can overcome
scarcity or that the interventionist state erodes their influence on attitudes and behavior. Macpherson's conception of possessive individualism is simply too restrictive. Contrary to Macpherson, persons motivated primarily by material or tangible drives are not necessarily
unpolitical; possessive individualism is the stuff of which factional
conflict and politics are made. Of course, the concept of ownership or
possession is not limited to the possessive individualist variant of liberalism in which property is construed as an end in itself. It is also an
aspect of the Jeffersonian republican strand of American political culture. Here, possession is an instrument or means for attaining the
independence or autonomy required of citizenship. Nonetheless, it
seems clear that the possessive individualist variant is predominant
and that appeals to Jeffersonian independence serve to rationalize
subcultural norms rather than give them force.[34] In all likelihood, the

practices of cooperatively owned or democratically managed firms would have to accommodate the norms of a political culture that values ownership. Such traditional liberal democratic bywords as *liberty* and *equality* (the latter understood as equal opportunity), not *fraternity, community,* or *solidarity,* would likely be the relevant symbols. Because ownership or possessive individualist values do count, attempts to democratize the workplace will predictably be constrained by them, unless these values can be used instrumentally as incentives to organize and sustain democratic workplaces.[35]

An Instrumental Role for Possessive Individualism

The influence of the market and its possessive individualist values cannot be dismissed. Possessive individualism must be accounted for and utilized in a way that can support internal workplace democracy. For example, the success of the plywood cooperatives that Greenberg studied is largely attributable to the "pride in ownership" and "American dream" ideals of the members. In other words, self-interest *can* sustain cooperative efforts; it need not undercut them. In what specific ways can possessive individualism serve as a positive force in attaining the first objective of workplace democracy?

Corporate managers are notoriously shortsighted defenders of the quarterly report's bottom line, not farsighted proponents of the firm's growth and stability. They often practice "paper entrepreneurialism," buying and selling assets through acquisitions and divestments rather than engaging in research and development.[36] Would worker-owned or worker-managed enterprises behave any differently? With the exception of cases that fail because they are undercapitalized or because an adversarial labor-management culture of prior corporate ownership pervades the worker-managed effort (see the discussion earlier in this chapter), worker-owned or worker-managed firms appear to be no less, and in some cases more, efficient and productive than their corporate predecessors and counterparts are. The successes are attributable in large part to workers having a greater vested interest or stake in the success of the firm.[37] This suggests that if the experiments increase and public acceptance is sustained, investors may have more incentive to invest in these concerns than in traditionally managed firms, thereby contributing to adequate capitalization. In short, successes may provide tangible incentives for investors in a possessive individualist world. (The growth of "ethical" mutual funds provides support.)

A related problem could be alleviated by increasing capital through outside investment, but the potential for an outside, nonworker take-over would also increase. Some successful cooperatives are faced with the problem that the values of ownership shares, which appreciate beyond a certain limit, restrict recruitment of new workers who find share costs prohibitive.[38] If the legal framework of the firm were modified to permit stock or share splits, as traditional corporations do to raise equity, share purchases would be more readily accessible to new workers and outside investors. This, however, would increase the risk that control of the firm, originally vested in worker ownership or management, could be acquired by outside investors and other corporations. To prevent this, the firm could require that a controlling percentage of shares or stock be held by membership.[39]

In practice, a reliance on investors' possessive individualist values is not very different from economic democrats' proposals to encourage local community ownership of once corporate-controlled production facilities.[40] Both local communities and outside investors serve as the sources of capitalization for workers, who presumably retain their incentives to ensure efficiency and productivity. These incentives are predicated on their stake in economic success—granted that in community-owned firms there is likely to be some overlap (and cross-pressures) among local citizens who also are workers.[41] This strategy is not out of line with others that sustain the value of ownership.

One such strategy is provided by Robert A. Dahl. He rejects the theoretical argument underpinning possessive individualism, that property is an inalienable right. He argues that the inalienability of property cannot be sustained because it conflicts with a more fundamental inalienable right, the right to self-governance (in firms).[42] Instead, possession must be justified instrumentally or in terms of whether it enhances the right to self-governance. Although the Jeffersonian republican notion of a balanced or self-regulating economy, which would moderate possessive individualist drives, was rendered inadequate with the advent of "corporate capitalism," its utilitarian or instrumental conception of ownership remains significant.[43] The instrumental value of property can be used to "entail a *shift* of ownership from stockholders to employees," with employee ownership ranging from worker cooperatives to social ownership. Dahl's argument partly rests on the distinction between effective control and nominal ownership.[44] Since stockholder ownership is nominal because effective control is delegated to corporate management, and since corporate governance is at odds with the right to self-governance, a shift to employee ownership would not violate the instrumental right to the possessions necessary to life, which is not at stake for stockholders. Employee-owners could then exercise effective control over—or as—managers.[45] In effect, Dahl's proposal sustains the value of ownership—recognizing it as a central element in the political culture—and uses it as an incentive to develop democratic workplaces.

The preceding considerations can mitigate some of the practical constraints that limit democratization in the workplace. Whether these also can support the second objective of workplace democrats remains to be seen. Writers who intertwine the two objectives of workplace democracy tend to emphasize the extent to which democratic workplaces can encourage broader mass participation, as if the boundaries of participatory units could be expanded by moving from the center to the outer limits of a series of concentric circles.[46] They emphasize the roles of workplaces as molders and educators of individual democratic citizens who participate in elections. Their faith that participatory values can be transferred to the larger political system is, however, insufficient as long as the possessive individualist values that help define both political citizenship and corporate membership are discounted. They risk relegating the participatory aims of workplace democracy to the realm of idyllic proposals that lack a program of action—an area in which too much political theory finds itself when it confronts the constraints of the political system and contemporary political practices.

By contrast, the analysis here provides a different basis for understanding how democracy can be expanded to the political system and to the state. It suggests that democratized organizations, such as workplaces, can play legitimate democratic roles as functional constituency organizations within an interest group liberal society. It is *not* suggested here, however, that efforts to attain workplace democracy's first objective should be undertaken independent of efforts to attain the second objective, the transmission of democratic practices to the larger political system. Although the two are conceptually distinct, a fully developed theory of workplace democracy must incorporate both objectives, for they are reciprocal or mutually reinforcing. A theory of workplace democracy must provide linkages with its institutional and cultural contexts and explain the roles of democratized functional constituencies within a broader theory of the state. The extent to which this is feasible is considered in the remaining chapters.

NOTES

An earlier version of this chapter appeared as "Workplace Democracy and Possessive Individualism" in *Journal of Politics* 52 (Feb. 1990). Used by permission of the University of Texas Press.

1. Robert A. Dahl, *A Preface to Economic Democracy* (Berkeley: University of California Press, 1985); Kenneth M. Dolbeare, *Democracy at Risk: The Politics of Economic Renewal*, rev. ed. (Chatham, N.J.: Chatham House Publishers, 1986); Edward S. Greenberg, *Workplace Democracy: The Political Effects of Participation* (Ithaca, N.Y.: Cornell University Press, 1986); Robert E. Lane, "From Political to Industrial Democracy?" *Polity* 17 (Summer 1985): 623–48; C. B. Macpherson, *The Rise and Fall of Economic Justice* (New York: Oxford University Press, 1987).

2. For example, Martin Carnoy and Derek Shearer, *Economic Democracy: The Challenge of the 1980s* (Armonk, N.Y.: M. E. Sharpe, 1980); Dahl, *Preface to Economic Democracy;* cf. Macpherson, *Rise and Fall of Economic Justice*, chap. 3.

3. The law of Whig compensation and the Horatio Alger myth in Louis Hartz, *The Liberal Tradition in America* (New York: Harcourt, Brace and World, 1955), effectively illustrate these values. See also Hartz's description of "Americanism" as the "bizarre fulfillment of liberalism" (284–309).

4. In addition to the citations following this note, useful reviews of the literature on participatory and workplace democracy are in Greenberg, *Workplace Democracy;* Ronald M. Mason, *Participatory and Workplace Democracy* (Carbondale: Southern Illinois University Press, 1982); Dennis F. Thompson, *Political Participation* (Washington, D.C.: American Political Science Association, 1977).

5. Peter Bachrach, *The Theory of Democratic Elitism* (Boston: Little, Brown, 1967), 92; see also chap. 7.

6. Carole Pateman, *Participation and Democratic Theory* (Cambridge: Cambridge University Press, 1970), 110; see 104–11. Unlike the pluralists, Pateman draws on the "classical" democratic theorists to develop operational propositions about efficacy and participation. See ibid., 22–44.

7. Ibid., 53–66, 97–111; Bachrach, *Theory of Democratic Elitism*, 103–5. Support for their hypothesis that political efficacy, developed in the workplace, can be generalized to the political system is developed in J. Maxwell Elden, "Political Efficacy at Work," *American Political Science Review* 75 (Mar. 1981): 43–58, at 52–56. It is central to Mason, *Participatory and Workplace Democracy*, chaps. 3–4, where it is labeled the "proximity hypothesis." Weaknesses of the hypothesis are explored in Edward S. Greenberg, "Industrial Democracy and the Democratic Citizen," *Journal of Politics* 43 (Nov. 1981): 964–81; Greenberg, *Workplace Demcracy.*

8. C. B. Macpherson, *The Life and Times of Liberal Democracy* (New York: Oxford University Press, 1977), 104, 114. The theory of developmental democracy underlies Macpherson's view of liberal democracy (see ibid., chap. 3). This conception of democracy is shared by Bachrach, *Theory of Democratic Elitism*, chap. 1, esp. 3–7, and chap. 7, esp. 99–106, and Pateman, *Participation and Democratic Theory*, chaps. 2, 6.

9. Macpherson, *Life and Times*, 97.

10. Gar Alperovitz and Jeff Faux, *Rebuilding America* (New York: Pantheon Books, 1984); Samuel Bowles, David M. Gordon, and Thomas E.

Weisskopf, *Beyond the Waste Land* (Garden City, N.Y.: Anchor Books, 1984); Carnoy and Shearer, *Economic Democracy.*

11. Keith Bradley and Alan Gelb, *Worker Capitalism* (Cambridge, Mass.: MIT Press, 1983); Arthur Hochner, Cherlyn S. Granrose, Judith Goode, Elaine Simon, and Eileen Appelbaum, *Worker Buyouts and QWL* (Kalamazoo, Mich.: W. E. Upjohn Institute for Employment Research, 1988); Thomas A. Kochan, Harry C. Katz, and Nancy Mower, *Worker Participation and American Unions* (Kalamazoo, Mich.: W. E. Upjohn Institute for Employment Research, 1984); Frank Lindenfeld and Joyce Rothschild-Whitt, eds., *Workplace Democracy and Social Change* (Boston: Porter Sargent, 1982); Robert N. Stern, K. Haydn Wood, and Tove Helland Hammer, *Employee Ownership in Plant Shutdowns* (Kalamazoo, Mich.: W. E. Upjohn Institute for Employment Research, 1979); William Foote Whyte, Tove Helland Hammer, Christopher B. Meek, Reed Nelson, and Robert N. Stern, *Worker Participation and Ownership* (Ithaca, N.Y.: ILR Press, 1983); Warner Woodworth, Christopher Meek, and William Foote Whyte, eds., *Industrial Democracy: Strategies for Community Revitalization* (Beverly Hills, Calif.: Sage Publications, 1985); Daniel Zwerdling, *Workplace Democracy* (New York: Harper and Row, 1984).

12. This follows the typology of Zwerdling, *Workplace Democracy,* 2–8.

13. Ibid., vii–x; cf. Paul Bernstein, "Necessary Elements for Effective Worker Participation in Decision-Making," in *Workplace Democracy and Social Change,* ed. Lindenfeld and Rothschild-Whitt, 51–81; Kochan, Katz, and Mower, *Worker Participation and American Unions.*

14. See Warner Woodworth, Christopher Meek, and William Foote Whyte, "Theory and Practice of Community Economic Reindustrialization," in *Industrial Democracy,* ed. Woodworth, Meek and Whyte, 297–304; Frank Lindenfeld, "Workers' Cooperatives: Remedy for Plant Closings?" in *Workplace Democracy and Social Change,* ed. Lindenfeld and Rothschild-Whitt, 337–52. See also Gar Alperovitz and Jeff Faux, "The Youngstown Project," in *Workplace Democracy and Social Change,* ed. Lindenfeld and Rothschild-Whitt, 353–69; Alperovitz and Faux, *Rebuilding America;* Bradley and Gelb, *Worker Capitalism;* Bradley and Gelb, "Employee Buyouts of Troubled Companies," *Harvard Business Review* 63 (Sept.–Oct. 1985): 121–30.

15. For example, the case of Hyatt-Clark Industries. See Thomas J. Lueck, "A Noble Experiment Goes Bankrupt," *New York Times,* May 3, 1987; "When Workers Get in the Takeover Game," *U.S. News and World Report,* June 8, 1987.

16. Tove Helland Hammer, Robert N. Stern, and Michael A. Gurdon, "Workers' Ownership and Attitudes towards Participation," in *Workplace Democracy and Social Change,* ed. Lindenfeld and Rothschild-Whitt, 87–108, at 90–93, 101–2, 106–7. See also Harley Shaiken, "When the Computer Runs the Office," *New York Times,* Mar. 22, 1987.

17. Hammer, Stern, and Gurdon, "Workers' Ownership and Attitudes towards Participation," 106–7; cf. Edward S. Greenberg, "Industrial Self-

Management and Political Attitudes," *American Political Science Review* 75 (Mar. 1981): 29–42; Christopher Eaton Gunn, *Workers' Self-Management in the United States* (Ithaca, N.Y.: Cornell University Press, 1984), esp. 168–76, 198–212; Zwerdling, *Workplace Democracy*, 103–4.

18. Lindenfeld and Rothschild-Whitt, *Workplace Democracy and Social Change;* Samuel Bowles, "The Production Process in a Competitive Economy," *American Economic Review* 75 (Mar. 1985): 16–36. These problems are anticipated in Bachrach, *Theory of Democratic Elitism*, 101, n. 8; cf. Sidney Verba, *Small Groups and Political Behavior* (Princeton, N.J.: Princeton University Press, 1961), chap. 10. Predictably, unions divide over the desirability of different types of worker participation. See Kochan, Katz, and Mower, *Worker Participation and American Unions;* Jacob M. Schlesinger, "UAW Girds for Scrappy Debate on 'Joint Cooperation,'" *Wall Street Journal*, Apr. 10, 1987; "Unions Join Management in Partnerships to Survive," *Investor's Daily*, Dec. 12, 1990; Zwerdling, *Workplace Democracy*, 167–81. For a case of successfully attained managerial objectives, see John Merwin, "A Tale of Two Worlds," *Forbes*, June 16, 1986, 101–6.

19. See Elden, "Political Efficacy at Work." On the mixed evidence about managerial objectives and democratic effects, see Kochan, Katz, and Mower, *Worker Participation and American Unions*, chaps. 2, 4–7; Richard E. Walton, "From Control to Commitment in the Workplace," *Harvard Business Review* 63 (Mar.–Apr. 1985): 77–84; cf. Robert Drago, "An Analysis of Why Quality Circles Fail," paper presented at the American Political Science Association annual meetings, Washington, D.C., 1986.

20. See the argument in Alperovitz and Faux, *Rebuilding America*, and the cases in Kochan, Katz, and Mower, *Worker Participation and American Unions*, and in Woodworth, Meek, and Whyte, *Industrial Democracy*, esp. chaps. 5–8, 11–12 (but in reference to chap. 12, see Lueck, "Noble Experiment").

21. Cited in Whyte et al., *Worker Participation and Ownership*, 136.

22. For a survey of capitalization and investment problems, see Corey Rosen, "Financing Employee Ownership," in *Industrial Democracy*, ed. Woodworth, Meek, and Whyte, 261–75; Bradley and Gelb, *Worker Capitalism*, chaps. 4, 8; Whyte et al., *Worker Participation and Ownership*, chap. 6. On the remaining points, see J. David Edelstein, "The Origin, Structure, and Problems of Four British Producers' Cooperatives," in *Workplace Democracy and Social Change*, ed. Lindenfeld and Rothschild-Whitt, 199–219; David Ellerman, "On the Legal Structure of Workers' Cooperatives," in *Workplace Democracy and Social Change*, ed. Lindenfeld and Rothschild-Whitt, 307–13; Alperovitz and Faux, "The Youngstown Project." See also Lueck, "Noble Experiment"; Louis O. Kelso and Patricia Hetter Kelso, "Why Owner-Workers Are Winners," *New York Times*, Jan. 29, 1989. In some instances, worker-guided cooperatives lack sufficient skills and resources to make adequate decisions in the capital and investment markets; for a case in point, see Hesh Kestin, "High Marx, low marx," *Forbes*, Jan. 26, 1987, 35–36.

23. Robert A. Dahl, *Dilemmas of Pluralist Democracy* (New Haven, Conn.: Yale University Press, 1982), 198–202; Alperovitz and Faux, *Rebuilding America*, 143–47; Barry Bluestone and Bennett Harrison, *The Deindustrialization of America* (New York: Basic Books, 1982); cf. Bowles, Gordon, and Weisskopf, *Beyond the Waste Land*.

24. Certain aspects of hierarchy—for example, job classifications and work rules—can be negotiated, and job vouchers could be used to mitigate forced mobility. On the latter, see Robert B. Reich, *The Next American Frontier* (New York: New York Times Books, 1983), 239–40. These issues are reconsidered in chapter 8 in the context of expanding democracy from the workplace to the political system.

25. See Edward S. Herman, *Corporate Control, Corporate Power* (New York: Cambridge University Press, 1981), 283–89.

26. Macpherson, *Life and Times*, 22, both quotes. See also Macpherson, *Rise and Fall of Economic Justice*, chap. 1, and chap. 5, 73–74; Pateman, *Participation and Democratic Theory*, 103–11.

27. Bowles, Gordon, and Weisskopf, *Beyond the Waste Land*, 384–85; see also 293–94.

28. Each view has its negative counterpart: for the first, that higher wages discourage participation by encouraging consumer-leisure activities; for the second, that militant activism can be countered by layoffs, "givebacks" to maintain job security, plant closings through capital mobility and capital strikes, and so forth. See Alperovitz and Faux, *Rebuilding America*, 99–109, 143–47; Bradley and Gelb, *Worker Capitalism;* Drago, "Why Quality Circles Fail"; Dahl, *Preface to Economic Democracy*, 120–33; Kochan, Katz, and Mower, *Worker Participation and American Unions*, chap. 3; Stern, Wood, and Hammer, *Employee Ownership in Plant Shutdowns*.

29. Dahl, *Preface to Economic Democracy*, 94–110; Greenberg, "Industrial Democracy," and "Industrial Self-Management"; Hammer, Stern, and Gurdon, "Workers' Ownership and Attitudes towards Participation," 106–7. See Lane, "From Political to Industrial Democracy?" for both support and objections. For a dissent, see Elden, "Political Efficacy at Work," and the research cited therein.

30. Macpherson, *Rise and Fall of Economic Justice*, 15–16; see also 65–75.

31. Norman Furniss and Timothy Tilton, *The Case for the Welfare State* (Bloomington: Indiana University Press, 1977), esp. chaps. 7–8; Theodore J. Lowi, *The End of Liberalism*, 2d ed. (New York: W. W. Norton, 1979), chap. 8.

32. Greenberg, "Industrial Self-Management," 41, and "Industrial Democracy," 977–81. See Greenberg, *Workplace Democracy*, for an overview. See also Zwerdling, *Workplace Democracy*, 101–4; cf. Lane, "From Political to Industrial Democracy?" For an assessment of the positive and negative aspects of the sorts of constraints Greenberg mentions, see Dahl, *Preface to Economic Democracy*, 96–107, 116–33.

33. Greenberg, "Industrial Democracy," 975, 977–78. The last point,

suggested by a critic, represents a minor adjustment to Greenberg's hypothesis. It is plausible and further supports the significance of possessive individualist values. The educative role of the market both precedes and is reinforced by the cooperative experience.

34. In American political thought, this is traditionally seen as a clash between Hamiltonian and Jeffersonian ideals; see Dolbeare, *Democracy at Risk*, 25–27. For a more complex account, see J. R. Pole, *The Pursuit of Equality in American History* (Berkeley: University of California Press, 1978), chap. 5. For an interesting assessment of how liberal or possessive individualist values can be both at odds and compatible with democratic and communal values in the public mind, see Herbert McClosky and John Zaller, *The American Ethos* (Cambridge, Mass.: Harvard University Press, 1984), esp. chaps. 7–9. A now dated secondary analysis of survey data stresses the predominance of possessive individualism. See Donald J. Devine, *The Political Culture of the United States* (Boston: Little, Brown, 1972).

35. On these points, see the discussions in Robert N. Bellah, Richard Madsen, William M. Sullivan, Ann Swidler, and Steven M. Tipton, *Habits of the Heart* (New York: Harper and Row, 1985), about individualism and justice (22–26) and the dilemmas of "Wayne Bauer" (17–20, 190–91, 203–7, 214–18). See also Greenberg's circumspect conclusions in "Industrial Democracy," 980–81.

36. Reich, *Next American Frontier*, chap. 8; Alperovitz and Faux, *Rebuilding America*, 95ff.; cf. Dahl, *Preface to Economic Democracy*, 105fn., 109–10. A good case in point is how U.S. Steel used the 1981 Economic Recovery and Tax Act (ERTA), presumed to stimulate investment in new technology (electric furnaces) through tax incentives, to purchase Marathon Oil and, not incidentally, to enhance the bottom line with accelerated cost recovery system rules applied to Marathon's reserves. Throughout the 1980s, the "mergers and acquisitions mania" (as it was dubbed by the financial press) was funded by "junk bonds," whose interest payments frequently cut into reinvestment and recapitalization opportunities and dividend increases for stockholders. Virtually any issue of *Barron's, Business Week, Forbes*, and the *Wall Street Journal* addressed this.

37. See the survey in Dahl, *Preface to Economic Democracy*, 119–33. See also Alperovitz and Faux, *Rebuilding America*, chap. 6; Bradley and Gelb, *Worker Capitalism*; Marie Howland, "The Causes of Plant Closures: Implications for State and Local Development," *Business Outlook for West Michigan* 3 (undated reprint); Hochner et al., *Worker Buyouts and QWL*; Lindenfeld and Rothschild-Whitt, *Workplace Democracy and Social Change*, chaps. 7, 8, 10; Stern, Wood, and Hammer, *Employee Ownership in Plant Shutdowns*; William Foote Whyte and Joseph Blasi, "The Potential of Employee Ownership," in *Industrial Democracy*, ed. Woodworth, Meek, and Whyte, 181–94.

38. Dahl, *Preface to Economic Democracy*, 140, cites Ellerman's estimates of $60,000–80,000 per share in successful firms. See also Zwerdling, *Workplace Democracy*, 102–3.

39. See Ellerman, "On the Legal Structure of Workers' Cooperatives," 303–5; Rosen, "Financing Employee Ownership." Placing a limit on outside ownership would be in principle similar to the "limit" of 50 percent of available stock that James Gibbons placed on himself in establishing International Group Plans as a worker self-managed insurance firm. See Daniel Zwerdling, "At IGP, It's Not Business as Usual," in *Workplace Democracy and Social Change*, ed. Lindenfeld and Rothschild-Whitt, 221–40.

40. Alperovitz and Faux, *Rebuilding America*. See also Woodworth, Meek, and Whyte, *Industrial Democracy*, passim.

41. For some of the issues to resolve between employee and community control, see Ellerman, "On the Legal Structure of Workers' Cooperatives," 302–3ff.; Rosen, "Financing Employee Ownership," 262–67.

42. Dahl, *Preface to Economic Democracy*, 62–83; see also 22–31. See also Dahl, *Dilemmas of Pluralist Democracy*, 198–202.

43. Dahl, *Preface to Economic Democracy*, 62–73.

44. Ibid., 112–13, 140–52. Here he follows Adolph A. Berle and Gardiner C. Means, *The Modern Corporation and Private Property* (New York: Macmillan, 1932).

45. The control-ownership distinction is elaborated in Dahl, *Preface to Economic Democracy*, 54–56, 117–20. Dahl recognizes that the functional *role* of stockholders (providing equity) is separable from their *rights* as owners: "In principle, the task of supplying capital to enterprises can be separated from the rights of ownership and control" (79). But he dismisses this role a bit too easily by presuming that they inevitably go together (79–81, which rests on the broader criticisms of inalienable property rights). The previously suggested strategy to capitalize on investor incentives combines the role of providing equity with the value of (self-interest in) ownership, but it requires that control be vested in employees (say with 50-plus percent of shares)— which is precisely what Dahl attempts to provide (112–13).

46. For example, Mason, *Participatory and Workplace Democracy*, chap. 7.

CHAPTER 8

Participatory Theory and the Political System

Participatory theorists stress a positive relationship between democratic participation in the workplace and democratic participation in the larger political system. The expected correlation between workplace and political participation has been labeled the *proximity hypothesis*. It assumes that people will be encouraged to participate as citizens in the polity after they experience democracy in the workplace and that the benefits of workplace democracy will be cumulative and lead to an increased democratization of the state.[1] The proximity thesis or a variation of it is important also for other theorists of liberal democracy who are troubled by civic apathy and an apparent decline in democratic commitments and citizens' political participation. While participationists can cite increasing evidence in support of the thesis, significant restrictions remain.

The most obvious constraint on the proximity thesis derives from the corporatist perspective on associational membership, namely, that *because* citizens define themselves and their roles through their corporate membership, the traditional political process is largely irrelevant. Several decades ago, some scholars viewed this development with alarm. Andrew Hacker warned that the traditional liberal democratic rationale for citizenship had become untenable, displaced by "corporation citizenship." Hacker's principal concern was with the middle or managerial class, not the working class, in part because the former sets the terms of membership for the latter. The corporation had elevated the middle class to positions of status and influence. After World War II, however, it became apparent that individuals were being "uprooted" by the modern corporation. It had broken down sectional differences and created a "nation" by moving its workers between geographic jurisdictions and by shaping urban life in its image. National and local governments could no longer provide an environment for participation and membership. The corporate community and corporate citizenship had replaced traditional jurisdictions and had undermined "the need for political participation on the part of the very people who have always been the prime participants in the political process."[2]

Hacker concluded his assessment on an exceedingly pessimistic note. He believed the abandonment of traditional politics for corporate citizenship would have significant consequences. The middle class, in his view, was the traditional source of political leadership, but as it neglected political for corporate life, the nation would face a vacuum of political leadership. The sorts of individual interests and one's sense of having a stake or vested interest in political life, which James Madison had envisioned as the basis for an active citizenry, were being downgraded and displaced by interests delineated by corporate membership. Because corporate citizenship is nondemocratic, corporate members would be encouraged to put their faith in perhaps responsive, but democratically unaccountable corporate leaders. Corporate interests, not citizens' interests, would invariably shape and define the nation's politics.[3]

Many of Hacker's concerns anticipated subsequent criticisms of interest group liberalism. The defenders of the world shaped by corporate life see positive virtues in the problems Hacker encountered, however. Robert B. Reich, the neoliberal advocate of industrial policy, underscores the possibilities when the corporation replaces "geographic [political] jurisdictions. . . . And all citizens . . . become employee members of some business enterprise." Reich believes that workplace participation might help develop a sense of corporate "civic virtue" because workplaces are "where people experience authority most directly and learn the practical realities of collective action" and that corporate leadership can be induced to promote social justice and economic change.[4] Reich is clearly more sympathetic to the values of participatory theorists than are other advocates of corporatist industrial policies.[5] Since the corporation, not the community, is the center of politics for him, his commitment to participatory ideals is necessarily limited, however. It encompasses only corporate "civic virtue" (hence the quotation marks) because individuals' "civic" expectations and responsibilities will be shaped by corporate practices and employee needs, not by the interactions of citizens in the political arena and their connections with public authority and its institutional practices. The demise of political citizenship and civic virtue is not to be lamented, however; in the minds of Reich and other corporatists, the corporation provides a more than adequate alternative.

The centrality of so-called corporate citizenship and the irrelevance of traditional citizen politics, which corporatists recognize as defining features of contemporary politics, are significant constraints on the possibilities for participatory ideals. Although many of the practical constraints limiting democratization *within* the workplace can be alleviated, chapter 7 revealed that possessive individualism and the market are independent or intervening factors relative to workplace democratization efforts, not external factors or "dependent variables" that vary with the extent of workplace democratization. That they tend to override the significance of democratic values inculcated in relatively democratized workplaces is evident when workers decline to become politically active outside the workplace but defer to their corporate representatives, particularly when their economic well-being is at stake.[6] American political ideals about consent, representation, and electoral accountability inform efforts to create democracy within workplaces. They are important ideals, but they are frequently subordinated to economic ideals of equal opportunity and individualism, which reflect the pervasiveness of possessive individualism and the role of the market.[7] To postulate the proximity thesis without facing up to such constraints as these risks circularity, if not simply question begging.

The proximity thesis is limited also by the sheer scale and hierarchical characteristics of the modern corporation. To recapitulate observations from the preceding chapter, a reduction in the size of organizations and a degree of voluntary membership for workers are appropriate goals for participationists. They are problematic, however. In general, the modern corporation is a large-scale organization arranged along hierarchical lines, bureaucratized and involuntary inasmuch as employees are "functionaries" or interchangeable components. It has identifiable interests that are independent of member interests, and it is guided by managerial discretion, which need not rest on consultation or negotiation with all relevant members. Employers also have discretion about whom they will employ where and under what circumstances, whereas employees simply must work. Economies of scale are often used to justify these arrangements and any necessary trade-offs of equity for efficiency.[8]

Many laissez-faire advocates discount these observations and deny employment is involuntary. They claim economic relationships are grounded in voluntary actions because "citizenship" in a corporation is constrained only by a series of contractual agreements between employer and employee that are permissible because of their mutual willingness to engage in contractual negotiations in the first place.[9] By contrast, citizenship in the state is not voluntary in most important respects. Citizens of a state may not simply leave. The physical, emotional, and economic costs may be prohibitive; successful abdication of one country for another depends on the recipient country's willingness to accept new members; leaving with nowhere to go imposes the legal status of nonperson (witness the plight of Palestinian refugees) for there is no "going back" to a "state of nature," as the social contract theorists made clear.

In fact, however, organizational scale and criteria for corporate membership are seldom subject to negotiation between employers and employees. Moreover, there are virtually as many practical constraints on economic mobility as there are on political mobility. The specific sorts of constraints that effectively limit political mobility (physical, emotional, economic) also serve to constrain the mobility of employees. Further, in one crucial respect, political citizenship has certain voluntary qualities that do not apply to "corporate" citizens. In relatively large federal systems, citizens may freely move from one jurisdiction to another and retain their basic rights as citizens. Employees, however, simply do not carry "rights" to "citizenship" in moving from firm to firm within the same sector or from one sector to another (in moving, say, from Bethlehem to Inland Steel or from "low tech" assembly line work to "high tech" service work, to push the federalism analogy to extremes). For these sorts of reasons, adherence to certain democratic norms is required of governments and politics but not of economic organizations and relationships: "citizens have a claim on government for representation and responsiveness that does not exist as a democratic *right* in the economic marketplace."[10] Because employees do not have these guarantees, the purported voluntary character of economic membership is an inappropriate claim. Although political citizenship is highly constrained, economic membership proves to be even less free than political citizenship in terms of the basic guarantees assigned to the status of citizen.

Workplace Democracy and the Political System

The contribution that workplace democracy can make to political democracy appears to be problematic. Workplace democracy constitutes a theoretically satisfying approach to resuscitating democratic participation, but its development as a viable approach to democratic renewal is limited by the extent to which political institutions and practices—and the political culture—are supportive, that is, already embody and sustain minimal democratic norms and practices. Some workplace democrats acknowledge this and argue that a culture and institutions supporting democratic participation are required or, in their absence, that workplace democratization can be advanced by political or economic crises and movements underscoring the failures of existing institutional arrangements.[11] The potential relationships between democratic workplaces and political culture and institutions will be sketched out in more detail later. The second factor—crises and movements—seems remote for reasons to be explored now.

Several proponents of economic democracy believe the failures of existing economic and political practices presage worsening crises for the political economy that justify their proposed alternatives for conducting economic policy and reforming political arrangements. They further believe these changes can occur through mass-based movements. One position envisions quasi-populist, grass-roots movements generated by individuals committed to and capable of acting out democratic reforms at state and local levels. These movements could acquire majority status incrementally. Another postulates changes through electoral transformations. In this scenario, the left wing of an increasingly polarized electorate may attain sufficient organizational status—perhaps as a "party within a party" (Democratic)—to win elections, secure representation, and influence public policy. A third position foresees movements developing out of changes in public opinion and ultimately in voting patterns. These changes would be based on gradual popular recognition that the costs of corporatism need not be sustained and that the benefits of economic democracy are appropriate and viable.[12]

There are more or less historical parallels or precedents for these possibilities. For the first, there are the populist, farmer-labor, and progressive movements at the turn of the century. For the second, there are the electoral transformation of the 1930s and, very tentatively, the civil rights, antiwar, and often envisioned student-labor-feminist-minority coalition of the 1960s (and "Rainbow Coalition" of the 1980s?). For the third, there is the institutionalization of the 1930s electoral transformation under the auspices of the second New Deal. Mass-based movements seem unlikely independent causes of change, however. They may emerge as by-products of the first factor: cultural and institutional changes that support democratic participation. But the likelihood of movement-induced change seems remote, if for no other reason than the simplistic one that virtually every significant popular movement in the twentieth century became co-opted as pluralism evolved into interest group liberalism. A case in point is the War on Poverty. This was stimulated by, among other things, grass-roots activism and such popular works as Michael Harrington's *The Other America* and Harry Caudill's *Night Comes to the Cumberlands* (as well as by Democratic presidents seeking to shore up a declining New Deal coalition). Once institutionalized by the Great Society, however, the movement, in effect, became a respectable "poverty lobby."[13]

The moral? Movement politics presupposes supportive institutional changes. Granted this is an assertion, and the fact that major movements often do contribute to significant policy and attitudinal changes may appear to belie it (the civil rights movement is perhaps the preeminent contemporary example). It is based on a plausible assumption, though: changes in both political culture and institutional practices precipitate collective action, not the other way around. Otherwise, if movement-induced change is given center stage instead of a peripheral role, advocates of workplace democracy may tend to downplay the relationships between their values and the political culture and institutional practices that seem so problematic. This tendency is altogether too evident in much of the literature that, in effect, romanticizes participatory democracy and community and downplays the instrumental role of the sorts of material incentives that possessive individualism incorporates.

What, then, of the relationship between democratic workplaces and the broader contexts of political culture and political practices and institutions? Even where workplace democratization is successful, it is not obvious that even the more *politicized* citizens of democratic workplaces would extend democratic principles to those outside the firm. A high degree of homogeneity and conformity pervades small constituencies. There, minorities, fearful of face-to-face antagonism and isolation, submerge their values within a group consensus, and outsiders (future members) exclude themselves for similar reasons.[14] This would seem all the more likely to occur when group members are motivated by purposive and solidary incentives rather than material incentives.[15] The problem is a contemporary variation on Madison's views on the relationship between constituency size and factions: small constituencies are likely to be dominated by factions, larger ones less so.[16]

Even if the problem of conformity could be overcome in the workplace, say through appropriate procedural safeguards, the factional behavior of the organization relative to the larger political system remains a problem, particularly where members find themselves facing an adversarial or possessive individualist culture. Madison argued that the problem of faction could be alleviated throughout the national state by the system of federalism. Some such provision is necessary so that the participationists' *presumption* that democratic workplaces will contribute to democracy in the state is not belied or dismissed as simplistic. It must be shown how democratic values learned in democratic workplaces can be transferred to the domain of public politics and how constraints limiting this can be overcome. In other words, theories of workplace democracy must be incorporated within a broader institutional theory of the relationship between the workplace and the state. This proposition requires that the broader political theory account for the influential role of possessive individualism characterizing much of the political culture. For example, popular representation, electoral accountability, and institutional guarantees of due process and civil liberties in firms are compatible with both possessive individualist values and workplace democracy objectives. Two tentative recommendations along these lines by Robert Dahl and Jane Mansbridge warrant consideration. Dahl stipulates a regulatory framework for democratic firms, and Mansbridge suggests "consociational democracy" as a linkage for unitary (local) and adversarial (systemic) democracy.[17]

Dahl proposes that democratic enterprises exist in a regulatory framework that sustains, for interfirm relations and the political system, his criteria for procedural democracy to be met in firms. This is similar in outline to Theodore Lowi's proposal to resuscitate the rule of law through democratic representation and legislative deliberation and thereby to displace the corporatistlike politics of interest group liberalism.[18] Both proposals harken back to Madisonian theory since they presuppose that relevant subnational constituencies—firms in Dahl's case and state and local jurisdictions in Lowi's—will behave like factions. Dahl's point in particular is germane because he rejects the assumption that a system of self-governing firms, in and of itself, will approximate the Jeffersonian ideal of a self-regulating social order. That ideal is similar to, if it does not underlie, the assumption of many workplace democracy advocates that democratic workplaces will contribute to the democratization of the state without additional provisions.[19] By stressing the need to integrate theories of democratic workplaces within a regulatory framework that is compatible with traditional conceptions of the liberal state, Dahl points to the importance that theories of the political system have for theories of workplace democracy.

Likewise, Mansbridge suggests that the theory of consociational democracy might provide a basis to link or integrate small-scale democratic institutions (unitary democracies) with a national process of interest group politics (adversary democracy). Like Dahl, who is skeptical that democratic workplaces can be collectively self-regulating, Mansbridge doubts the feasibility—and the desirability—of attempting to emulate small-scale democracy at the national level:

> adversary democracy has its own ideals, which, although less emotionally inspiring than unitary ideals, will still appeal to the citizen's sense of equity. Nations organized primarily as adversary democracies have not generally faced up to the radical implications of the central adversary principle that each citizen's interests deserve equal protection. . . . In no adversary democracy would it be in the interests of those who now have greater power to begin to protect all citizens' interests equally. . . . Taking adversary ideals seriously would go a long way toward relieving the simple self-interested focus of adversary politics.[20]

Consociationalism can provide the bridge between direct discussion and consensus building, on the one hand, and interest group (or constituency) conflict mediation and resolution, on the other, "without insisting that on most matters all . . . citizens have a common interest."[21] In a very real but unstated sense, Mansbridge attempts to link the ideals of workplace democracy, the earlier republican ideals that federalism was thought to sustain, and the twentieth-century pluralist or interest group liberal practice of organized interest politics.

Philosophically at least, Mansbridge is not promoting consociationalism in the same way that industrial policy advocates adopt corporatism. Her position stresses the bargaining *process* and subsystem autonomy; theirs emphasizes the *resultant* consensus and authority for decisions.[22] Nonetheless, the bargaining process envisioned is a bargaining process built around functional constituencies. This recommendation and Dahl's imply a second requirement for successfully incorporating theories of workplace democracy within a broader institutional theory of the relationship between the workplace and the state. It is the requirement to emphasize the roles of workplaces as functional constituency organizations instead of their roles as molders and educators of individual democratic citizens who participate in elections. It is necessary to reconcile the public roles of these organizations, whose existence as political constituencies introduces functional inequalities and differential claims on public resources, with traditional notions of equal citizens and majority consent.

Toward Democratic Functional Constituencies

Participatory theorists disagree about appropriate strategies for developing democratic constituencies and about the likely outcomes or by-products of more or less democratized workplaces. Some writers—notably Peter Bachrach, C. B. Macpherson, and Carole Pateman—believe that participants in democratic workplaces are better equipped than members of undemocratic organizations to fulfill their roles as public citizens. Their proximity hypothesis holds that democratic values learned in the workplace should awaken the civic consciousness of individuals and motivate them to participate in such traditional political forums as elections. In this way, democracy within the political system can be expanded and the accountability of public officials enhanced. Other writers are skeptical of the proximity hypothesis. Dahl and Mansbridge, for example, think that the pluralistic and institutional constraints of the political system—adversary democracy, in Mansbridge's parlance—cannot be as easily overridden as advocates of the proximity hypothesis hope.

Many advocates of workplace democracy lack a theory of the state—or, more accurately, they assume that the state is divorced from, if not at odds with, the possessive individualist values that pervade American political culture. But democratized workplaces frequently reflect and reinforce these values rather than contribute to a form of political democracy as measured by egalitarian and cooperative standards. Theories of institutional linkage that are compatible with possessive individualist values are therefore necessary. Both the regulatory framework of Dahl (or Lowi) and the consociational bridge of Mansbridge rely on possessive individualist urges manifested in factional behavior, federalism as an institutional theory of factional constraint and accommodation, and the ideal of local democracy believed protected by federalism. Their proposals provide suggestive avenues for incorporating theories of workplace democracy within a theory of the political system. To be sure, they also are compatible with interest group liberal or corporatist practices, but these practices prevail partly because of a lack of countervailing democratic constituencies. The difficulty lies in justifying functional constituencies as legitimate actors in the political process.

Dahl's and Mansbridge's strategies attempt to link the ideals of participatory theory with the organized interest politics of pluralism or interest group liberalism. They underscore an implicit theme throughout this and the preceding chapter: a *viable* theory of workplace democracy promises not a radical transformation of American politics but realizable adjustments to contemporary practices that are in keeping with the pluralism and liberalism of the polity. Possessive individualist values, which are reinforced by institutional and political practices, must be incorporated, not discounted, in the design of participatory theories of democracy. A straightforward proposition follows from this theme: the success of workplace democracy will ultimately be measured by *the extent to which more or less democratic workplaces serve as constituent organizations for their members' interests*—interests shaped largely by possessive individualist values—*and take on the roles of constituency organizations in the political arena.* These democratic organizations can select or influence public officials to serve as their representatives, or they can engage in public policy-making with other functional interests and with representatives of the government (or a combination of the two). In these ways, such organizations can provide the basis for advancing and defending members' tangible interests in the larger political arena against similarly constituted and elite-dominated organizations.

This proposition can be labeled the *democratic functional constituency* thesis, or DFC. It suggests principally that democratic workplaces bargain, as functional constituencies, with other functional constituencies in an interest group liberal or corporatist fashion. This may appear to contradict a recurrent theme of participationists: that democratized workplaces can renew civic consciousness of worker-citizens and contribute to enhanced political system democracy through elections and popular representation. There is no contradiction. Workers in their constituency roles differ from workers in their public or civic roles. Individual workers may have learned democratic values and may seek to extend them to the political system through voting and other legitimate—and usually individualized—means (for example, campaign contributions, interest group affiliation). These individuals, however, also may be cross-pressured, co-opted, or alienated and may "unlearn" their participatory values, thus forestalling hopes of rejuvenating effective popular participation. Their roles in the public arena are not hereby disregarded. But since the interests workers have to defend are their interests *qua* workers, not their interests as isolated individuals, it is appropriate to focus on the functional constituency in the political system, not on the civic role of the individual worker.

The differences between these two general positions—the proximity hypothesis and the DFC—echo the early strategic (and philosophic) divisions between Fabian and guild socialists over legislative (popular) representation as opposed to functional representation and over how far to democratize which constituents, citizens or workers.[23] The proximity hypothesis and the DFC are not at odds; they are complementary. Like their industrial and economic democracy counterparts, both approaches to participatory theory posit the workplace—

that is, the functional unit—as the central unit of jurisdiction for peoples' lives. The two approaches do diverge over strategy: how participatory values are to be implemented in developing political democracy. Advocates of the proximity hypothesis place the burden of proof for enhanced democratization on a highly optimistic prescription for deriving broad political participation from values developed in the workplace, and they assume, too easily, political system conditions that facilitate democracy. The DFC assumes that the values and political practices constraining the fulfillment of the proximity hypothesis can be used advantageously by democratic functional constituencies. Workers who have sufficient interest in their livelihoods and democratic decision-making mechanisms in the workplace may or may not extend individualized democratic participation to the political system, but they are in positions to prevent the breakdown of the conditions that empower them and to minimize the co-optative effects of cross-pressured individualized participation.

The DFC, however, poses difficult problems within the context of liberal democratic theory that the proximity thesis seems to avoid. A cautionary note is therefore in order. Workplaces may serve as the significant democratic forums for their members, and democratic workplaces built on possessive individualist values may be viable as mechanisms for aggregating and articulating members' interests. Workplaces, however, are functional jurisdictions. They exist in a broader social, political, and economic context set by liberal democratic theory (not to be confused with interest group liberal practice). That context traditionally vests political legitimacy in the free (voluntary) consent given by individual citizens—thus the juridical criterion, "one person, one vote." If democratic workplaces are to bargain and negotiate with other functional interests, that proposition implies another, the flip side of the coin so to speak: by what authority do functional units undertake political or public action on behalf of their constituents? Public authority gains its authority through consent and popular representation, and only public authority can sanction (or, stated negatively, default to) corporatist or interest group liberal negotiating forums.

Although the Constitution recognizes geographic jurisdictions, these were designed to extend and enhance the principle of popular representation, not to provide functional alternatives to it, as some detractors claimed. Both Madison and Jefferson viewed state and local representation as extensions of the principle of popular representation, not as functional alternatives, as some Anti-Federalists argued and as Calhoun would later argue.[24] The very existence of functional jurisdictions, however, poses differential claims on public authority. The theoretical constraints on democratized workplaces are therefore analogous to, and in some instances identical with, the constraints facing corporatist modes of restructuring the political economy. A key difference is that democratized workplaces are not organizations for top-down elite management or control and that they need not be deployed (or co-opted) in a strategy to alleviate the so-called governability crisis, as corporatism frequently is perceived to do.[25] To overcome or to resolve these constraints, a theory of workplace democracy must reconcile the public roles of its functional organizations—and the distinctions and priorities, that is, inequalities, that such organizations imply—with traditional notions of equal citizens and majority consent. The burden of proof is on theories of the political system more than on theories of workplace democracy, for democratic workplaces must be incorporated within a broader institutional theory that spells out the ground rules for relationships between the workplace, and other functional jurisdictions, and the state. The next chapter describes the basic ground rules that must be established for relationships between legislative bodies (public authority) and democratic functional units (workplaces) to permit or to legitimate publicly binding actions by functional jurisdictions.

NOTES

1. C. B. Macpherson, *The Life and Times of Liberal Democracy* (New York: Oxford University Press, 1977), 104; Carole Pateman, *Participation and Democratic Theory* (Cambridge: Cambridge University Press, 1970), 44, 103–11. The thesis is explicated in Ronald M. Mason, *Participatory and Workplace Democracy* (Carbondale: Southern Illinois University Press, 1982), chaps. 3–4. It is tested in Edward S. Greenberg, *Workplace Democracy: The Political Effects of Participation* (Ithaca, N.Y.: Cornell University Press, 1986).

2. Andrew Hacker, "Politics and the Corporation," in *The Corporation Take-Over,* ed. Hacker (Garden City, N.Y.: Doubleday, 1964), 239–62, at 251–52, 261.

3. Ibid., 254–59.

4. Robert B. Reich, *The Next American Frontier* (New York: New York Times Books, 1983), 248–49, 251; see also 246–54, 280–82.

5. See chapter 6, herein, note 38.

6. See chapter 7, note 17. Edward S. Greenberg, "Industrial Democracy and the Democratic Citizen," *Journal of Politics* 43 (Nov. 1981): 964–81, argues that members of participatory firms are more inclined to be activist in

local politics, though not in such traditional forms of participation as voting and party politics, and that workplace participation encourages this activism (not the other way around), but he also points out that this activism is based on possessive individualist values and incentives.

7. On the distinction between public values and economic ideals as private values, see the interesting exchange between Philip Green and Robert A. Dahl, "What Is Political Equality?" *Dissent* 26 (Summer 1979): 351–68, esp. Green, passim, and Dahl, 365–67. See also Dahl, "On Removing Certain Impediments to Democracy in the United States," *Political Science Quarterly* 92 (Spring 1977): 1–20. More generally, see chapter 7, note 35.

8. Robert H. Salisbury, "Interest Representation: The Dominance of Institutions," *American Political Science Review* 78 (Mar. 1984): 64–76, at 67–70, 75; Charles E. Lindblom, *Politics and Markets* (New York: Basic Books, 1977), 45–50, 176–77.

9. George Gilder, *Wealth and Poverty* (New York: Bantam Books, 1981); Robert Nozick, *Anarchy, State, and Utopia* (New York: Basic Books, 1974); cf. Lindblom, *Politics and Markets*, 47.

10. Douglas Yates, Jr., *The Politics of Management* (San Francisco: Jossey-Bass Publishers, 1985), 12. See also Robert A. Dahl, *A Preface to Economic Democracy* (Berkeley: University of California Press, 1985), 113–16; Hacker, "Politics and the Corporation," 249–53, 258–59.

11. Christopher Eaton Gunn, *Workers' Self-Management in the United States* (Ithaca, N.Y.: Cornell University Press, 1984), chap. 8; Ronald M. Mason, "Constraints upon Workplace Democracy in the United States," paper presented at the Midwest Political Science Association annual meetings, Chicago, Ill., 1986.

12. On the first, see Martin Carnoy and Derek Shearer, *Economic Democracy: The Challenge of the 1980s* (Armonk, N.Y.: M. E. Sharpe, 1980), chaps. 9–10; the second, Kenneth M. Dolbeare, *Democracy at Risk: The Politics of Economic Renewal*, rev. ed. (Chatham, N.J.: Chatham House Publishers, 1986), chaps. 9–12; the third, Samuel Bowles, David M. Gordon, and Thomas E. Weisskopf, *Beyond the Waste Land* (Garden City, N.Y.: Anchor Books, 1984), 385–90, to which cf. Macpherson, *Life and Times*, 98–108.

13. See Theodore J. Lowi, *The End of Liberalism*, 2d ed. (New York: W. W. Norton, 1979), chap. 8. On the institutionalization of movements, see Lowi, *The Politics of Disorder* (New York: W. W. Norton, 1971).

14. Jane J. Mansbridge, *Beyond Adversary Democracy* (New York: Basic Books, 1980), 278–89; cf. 163–82; Mansbridge, "Fears of Conflict in Face-to-Face Democracies," in *Workplace Democracy and Social Change*, ed. Frank Lindenfeld and Joyce Rothschild-Whitt (Boston: Porter Sargent, 1982), 125–37. On the problem of outsiders and recruitment, see Joyce Rothschild-Whitt, "The Collectivist Organization: An Alternative to Bureaucratic Models," in *Workplace Democracy and Social Change*, ed. Lindenfeld and Rothschild-Whitt, 23–49, at 38–45.

15. See Robert H. Salisbury, "An Exchange Theory of Interest Groups," *Midwest Journal of Political Science* 13 (Feb. 1969): 1–32; Terry M. Moe, *The Organization of Interests* (Chicago: University of Chicago Press, 1980); Mancur Olson, Jr., *The Logic of Collective Action* (New York: Schocken Books, 1968).

16. *Federalist 10*. See the excellent assessment of the problem in Grant McConnell, *Private Power and American Democracy* (New York: Alfred A. Knopf, 1966), 102–18.

17. Dahl, *Preface to Economic Democracy*, 91–92, 98–110; Mansbridge, *Beyond Adversary Democracy*, 264–69, 293–98.

18. Procedural criteria are discussed in Dahl, *Preface to Economic Democracy*, 56–62; see also Dahl, "On Removing Certain Impediments to Democracy."

19. On factional behavior, see Dahl, *Preface to Economic Democracy*, 99–100, 108–10. On self-regulation, see ibid., 104–5, cf. 65–71.

20. Mansbridge, *Beyond Adversary Democracy*, 296.

21. Ibid., 298; see also 264–69, 293–98.

22. Consociational democracy and corporatism are frequently conflated; consociationalism is viewed as a liberal or moderate version of liberal or societal corporatism. For attempts to clarify confusions, see Gabriel A. Almond, "Corporatism, Pluralism, and Professional Memory," *World Politics* 35 (Jan. 1983): 245–60; Frank L. Wilson, "Interest Groups and Politics in Western Europe," *Comparative Politics* 16 (Oct. 1983): 105–23.

23. For a brief discussion, see Pateman, *Participation and Democratic Theory*, 36–41. See also Robert A. Dahl, "Workers' Control of Industry and the British Labor Party," *American Political Science Review* 41 (Oct. 1947): 875–900.

24. See, for example, Adrienne Koch's discussion of Madison's position in the controversy over the Alien and Sedition Acts in her *Jefferson and Madison: The Great Collaboration* (New York: Oxford University Press, 1950), 184–211. See also Jefferson's arguments for an extensive and democratic system of wards in Merrill D. Peterson, ed., *The Portable Thomas Jefferson* (New York: Viking Press, 1975), 537–38; exerpts in Saul K. Padover, ed., *Thomas Jefferson on Democracy* (New York: New American Library, 1939), 18, 39–42.

25. With respect to political settings more receptive to formalized corporatism than the United States, Stewart Clegg argues that workplace democratic participation within the political system is likely to be sanctioned by state-guided corporatism. See "Organizational Democracy, Power and Participation," in *Organizational Democracy and Political Processes*, ed. Colin Crouch and Frank A. Heller (New York: John Wiley and Sons, 1983), 3–34, at 19–20. Corporatism as a method of control to enhance governability and elite interests is stressed by Schmitter and Panitch, among others; see chapter 6 herein.

CHAPTER 9

Democratic Functional
Constituencies and Liberal Norms

Civic participation, popular representation, and public accountability
are central principles of the Madisonian or constitutionalist tradition.
Today, however, they are not highly valued, or they are given only
token acknowledgment in American politics. Their decline has been
attributed to several interrelated factors. At this point it may be useful
to recapitulate the more salient ones discussed in earlier chapters.

• Pluralism arguably has been the dominant twentieth-century public philosophy. Pluralist theory is a response to the ostensible inadequacies of the Madisonian model, a caricature of Madison's theory
which takes for granted that the political apathy of citizens and their
deference to interest group leadership are the natural stuff of politics.
Pluralism attempts to remedy these deficiencies with a theory that
reduces politics to interest group representation and accommodation.

• The theory and practice of pluralism has evolved to the point that
any pretense for the authoritativeness of public institutions has effectively been abandoned. Interest group liberalism, a term that characterizes the "logic" of mature pluralism, brings politics full circle to the
dilemma posed by Madison: the problem of faction. In undermining
public institutions and delegating authority to private interests, however, it legitimates rather than controls the role of faction. The "public
interest" is a function of organizational objectives, not deliberations
by public representative bodies.

• The costs of these developments are significant. Madison's hopes
that civic participation and popular representation would be the pivot
upon which the new government would turn have been belied. Moreover, it is unlikely these principles can be restored, at least not in the
same terms that Madison envisioned. Citizens' commitments to their
economic or functional jurisdictions and the actual roles of these organizations appear to be so well institutionalized that any return to

the sorts of conditions that made the Madisonian principles realistic, in the founders' eyes, is highly improbable. The inadequacies of the argument for revitalizing the rule of law are indicative of this.

• Corporatist scholars have proposed one solution to the patholo-gies of interest group liberalism. Although the solution is rooted in the realities of group and organizational jurisdictions and predicated on a need to enhance governability, it is unsatisfactory from the stand-points of both civic participation and public accountability.

• Participatory theorists have posed a different sort of solution, one that makes a plausible case for the development of democracy within functional jurisdictions and one that is much more compatible with democratic principles. It is not self-evident, however, that the demo-cratic functional constituency thesis, or DFC, can be made compatible with the Madisonian principle that corporatism fails to satisfy: the public accountability required of elective institutions. It must be shown that the DFC does not contradict and may even enhance the inclusive, egalitarian requirements of popular representation. It must not exclude others or be simply a form of privilege for functional con-stituencies that happen to be democratically organized and governed at the expense of individuals not so privileged.

• Notwithstanding the anticipated pitfalls encountered in the ar-gument for the DFC, it should not be dismissed too easily. The alter-native is interest group liberalism and its maturation in a form of corporatism. Under these, the constitutionalist or Madisonian re-quirements for popular representation and public accountability con-tinue to be eroded and reduced to symbolic exercises. This is no alternative.

The proximity thesis proposes that citizens can promote political system democracy if the values they gain from workplace participa-tion motivate them to participate in popular elections and other civic forums. It raises few difficulties of a *theoretical* nature. The more sa-lient issues are *practical:* cross-pressures, co-optation, and the like, mentioned in the preceding chapters, may undo the educative effects of democratic workplaces. By contrast, the democratic functional constituency thesis emphasizes the organizational role of the work-place constituency in politics. The DFC proposes that these constitu-ent organizations or jurisdictions can play significant political roles, as democratic organizations, in the development, or redevelopment, of real democratic representation in the political system. As such, unlike the proximity thesis, this proposition raises certain *theoretical* difficulties.

Aside from its normative virtues, the concept of popular representation has one important practical virtue: it is neat. It assumes the juridical guideline of one person, one vote.[1] Any proposal for the representational roles of functional jurisdictions, democratic or otherwise, is inherently messy or complex. Functional jurisdictions are principally corporate units, but by extension an argument for them must include the other sorts of interest associations (ethnic, religious, and geographic, for example) through which people define their civic roles. The workplace may provide the primary context for one's political identity and help shape one's values. For many citizens, it is the organizational jurisdiction for their political activities. But on what grounds are its authority and its various roles sanctioned? In some situations, the representational roles of functional institutions may parallel, perhaps supersede, the traditional roles of elective institutions. In others, these institutions may provide the basis for citizen participation in traditional electoral politics. The complexity of identifying, legitimating, and assigning roles to diverse types of functional jurisdictions, coupled with the overlapping activities of these and elective institutions, compounds the sorts of problems that are thought to be resolved in theories of popular representation.

In short, how can legitimacy be granted to the public roles of functional constituency units within the framework of liberal democratic theory? The dilemma for the DFC thesis is how—or whether—the requirements necessitated by functional jurisdictions can be reconciled with those of liberal democracy, particularly its procedural norms.

This chapter spells out the considerations necessary to reconcile the DFC with certain procedural liberal democratic principles. These principles, if developed and put into practice, permit democratic functional constituencies to be assigned legitimate roles within the framework of popular representation. In some instances, the feasibility of the principles is straightforward; in others, it is problematic, even tenuous. In the end, no new "theory" of democracy is developed, however desirable that might be, because the conditions for realizing each of the principles cannot fully be met. These practical liabilities of restoring real democratic representation by the DFC are examined in the concluding chapter.

Criteria for Functional Constituencies

Logically, democratic functional constituency organizations can undertake three roles, either independently or simultaneously. First, they can be the primary linkage mechanism between organizational members and public officials by serving as the electoral jurisdictions for their members in lieu of traditional geographic jurisdictions for popular representation. This would require a constitutional amendment and inordinately complex calculations to determine at what point individuals abandon traditional electoral venues for functional ones. (Theoretically, the calculations could lead to the conclusion that all geographic jurisdictions be abandoned in favor of functional ones.) The creation of functional jurisdictions as the electoral venues for elective legislatures is a theoretical possibility but not a likely one, and it is not henceforth included in the discussion. Under the criteria specified shortly, the assignment of roles for DFCs must be made by elective legislatures based on public interest standards they establish, and it is improbable that they would act to transform radically the basis for their elective status. Instead, it is more plausible to assume they would assign or delegate representational and policy-making roles to specific functional constituencies for specific types of activities, as suggested by the following two roles for DFCs.

Second, democratic functional constituencies can serve as linkage mechanisms for influencing public officials to act on behalf of the membership's interests; that is, they can seek to gain access to decision makers, lobby, and engage in the usual practices of bargaining for influence and accommodation prescribed by pluralists. Although this role is part and parcel of pluralism, the assertion that functional organization elites must represent their membership distinguishes the argument for democratic functional constituencies from interest group liberal elitism. It also hinges on the third role.

Third, they can engage in policy initiation, policy-making, and policy implementation with public officials and other functional interest organizations in the formal manner of corporatism; that is, they can acquire authority for these activities under explicit delegations by legislative bodies. Interest group liberalism and corporatism do not pretend to be legitimated within the framework of liberal principles. Rather, they serve to undermine the criteria for legitimacy required by liberal theory. The third role is thus crucial. If it can be justified, then the claims on behalf of membership representation made when DFCs fulfill the second role can also be justified and carry greater weight than the practices of interest group elites under interest group liberalism or corporatism.

A starting point is in an argument Charles Anderson made to challenge corporatist theorists, which received only scant acknowledgment by them. Anderson argues that an attempt to reconcile the representational roles of functional organizations with liberal norms can be undertaken only if certain minimal and stringent liberal democratic principles are incorporated in the process of designing corporatist arrangements. He stipulates, first, a public interest criterion to justify representation by functional organizations and, second, the proviso that the actions of these bodies conform to the criterion, that is, "the decisions taken by bodies structured on functional lines are not rendered legitimate by virtue of the principle of representation on which they are based but by the conformity of their decisions to some substantive criterion of public action."[2] Anderson further stipulates, almost as a corollary of the first proviso, the requirement of organizational democracy. The criteria serve as the basis for the argument that follows.

The first criterion pertains to the *grounds for incorporating interest representation.* Even if functional units (workplaces) are democratized, should they "count" in the political process, and if so, count as what or for what? The second pertains to the *guidelines for decisionmaking outcomes.* If a decision role for democratic functional units is granted, are these units authorized to promote ends as they define them, or are they constrained by—that is, must they be in conformity with—prior guidelines? The principles are more complex than they first appear to be. They serve as a skeletal framework that will be fleshed out in the following paragraphs. The principles are similar in intent to the rule of law framework proposed by Theodore Lowi, a similarity Anderson noted when he proposed them. They are also consistent with Robert Dahl's criteria for procedural democracy. Anderson's principles can be refined by integrating them with certain of Lowi's principles (the requirement that public purpose be articulated in law produced by legislative deliberation) and Dahl's (the requirements of equality, effective participation, public control of the agenda, and inclusiveness). The result is a framework of four basic principles that should guide the design of arrangements for decision making by functional jurisdictions.[3]

First, *delegations of authority,* which authorize the public roles of functional organizations, *are permissible only when granted on the grounds of explicit public interest standards.*

Second, *public interest standards or guidelines must be established by legislative deliberation,* that is, by the actions of popularly elected representative bodies.

Third, *the actual decisions taken by functional organizations must conform to the public interest guidelines established by legislative deliberation.*

Fourth, *functional organizations must be governed internally by democratic procedures.*

The first two principles establish the grounds for incorporating functional bodies as legitimate representative institutions or representatives of their constituents. That is, only properly authorized bodies can have legitimate public roles. On what grounds are organizations "properly authorized," though? The first two general principles suggest necessary conditions for functional representation.

In liberal theory, public authority may legitimately be delegated to administrative agencies and private interests under a variety of circumstances. Whatever specific policy problems occasion the delegation, the first two principles should govern it. The delegation must be granted to secure public ends, and public ends must be established through legislative deliberation, that is, through deliberations based on popular representation.[4] It should be expected that specific delegations of authority will be made primarily on pragmatic, not normative, grounds. The objectives to be secured through delegations of authority, however, must be sanctioned by popular consent, that is, by the public's elected legislative body. Further, not all delegations of authority need be granted by direct legislative acts, since subsequent subsidiary delegations can be permitted under prior ones. But public purposes, or the public interest criteria guiding delegations, must be the result of direct legislative action.

The first two criteria are in keeping with a basic tenet of liberal democratic theory, namely, that governmental legitimacy rests on public consent exercised through popular representation. It is notoriously difficult, however, for legislatures consistently to specify clear and precise guidelines to govern their delegations of authority. Lowi's well-known proposal for juridical democracy, for example, seems to have gone largely unheeded by policymakers.[5] Lowi, Grant McConnell, and others have criticized contemporary explanations of the political process in part because these distort traditional liberal theory. They also have been concerned because the explanations make no effort to justify functionally based policy-making and representation as an alternative to traditional liberal norms. An acceptable theory of functional representation must supplement, but not supplant, the liberal democratic ideal of popular representation. For functional representation will be used to reinforce public interest criteria established through popular representation for those policy arenas in which the popularly elected legislature acknowledges it is desirable or necessary to delegate its decision-making authority. To summarize, the necessary conditions for functional representation require that the designation of appropriate functional interest constituencies be based on public interest standards articulated by popularly elected representatives in the legislative arena.

The third and fourth principles pertain to the actions of functional bodies sanctioned under the first two principles. That an organization has been properly delegated to act, under the preceding criteria, is a necessary condition, but it is not a sufficient condition for action. Instead, the third criterion requires action consistent with the legislative guidelines: *the actual decisions taken by functional bodies must conform to the criteria of public purposes.* This underscores the point that prior legislative authorization is a necessary but not a sufficient condition for action by functional organizations: "policies are not legitimate because they are made by a certain kind of representative body but because they conform to an explicit standard of public decision."[6] It is precisely the failure of interest group liberalism to meet this criterion that has concerned Lowi and McConnell.

Nor are the decisions of functional bodies legitimate simply because they meet the interests of the constituents represented in the decision-making body. Unions (or professional associations) may be authorized to *establish* tenure and promotion (or accreditation and licensing) guidelines because they represent the individuals under review more adequately than do other associations. They also may be authorized to *implement* the guidelines, that is, to conduct personnel evaluations, based on their expertise, proficiency, and so forth. These are necessary but not sufficient conditions for their actions. Legislative authorization must also include *standards that the legislature defines as a public interest,* under the second criterion, and these become *the ground rules for establishing and implementing the guidelines.* For example, tenure and promotion guidelines may be established to promote a public interest in employment stability (in which case seniority serves as a guideline), economic or other forms of productivity (expertise or meritocracy as a guideline), social or group equity (equal opportunity as a guideline), and the like.

The fourth principle is rooted in concerns similar to those voiced by McConnell in *Private Power and American Democracy:* the delegation of public authority to functional bodies or units amounts to a licensing procedure under which internal democracy ought be required, because organizations authorized to act on behalf of the public interest become agents of the state. Moreover, these publicly authoritative interests are involuntary associations in a variety of ways, and their constituents do not ordinarily have the freedom to reject their authority. Just as democracy is necessary to constrain the (involuntary) state, organizational democracy is necessary for these associations.[7] This principle is problematic at best, as will become evident shortly, partly because its status is contingent on the ways in which legislatures might address the other criteria.

The preceding criteria are minimal but stringent. They provide a framework in which both the *delegation* of public authority and the *public interest* criteria that underlie such delegations serve as the ground rules for actions by functional bodies. The next section takes up the issue of what sorts of standards a legislature must consider. The corollary issue of whether a legislature is politically capable of articulating public interest standards is addressed in the following chapter.

Delegating Authority and the Public Interest

How would a legislature establish public interest criteria and guidelines to constrain the activities of functional bodies? Any delegation of authority will involve substantive guidelines concerning which interests should have what sort of authority, and these guidelines will depend primarily on the discrete policy arena—at least in the initial effort. For example, a commodity price support system can be undertaken by delegating to agricultural interests the power to police acreage and weight allotments rather than giving them direct cash subsidies. The former alternative has the advantage of designating specific interests to be responsible for both costs and benefits of the program; the latter, the disadvantage of providing benefits to a narrow range of interests while imposing costs on a broad array of interests and ultimately the general public. As the preferred alternative evolves, however, other interests develop relevant claims on the policy: commodity brokers, suppliers, exporters, retailers, and consumers, all of which are affected by the results of the initial policy effort. Subsequent legislative oversight is likely to be influenced by these claims, producing other conflicting, and sometimes counterproductive, ancillary policies.

The preceding scenario may appear to pose intractable problems. It suggests the quagmire that characterizes contemporary agriculture policy developed under interest group liberal auspices since the 1950s.[8] The point to stress, however, is that the problems are preeminently practical ones, notwithstanding their apparent complexity. They are resolvable, in principle at least, if the substantive guidelines for identifying functional organizations are first predicated on the sorts of procedural democratic principles stipulated earlier. Substantive guidelines that designate functional interests and their activities in delegating authority should be consistent with these procedural guidelines. Appropriately constituted procedures raise thorny practical *and* theoretical problems. These include questions about the type of interest constituency, the scope of representation for the constituency, and the decision rules to be employed by functional bodies. Constituency type and the scope of representation involve principles of inclusiveness and equality: what type of constituency, which interests, who or what counts as equals. Decision rules pertain to principles of effective participation, control of the agenda, and, again, inclusiveness: voting and representation within the constituency as well as in the relationships between functional jurisdictions.

First, on *what grounds* do *which* functional interests have greater priority over others for inclusion within a particular scheme of functional representation? A logically prior question is, why functional jurisdictions in the first place, as opposed to popular or geographic ones? This question is not merely rhetorical since the preponderance of views in the liberal tradition inveighs against functional representation. As Elaine Spitz said in a pithy criticism, "Representing the will of the people through agencies they have not willed to join seems anomalous."[9] This is another way of alleging that functional representation presumes to "prefigure" individuals' interests, thereby violating liberal standards of individualism and nullifying the individualist grounds on which popular representation is justified.[10] In many ways, however, the criticism is misleading, as reflection on discussions of participatory theory and corporate citizenship in previous chapters suggests. Individuals may not frequently be voluntary members of functional organizations, but they are perhaps less frequently voluntary members of geographic jurisdictions, Spitz's preferred mode of organizing individual voters. Citizens are not prone to "vote with their feet," as candidate Ronald Reagan was fond of recommending in the 1980 presidential election. Further, they develop ties, loyalties, a sense of belonging to both types of jurisdictions. These may be reinforced by people's immobility, but they also help individuals reconcile themselves to their positions, that is, to rationalize their "choices."[11] The relevant question is whether these different types of constituencies can serve liberal democratic ends (and whether both, not solely functional ones, are required to be governed internally by democratic principles, an issue taken up shortly).

In view of these considerations, it is assumed here—with full recognition that this is a big assumption—that the principle of representation for functional constituencies can be accepted on grounds analogous to those that permit representation for geographic ones, as opposed to, say, "at-large" electoral jurisdictions. That is to say, functional units must be designed to extend the principle of popular representation. Although it appears to beg substantial questions, the assumption is consistent with the aims of most participationists, especially with such proposals as Robert Dahl's and Jane Mansbridge's, reviewed in chapter 8. It also requires that the corporatist-derived basis for functional constituencies be accommodated to democratic norms, not the other way around.

Spitz's criticism is that members of functional groups have no real choices about membership—for example, membership for ethnic minorities and religious groups is by birth or acculturation. For that matter, class structure dictates that some workers be union members, not executives. That is why the insistence on the fourth principle, the requirement of *democracy* for the internal governance of functional groups, is important. Insofar as group membership conveys interests that exceed the sum of individual interests—a sort of group or collective or "corporate" identity, for example—subordination of individual to group interests is warranted in the same way that traditional liberal democracy sanctions the subordination of individual interests to the public interest: through the democratic process. Moreover, the designation of a particular functional jurisdiction can be undertaken in the first place only by adherence to the second principle: criteria for selection are made through deliberations of elective legislative bodies. Even with these caveats, the designation of functional jurisdictions raises problems that geographic ones do not, and the requirement that these organizations adhere to democratic principles will remain questionable.

Geographic units of representation (state governments) are variable, based largely on historical circumstances that antedate the Constitution. Functional units, however, have no "natural" history guidelines. *Which* functional interests have greater priority over others for inclusion in an arrangement that provides for group representation? If a legislative body attempts to incorporate functional interests within a scheme of representation, it cannot avoid simultaneously designating specific functional interests. Virtually by definition, the concept of functional representation entails types, classifications, categories. In other words, the purposes of specific policies should provide reasonably clear guidelines for inclusion or exclusion.

Expediency and efficiency—and even rights—are common justifications for functional representation.[12] Such guidelines as these might enable legislators to include some interests and exclude others from deliberations about particular policy arenas. For example, agricultural interests superficially are not germane to problems facing basic industry, in which industry, labor, and investment banking have relevant stakes; industry and banking are not germane to educational policy; and so on. Nonetheless, lobbying by groups that believe they would be affected by the guidelines, albeit tangentially, might contribute to an inordinately complex process of establishing substantive guidelines. Agriculture does have a stake in international trade deficits that primarily affect industry; industry and banking have stakes in education (job training, technical and computer proficiency, mathematics and science curricula, and so forth).[13] In other words, the process of identifying legitimate functional interests could become bogged down in endless special pleading.[14] Some interest claimants could be assigned legitimate functional status more easily than others. Civil rights problems provide an analogy: the determination of "protected" or "suspect" classes based on histories of past discrimination. Historical practices that denied constitutional rights provide grounds for giving priority to women and ethnic minorities but not to left-handed or short/tall persons, for example. (Unless, of course, left-handed or short/tall people can mobilize evidence of constitutional deprivations.) The problem of assigning functional priority to some interests but not to others would require ongoing reevaluation of the status and claims of interests and would be particularly daunting to legislative bodies that historically had played the game of interest group liberal politics.[15]

Moreover, even if general substantive guidelines can help narrow the field of relevant interests for a given policy arena, these must be consistent with basic liberal procedural guidelines. Procedural guidelines of equality and inclusiveness in participation obviously would not suffice or aid legislators in selecting functional representatives. For example, unorganized service or technology workers and migrant farm laborers do not have the organizational resources to be recognized as functional interests that some unions and agricultural organizations (the Farm Bureau Federation, for instance) do. To apply egalitarian and inclusive guidelines to established functional interests only, ignoring nascent groups, movements, and the unorganized, is simply to beg the question. (This problem is similar to the pluralist dilemma of postulating that potential groups constrain organized interests.) Unlike geographic units of representation (and religious constituencies in consociational states) that precede constitutional design, functional interests evolve through time. Some antedate specific policy arenas, others emerged in response to them, and others are emerging. To assign public roles to some interests but not to others based on considerations of organizational development, longevity, and the like would be to apply principles of equality and inclusiveness arbitrarily.

Further, there are similar problems concerning the scope of representation in designating the appropriate constituency or constituencies for the functional unit. For the corporation, are workers the sole constituents? Workers and management? Workers, management, and stockholders? Workers, management, stockholders, and consumers? These plus community representatives? Should suppliers and distributors be included?[16] Once constituencies are identified, the list goes on. Should constituency members simply vote their interests in popular elections for the legislature? Should they aggregate their votes in an effort to ensure that elected representatives represent their interests? Under a hybrid system of popular and functional democratic representation, voters in popular elections may or may not make choices that reflect their functional interests when they elect legislative representatives.

Finally, there is the problem of internal decision rules necessitated by the fourth principle of organizational democracy. What are appropriate procedural guidelines for determining how representation is to be exercised both *between* and *within* functional bodies or for weighing interests? As to the first—relationships between functional interests, as in typical corporatist interest intermediation—*equality* suggests one vote per interest; *inclusiveness,* a rule of proportionality based on membership (size); and *"functional priority,"* a rule of proportionality based on contribution—for example, that votes for capital and labor should be inverse to membership in each, since capital provides the basis for work. (The obvious variation is that votes for capital and labor should be proportionate to membership, since labor provides the basis or "value" for capital accumulation.) In principle, the voting "weight" allotted to a particular functional constituency would be determined with the articulation of public interest guidelines. The parenthetical caveat, however, suggests that a significant amount of ideological conflict would be incurred as the legislature undertakes this effort.

As to the second—the related problem of democratic representation within jurisdictions—there may be no obvious or all-encompassing solution. The first two principles advanced earlier (public interest standards, established by legislative deliberation) do not of themselves preclude the possibility that democratic sanction can be given to decisions taken by undemocratic organizations or through nondemocratic means. Legislators might want to delegate responsibilities to, or license, associations for their technical expertise in implementing the public interest, and requirements of expertise and democracy may be incompatible within the organization. The issue in such an instance would be whether the (undemocratic) organization is accountable for acting as it is authorized or delegated to act, that is, does it act in accordance with public interest criteria? Similarly, legislators may permit organizations to waive open meetings or sunshine requirements to enable personnel decisions to be conducted in a manner that protects the privacy of persons being evaluated. The extent to which personnel decisions adhere to democratic procedures may further be affected by the public interest objectives sought. Equal opportunity guidelines to promote social or group equity (to cite an example previously noted) would seem to necessitate some form of open or public decision-making process, as would meritocracy to promote productivity. But reliance on seniority to promote employment stability might not. In all such situations, however, the enabling authorization should incorporate procedures for appeal in cases of adverse decisions. Where undemocratic or nondemocratic procedures are permitted, these would be exceptions to the general rule requiring internal democracy. The likelihood of realizing the rule when no contingent exceptions are claimed is another matter, though.

In principle, attempts to develop solutions for the preceding problems should not be controversial for participationists. (Nonetheless, it is instructive to recall G. D. H. Cole's admonition against overdemocratization of the organization lest it undermine the longer-term objectives of attaining national democracy if democratic haggling and bargaining in organizations undercut their efficiency.) [17] For their corporatist counterparts, however, such efforts are controversial. A pertinent question, therefore, is whether functional interest groups incorporated within the policy process are democratic and representative of membership or whether the interests represented are those of organizational leadership.

The practice of corporatist arenas, in which membership compliance with the terms of agreements reached through elite negotiation is sought, provides a cautionary context.[18] Interest group elites may accede to certain membership demands (articulated democratically or not), but they do so primarily to obtain organizational objectives defined by the leadership. In return for this status, they can provide their counterpart elites with guarantees to constrain or discipline the organization. In other words, without further qualifications, legislative bodies can legitimate and provide criteria to guide functional representation and decision making involving organizations that are undemocratic and unrepresentative of their membership. There are, however, further qualifications.

Whether the functional organizations, deemed to have a legitimate role in public deliberations, are democratic and representative and whether the decisions taken in public deliberations conform to public interest criteria established by the legislature appear to be two entirely different questions. But are they? Legislative deliberations that establish public interest criteria to guide functional decision-making bodies should in principle incorporate, as a subsidiary criterion, the requirement that the representative associations be governed internally by democratic procedures. This is akin to saying that the legislature adopt "original position" assumptions in establishing the "contract" for publicly binding deliberations by the functional representatives.[19] The legislature would thereby require internal democracy in organizations, as a mechanism for minimizing harm for the "least advantaged" (lack of representation, in this case). Theoretically, legislatures should follow this line of reasoning if they are constituted according to the principles of popular representation and the equality of citizens in selecting their representatives and not according to an interest group liberal "gerrymander"—for example, a legislative history of acceding benefits and authority to groups based on their organizational resources and strategic position. In other words, to adopt the requirement of internal democracy for functional units presupposes that the legislature itself operates under rule of law guidelines (see chapter 4). In practice, this is unlikely.

NOTES

1. This comment is not as simplistic as it may appear. Schemes of proportional representation and weighted voting, for instance, although often articulated as modifications of popular representation criteria, carry tacit functional premises. On the other hand, the formal incorporation of functional jurisdictions within the political process raises different issues than do the sorts of interest aggregation and vote trading (often justified on functional interest grounds) that preoccupy social choice theorists. Cf. William H. Riker, *Liberalism against Populism* (Prospect Heights, Ill.: Waveland Press, 1989).

2. Charles W. Anderson, "Political Design and the Representation of Interests," *Comparative Political Studies* 10 (Apr. 1977): 127–52, at 148; they are discussed at 143–45, 148–50. See the discussion in Robert A. Dahl, *Dilemmas of Pluralist Democracy* (New Haven, Conn.: Yale University Press, 1982), 68–80, 99–100.

3. Lowi's five requirements are summarized in chapter 4 herein. See also Robert A. Dahl, *A Preface to Economic Democracy* (Berkeley: University of California Press, 1985), esp. 56–62; Dahl, *Dilemmas of Pluralist Democracy;* Dahl, "On Removing Certain Impediments to Democracy in the United States," *Political Science Quarterly* 92 (Spring 1977): 1–20. Anderson's note about juridical democracy is in "Political Design," 150.

4. See James Q. Freedman, *Crisis and Legitimacy: The Administrative*

Process and American Government (New York: Cambridge University Press, 1978); see also Grant McConnell, *Private Power and American Democracy* (New York: Alfred A. Knopf, 1966); Theodore J. Lowi, *The End of Liberalism*, 2d ed. (New York: W. W. Norton, 1979).

5. See chapter 5, note 1.

6. Anderson, "Political Design," 149.

7. Ibid., 145; McConnell, *Private Power;* cf. Dahl, *Preface to Economic Democracy*. See the discussion in chapter 8 herein.

8. William P. Browne, *Private Interests, Public Policy, and American Agriculture* (Lawrence: University Press of Kansas, 1988).

9. Elaine Spitz, *Majority Rule* (Chatham, N.J.: Chatham House Publishers, 1984), 45. See her useful review of distinctions between popular, geographic and functional jurisdictions (constituencies), 42–58.

10. Anderson, "Political Design," 148. The charge is noted in the concluding section of chapter 1 herein.

11. Spitz argues for this in her discussion of geographic constituencies in *Majority Rule*, 52–59. Loyalty and belonging are central to unitary democracy; see Jane J. Mansbridge, *Beyond Adversary Democracy* (New York: Basic Books, 1980).

12. Rights-based justifications are associated with consociationalism, in which religious and ethnic minorities have claims often based on their existence preceding constitutional design, rather than with corporatism, more typically associated with economic interests. See Herman Bakvis, "Structure and Process in Federal and Consociational Arrangements," *Publius* 15 (Spring 1985): 57–69; Thomas O. Hueglin, "Yet the Age of Anarchism?" *Publius* 15 (Spring 1985): 101–12; Arend Lijphart, *Democracies* (New Haven, Conn.: Yale University Press, 1984).

13. See "Human Capital: The Decline of America's Work Force," special report, *Business Week*, Sept. 19, 1988, 100–41.

14. For a good case in point, see Bruce A. Ackerman and William T. Hassler, *Clean Coal/Dirty Air* (New Haven, Conn.: Yale University Press, 1981).

15. This is compounded by the explosion in the number of effective lobbying groups since the 1970s. For an analysis, see Jack L. Walker, "The Origins and Maintenance of Interest Groups in America," *American Political Science Review* 77 (June 1983): 390–406. For a survey, see Kay Lehman Scholzman and John T. Tierney, *Organized Interests and American Democracy* (New York: Harper and Row, 1985), 74–82.

16. These issues could be excluded from discussion here on the grounds discussed by David P. Ellerman, "The Employment Relation, Property Rights and Organizational Democracy," in *Organizational Democracy and Political Processes*, ed. Colin Crouch and Frank A. Heller (New York: John Wiley and Sons, 1983), 265–78, at 272–75. Workers, management, and stockholders (not to mention consumers, etc.) have their own jurisdictions. These jurisdictions are defined largely in terms of laws of ownership and control (in other

words, property). In a traditional corporation, the functional unit for the worker is the union; in a cooperative, it is the firm itself. Dahl's analysis of instrumental property, in *Preface to Economic Democracy,* represents an effort to change the worker's functional jurisdiction from stockholder-owned corporation to worker-owned cooperative. Decisions *between* these jurisdictions fall under considerations about internal decision rules addressed later in this chapter.

17. See Robert A. Dahl's discussion, in "Workers' Control of Industry and the British Labor Party," *American Political Science Review* 41 (Oct. 1947): 875–900, at 887–93, and the comment he attributes to Cole: "We cannot afford to risk failure and confusion by trying to be too 'democratic' at the very start" (888). This point is also discussed in Peter Bachrach, *The Theory of Democratic Elitism* (Boston: Little, Brown, 1967), 104–5, n. 10.

18. See chapter 6; Colin Crouch, "Pluralism and the New Corporatism: A Rejoinder," *Political Studies* 31 (Sept. 1983): 452–60; Leo Panitch, "The Development of Corporatism in Liberal Democracies," *Comparative Political Studies* 10 (Apr. 1977): 61–90; Panitch, *Social Democracy and Industrial Militancy* (New York: Cambridge University Press, 1976).

19. Cf. John Rawls, *A Theory of Justice* (Cambridge, Mass.: Harvard University Press, 1970).

CHAPTER 10

Real Representation:
Reordering Political Priorities

It is one thing to describe the guidelines that should govern legislative delegations of authority to democratic functional constituencies; it is another to see them put into practice. Ultimately, legislatures set the terms for democratic workplaces and other jurisdictions.[1] If legislatures do not follow the guidelines, it is unlikely they will impose them on others.

Consider Theodore Lowi's case for juridical democracy, discussed in chapter 4. In recent decades, perhaps the most vigorously promoted argument has been that Congress should do its work in promulgating and living by the sorts of guidelines described earlier. The argument has fallen on unhearing ears—which is not surprising considering congressional incentives. Congress as a legislative institution has been so weakened that its members have little incentive to seek change; as committee member allies of organized interests, they have many incentives to sustain interest group liberal or quasi-corporatist forms of policy-making. Further, critics point out that the restoration of the rule of law presupposes an active electorate imbued with civic consciousness, whereas citizens no longer have these civic virtues but instead attune their goals and allegiances to the corporate institutions in which their needs and values are defined. (This is the liability that supporters of the proximity hypothesis seek to remedy.)

Lowi initially proposed that the *Schechter* rule be restored as the judicial linchpin for juridical democracy. The Supreme Court invalidated the National Industrial Recovery Act in *Schechter Poultry Corp. v. United States*. The Court ruled against the National Recovery Administration's promulgation of codes of fair competition under the NIRA on several grounds, including overly broad delegation: "In view of the scope of that broad declaration [of general aims], and of the nature of the few restrictions that are imposed, the discretion of the

President . . . is virtually unfettered."[2] Under the *Schechter* rule, the Court would invalidate legislative delegations of authority that do not spell out the public purposes governing the delegation and do not provide clear and precise guidelines for administrative implementation. In other words, "a blanket invalidation under the Schechter rule is tantamount to a court order for Congress to do its own work."[3] The rule was affirmed in another 1936 case but for all practical purposes was subsequently ignored.[4] A 1974 Court opinion appealed to the *Schechter* rule in restricting the leeway granted the Federal Communications Commission to levy fees, but that decision drew this response from Justices Thurgood Marshall and William J. Brennan in a companion case:

> The notion that the Constitution narrowly confines the power of Congress to delegate authority to administrative agencies, which was briefly in vogue in the 1930's, has been virtually abandoned by the Court for all practical purposes, at least in the absence of delegation creating "the danger of overbroad, unauthorized, and arbitrary application of criminal sanctions in the area of [constitutionally] protected freedoms." . . . This doctrine is surely as moribund as the substantive due process approach of the same era—for which the Court is fond of writing an obituary . . . —if not more so.[5]

According to one legal scholar, although the constitutional founders were largely silent on the issue (probably because they believed Congress would more likely expand than parcel out its authority), "the propriety of delegating legislative power must now be regarded as having been settled by the practices of two centuries." The issue turns on the type of delegation and the competencies of Congress and the recipient institutions or parties, not simply on the blanket or all-or-nothing grounds that Lowi recommends.[6]

The assumptions underlying *Schechter* have proved to be unrealistic criteria. *Schechter* was an exception to a century-old tradition that permitted Congress to delegate authority to other branches, which are to "[fill] in the details."[7] Further, once the New Deal's positive state was entrenched, the standards were easily bypassed. It is simply difficult for Congress consistently to specify clear and precise guidelines for administrative agencies. Judicial intervention designed to force Congress to live by its constitutional guidelines has been infrequent or ineffective. (Infrequent, because the presumption of constitutionality usually prevails; ineffective, because the *Schechter* rule, for example, is ignored.) The Supreme Court has moved in a *Schechter*-like direction with its invalidation of the legislative veto, however. If adhered to, the Court's decision in *INS v. Chadha* would result in congressional behavior similar to its objectives in the *Schechter* case. Invoking the language of separation of powers, the Court asks Congress to act as a legislature, not to defer to executive branch policymaking. Thus far, however, the objectives of *Chadha*, like those of *Schechter*, seem to be sidestepped easily (for example, in Gramm-Rudman-Hollings).[8] In a similar vein, Lowi's proposal that presidential vetoes of legislation be based on constitutional justifications, not on executive policy preferences, would invariably result in executive vetoes of legislative vetoes (rationalized on grounds from *Chadha*) and executive vetoes of overbroad legislative delegations of authority. A president benefiting from delegations of authority, however, is not likely to veto these on constitutional grounds, particularly since current incentives encourage a plebiscitary leadership role rather than that of responsible partisan leader or "chief legislator."[9]

Constraints and Incentives for Public Accountability

The proposal for reestablishing the rule of law must be construed as a circular argument. It seems to presuppose that legislators (and presidents) can be motivated by the sorts of public interest or juridical values and incentives that adoption of the rule of law is designed to promote.[10] One might therefore conclude that the argument for the democratic functional constituency (DFC) thesis is circular as well, since legislative designation and implementation of the public interest criteria are contingent on the existence of incentives that legislators do not seem disposed to follow.

Circularity does not condemn the DFC and its legitimating criteria to irrelevance—unless one adopts a crude instrumentalist view of political theory. It certainly does temper expectations that normative principles can guide political life. An argument for the DFC and its criteria must acknowledge these restrictions. Having said that, in what ways can the principles be relevant or "meaningful"? One important test of relevance is to juxtapose the principles to the usually unarticulated ones that inform interest group liberal politics and to suggest tentative steps for reform. Another is to spell out—recapitulate really—how the principles can be construed to be consistent with certain liberal values, notably those articulated by Madison. The first is undertaken in the remainder of this section; the second, in the concluding section.

The practice of interest group liberalism is preeminently the practice of legislative authorization: the delegation of authority to interest groups and administrative agencies. Delegation minimizes the constituency losses that attend legislative decision making and maximizes the accommodation of group claims. In the process, legislators can reduce their political costs with their elective constituents because the coercive role of government is transferred to the relevant interests and their administrative clientele. Because the authorization is frequently imprecise about public interest objectives, ways and means to attain the objectives, and the status of subsequent actions by the beneficiary organizations, the issue of responsibility or accountability—who has authority, with what consequences, for whom—is frequently lost from view. From the perspectives of legislators and organizational leaders, corporatism represents a vast improvement over interest group liberalism; governability can be enhanced, and managers can be shielded from electoral pressures. From a liberal tradition or constitutionalist perspective, of course, the practice of legislative authorization is problematic and worse as the keystone of interest group liberalism. Economic writers have criticized the practice for somewhat different reasons, but their conclusions converge with the criticism of interest group liberalism.

Over two decades ago, both Friedrich A. Hayek and Andrew Shonfield—each from substantially different perspectives—voiced concerns about the inadequacy of appealing to prior authorization to meet constituency claims. According to Hayek, "The trouble with the widespread use of delegation in modern times is not that the power of making general rules is delegated but that administrative authorities are, in effect, given power to wield coercion without rule, as no general rules can be formulated which will unambiguously guide the exercise of such power."[11] Shonfield's concerns were expressed in his observations about large-scale institutions that, simply because they are effective and efficient, displace smaller, voluntary associations and bypass democratic procedures. He focused on the central problem for subsequent corporatist scholarship, the conflict between traditional democratic norms and the roles of private institutions that exercise public authority. Shonfield acknowledged that traditional pluralist assumptions about voluntary associations blinded scholars and public officials to the involuntary, coercive character of corporations and unions. His perspective on British politics presaged subsequent critiques of interest group liberalism by American scholars: "the British, for all their anti-corporatist tradition, allow effective power to slide into the hands of the corporations without subjecting them to public control—for the national doctrine insists that they are no more than free associations of individuals whose activities are essential to the emergence of a consensus."[12] Like Hayek, Shonfield viewed such delegations of authority to be inevitable when economic coordination and planning are undertaken by governments, but he cautioned that effectiveness, efficiency, and inevitability are not antidotes to the arbitrariness that concerns Hayek.[13]

Hayek would prefer the abandonment of government intervention in the economy, but in the absence of this, his preference, like Shonfield's, is clear. Such guidelines as public interest criteria should be articulated in or govern the legislative authorization—guidelines comparable to those stipulated in the preceding chapter. If the legitimacy of functional interest representation hinged solely on whether the pertinent interests could verify the source of their public roles in prior legislative deliberations, then most of the criticisms of interest group liberalism's delegation of public authority would be irrelevant, and claims on behalf of functional representation would be self-evident in the contexts of economic policy and administrative politics. Under these circumstances, democratic workplaces and other democratic functional constituencies could engage in interest group liberal or quasi-corporatist bargaining and accommodation with their elite-dominated, undemocratic counterpart organizations. Ultimately, however, the legitimacy of functional interest representation in policy-making must depend not only on legislative authorization that specifies which interests can act to attain public objectives but also on whether those organizations take action that conforms to legislative guidelines with explicit public interest criteria.[14] The previously surveyed weaknesses of the rule of law position indicates how unlikely this is.

If achieving the criterion of public ends established through legislative deliberation is unrealistic, on what grounds can the publicly authoritative roles of these interests be legitimated? One might simply argue that this question is not particularly significant since, in the modern, complex world, such delegations are inevitable.[15] Such a claim, however, begs the question; inevitability is not the same thing as constitutionality. Alternatively, one might argue that the legitimacy of private power is self-evident, rooted, for example, in Lockean types of beliefs about the sanctity of private property. That sort of claim has tremendous ideological force, since it echoes underlying values of the political culture reflected in the possessive individualism that affects efforts to democratize workplaces and in the claims for business influence and autonomy that guide the corporatist industrial policy framework. It also begs the question, since Locke established a public interest criterion for the use and regulation of private property among those adhering to the social contract.[16]

The second argument is, nevertheless, closer to the mark. It implies that the legitimacy of any public role for private power is dependent on peoples' beliefs and values, not that it is legitimate merely by default because of the complex or inevitable nature of modern politics. A popular presumption in favor of private power can, however, help rationalize its authority when it conflicts with, or requires dispensations from, the public authority of the state. Since popular presumptions need not be based on explicit justifications, the authority of private power is problematic in democratic theory. To recall Grant McConnell's criticism of pluralism, on what grounds or "by what principle" can private power's authority be legitimated?[17] The fact that presumptions favoring private power persist sheds light on why justifications for its public authority are absent.

Presumptions in favor of private power in conflicts between public and private sector values or, stated somewhat differently, the belief that the public authority or legitimacy of private power is self-evident, can work their way into the political culture in a couple of different ways. One is a reasoned or principled justification about the beneficial role of private power (or the danger of excessive governmental authority). It would be based on claims about inalienable rights and justified through the traditional liberal notion of "negative freedom." (Locke's "libertarian" side: government "*cannot take* from any Man any part of his *Property* without his own consent.") The other involves a process of rationalization that appears to be something of a corollary of the first. In this process, beneficiaries of private power are able to attribute societal benefits to their actions, and individuals come to believe that "everyman" can exert initiative and reap benefits without invoking public authority. In other words, the exercise of private power is a preferable functional alternative to public authority.[18] This would be based on claims about freedoms to exert capabilities on a par with others and justified through the notion of "equal opportunity." (Locke's "publick good" or utilitarian side: the "preservation of the property of all the Members . . . as far as is possible," property grounded on individuals' labor, which "*puts the difference of value* on every thing.")[19] In a sense, both are at work in the American political culture. The normative principles underlying the first, however, have tended to be obscured by the pragmatic benefits of the second.

These factors represent certain of the tacit assumptions undergirding interest group liberalism and corporatism. They constrain the likelihood of satisfactorily justifying the roles of democratic functional constituencies. Any attempt to overcome them must recognize that participatory theory and proposals to revitalize the rule of law cannot be considered in isolation from one another. Nor should these reform proposals be considered in isolation from the popular values that define the political culture and shape the state. Participatory theory proposals must account for, not disregard, such political culture phenomena as possessive individualist values that constrain the viability of democratic workplaces. One positive example in this regard is Jane Mansbridge's suggestion that consociational democracy can bridge the gap between unitary (local) and adversarial (systemic) democracy. Her proposal acknowledges the sorts of possessive individualist values and interest group roles that typify American politics, and, like Robert Dahl's instrumental analysis of ownership, it provides a basis for democratizing constituencies in an otherwise interest group liberal or quasi-corporatist setting.[20]

However, proposals to restore the rule of law, while accounting for possessive individualist values, frequently downplay the importance of mobilizing constituencies—understandably, since relevant constituencies currently are defined by the elitism of interest group liberalism or corporatism. For example, Lowi believes that the practice of legislative delegation and administrative discretion can be reversed and replaced with the rule of law "only if the leadership desires to reverse it."[21] Existing incentives for legislative leaders plainly make this a lame option, beholden as they are to the functional interests characterizing interest group liberalism. The restoration of the rule of law may therefore be infeasible under interest group liberal or corporatist auspices. Taken in conjunction with attempts to enhance participatory politics through democratized functional constituencies, it has greater viability, though. It is precisely such constituencies that can pressure legislators and provide them incentives for change, particularly considering the weakened and symbolic traditional electoral connection.

Participatory theory thus has its major practical relevance within this context of strategic options. The context does not preordain success, however. Democratic functional constituencies may also play negative roles. Insofar as these interests succeed in battles with their elite-dominated counterparts in the political arena, they may simply contribute to the further erosion of democratic accountability in the polity. It is important to remember that these associations are organized around the possessive individualist values of their constituent members (a central theme of chapter 7). They risk being co-opted and undermined if successes in a political arena of interest group bargaining must come at the expense of discounting democratic accountability in favor of economic or strategic gains.

Conclusions

Consent, popular representation, and electoral accountability remain important political ideals, even though they are frequently subordinated to economic goals and the power of corporate institutions. Such subordination was easily reconciled when the prevailing public philosophy was pluralist theory, for under pluralism the elitist and undemocratic nature of group politics was only vaguely recognized. As contemporary politics increasingly has become the politics of corporatism, and as it increasingly becomes recognized as that (encouraged in part by debates over economic or industrial policies and by efforts to enhance worker participation in corporations), the issues at stake are becoming more clearly drawn. Corporatism and its interest group liberal predecessor represent not an uneasy amalgam of the founders and Tocqueville, as pluralism did, but a contradiction of the principles of popular representation and public consent. Political ideals can live with the vagueness of pluralism; they require solutions to contradictions. Solutions can come in the form of pressures to restore the rule of law and democratize workplaces and communities—or, of course, in a rejection of old ideals in favor of new ones.[22]

It is not self-evident, however, that the DFC can serve as a solution to the contradiction. The scope and roles proposed for functional jurisdictions seem to challenge two core values of traditional liberalism: its defense of popular representation against class-based or economic interest representation; its individualist assumptions upon which political life is thought to be grounded. In the context of American liberalism, the notion of functional representation does not bring to mind Madison and the Constitution. It brings to mind such lost causes as John Adams's plea for a class-based system of representation, certain Anti-Federalist defenses of functional jurisdictions, and, most notorious, John C. Calhoun's defense of "concurrent majorities" based on their "peculiar institutions" against the "numerical majority," that is, against popular representation based on equal and individual citizens. Functional jurisdictions also appear to conflict with the individualist premises of the classical liberals and the criticism that individuals' values cannot be predetermined by functional categories—class, association, ethnicity, gender, or whatever.

The problem of whether functional interests can predetermine individual interests can be resolved, at least theoretically, if two conditions are met. First, functional jurisdictions must be shown to be the central or paramount jurisdictions for their members. Second, these jurisdictions must be organized along democratic lines; that is, they must abide by democratic principles in their decision-making practices and in the assignment of rights and responsibilities to members. Both conditions, of course, are central to participatory theories of workplace or industrial democracy. Both conditions, theoretically at least, transcend issues of ethnic or gender representation, since other democratized functional jurisdictions should account for these in adhering to democratic principles in decision making and in the assignment of membership rights and responsibilities. A democratically organized economic jurisdiction thus could not prohibit membership on ethnic or gender grounds. (It is for reasons such as these that many civil rights issues, such as affirmative action, which presuppose functional-like categories, are anathema to elitists but do not raise many qualms for participationists concerning how they square with individualism.) Part of the burden of this and the preceding chapters has been to argue that the first condition is met in contemporary political practices and that the second condition is met in certain circumstances and can be met in a significantly greater array of circumstances.

The problem of whether functional jurisdictions take precedence over or supersede popular ones, à la a Calhoun-like theory of concurrent majorities, appears to be more difficult, at least on the surface. In traditional liberalism, the public consent of citizens and popular representation provide the basis for legislative deliberation and ultimately for constitutionalism and the rule of law. At the same time, the traditional liberal position—most notably Madison's—presumes that popular elections (the vehicles for public consent) are meaningful, not symbolic exercises, and that popular representation is grounded on meaningful participation within the electoral constituency (in most instances, geographic units of representation). The earlier liberals held these views precisely because they made the following sorts of assumptions. First, they believed that local, territorial units were the natural and logical organizing centers of political activity—Madison's and Jefferson's local wards, for instance. Second, they believed that all citizens shared certain common values—a commitment to the Lockean priorities of lives, liberties, and estates, for instance. Third, they believed that the role of the state would be largely passive—the minimal or "nightwatchman" state or the state associated principally with "protective" functions (*protective democracy,* to use a term favored by scholars who interpret classical liberals from a twentieth-century perspective).[23]

However distant from or antithetical to popular representation and territorial jurisdictions the notion of functional jurisdictions may appear to be, it simply is not plausible to argue that traditional liberalism is wedded to the first of these *per se*. That is to say, traditional liberalism values electoral consent and popular representation as the best means for articulating the consent of individual citizens and for developing law (and not simply policy) that regulates the behavior of citizens in their capacities as citizens. The constitutional founders valued local jurisdictions because they would serve as the centers for civic participation and thus as the basis for popular representation. They did not foresee—they could not have foreseen—a highly mobile population for which electronic communication techniques transcend regional differences and for which one's agent of employment (the job market) is both the source of mobility and the resource for citizens' paramount interests.[24]

For a significant segment of the population, however, functional jurisdictions are the "functional equivalent" of traditional political or geographic ones. It is scholarly arrogance or, more charitably, a short-sighted lack of imagination to presume that a Madison would countenance the disenfranchisement of a significant portion of the citizenry simply on the grounds that they have disqualified themselves by virtue of their economic choices or the constraints placed on them by their employers. The jurisdictions of meaningful political participation and the sources of shared values for many citizens are their functional associations. It is more plausible to argue that these should be included with more traditional forums than to assert that they must be discounted—especially if functional organizations adhere to democratic principles in ways that meet, if not exceed, the adherence to democratic principles in the traditional venues. The participationists' faith in the educative value of democratic participation in relatively small units is more compelling than the pluralists' faith in the natural state of apathy for an electorate cued by their opinion elites to perform.

Nor is it plausible to argue that the modern, positive, welfare or regulatory state should be dismantled or deflated because it is a response to the needs of unrepresentative or nondemocratic functional interests and because it thereby undercuts the value premises of traditional liberal individualism and its minimal state. First, the democratic state of modern liberalism is a *modern, industrialized, and technologically advanced* democratic state—and the italicized adjectives make all the difference. State and society are deeply, inextricably, and irretrievably intertwined, and there is simply no going back to a "golden age" of an individualistic society and its minimal state.[25] (In this respect, neoconservatives are reminiscent of prerevolutionary colonial jeremiads against crown corruption and a loss of classical virtue.) Liberals may cite the importance of popular representation in criticizing the modern state and its excesses, but some form of functional representation is a feature of it—a fact of the political landscape. Second, and a corollary, it is better to acknowledge this reality and attempt to deal with it on its own terms than to rationalize by pretending it is compatible with and an improvement on traditional liberal norms—the pretensions of pluralism in assuming the group process updates outmoded features of the Madisonian model.

NOTES

1. This is stressed by David Ellerman, "On the Legal Structure of Workers' Cooperatives," in *Workplace Democracy and Social Change,* ed. Frank Lindenfeld and Joyce Rothschild-Whitt (Boston: Porter Sargent, 1982), 299–313, at 307–13, in his analysis of laws of property that facilitate governance in a traditional corporation but limit access to and control over capital by cooperative ventures.

2. 295 U.S. 495 (1935). An antecedent opinion, ruling that legislative delegation failed to set adequate standards to guide the executive branch, is in *Panama Refining Co. v. Ryan,* 293 U.S. 388 (1935).

3. For a defense of the *Schechter* rule, see Theodore J. Lowi, *The End of Liberalism,* 2d ed. (New York: W. W. Norton, 1979), 300–302, quotation from 300.

4. *Schechter* was affirmed in *Carter v. Carter Coal Company,* 298 U.S. 238 (1936).

5. The 1974 case is *National Cable Television Assn., Inc. v. United States,* 415 U.S. 336 (1974), at 341–43. Marshall's opinion, joined by Brennan, is in *Federal Power Commission v. New England Power Co.,* 415 U.S. 345 (1974), at 352–53 (bracketed word in the original).

6. For discussion see James Q. Freedman, *Crisis and Legitimacy: The Administrative Process and American Government* (New York: Cambridge University Press, 1978), 78–88ff., quotation from 79. See also Alfred H. Kelly and Winfred A. Harbison, *The American Constitution: Its Origins and Development,* 5th ed. (New York: W. W. Norton, 1976), 693–709.

7. *Wayman v. Southard,* 10 Wheaton 1, 46 (1825).

8. *INS v. Chadha,* 103 U.S. 2764 (1983). (The popular press tended initially to view *Chadha* as expanding the power of the presidency at the expense of Congress.) For discussion, see James L. Sundquist, *Constitutional Reform and Effective Government* (Washington, D.C.: The Brookings Institution, 1986), chap. 8, esp. 218–24; Louis Fisher, *The Politics of Shared Power* (Washington, D.C.: Congressional Quarterly Press, 1987), 94–104. Gramm-Rudman-Hollings (formally, the Balanced Budget and Emergency

Deficit Control Act of 1985) brings in the equivalent of a legislative veto through the back door or covertly. It requires various across-the-board program cuts but exempts such significant entitlement programs as social security and veterans' compensation. For a useful brief discussion in the context of other approaches to budgeting, see Irene S. Rubin, "Budget Theory and Budget Practice: How Good the Fit?" *Public Administration Review* 50 (Mar.–Apr. 1990): 179–89.

9. For the last point, see Richard F. Bensel, "Creating the Statutory State: The Implications of a Rule of Law Standard in American Politics," *American Political Science Review* 74 (Sept. 1980): 734–44, esp. 736, 742–44.

10. See William E. Connolly, *The Public Interest* (Washington, D.C.: American Political Science Association, 1977), 50–51; the discussion in chapter 4 herein.

11. Friedrich A. Hayek, *The Constitution of Liberty* (Chicago: Henry Regnery, 1960), 211–12.

12. Andrew Shonfield, *Modern Capitalism* (New York: Oxford University Press, 1965), 163. On the role of organized institutions as opposed to voluntary associations in the United States, see Robert H. Salisbury, "Interest Representation: The Dominance of Institutions," *American Political Science Review* 78 (Mar. 1984): 64–76.

13. Shonfield, *Modern Capitalism,* 161–63, 230–36.

14. For a useful discussion of the rationale underlying these points, see Hanna Pitkin, "Obligation and Consent—I and II," *American Political Science Review* 59 (Dec. 1965): 990–99; 60 (Mar. 1966): 39–52. She argues that the doctrine of past consent (here analogous to prior authorization) is inadequate and should be superseded by a theory of consent based on the "nature of the government," where the nature of the government would be judged by its substantive acts and procedural guarantees (here analogous to the public interest criterion and its corollaries).

15. As does, for example, A. Lee Fritschler, *Smoking and Politics,* 3d ed. (Englewood Cliffs, N.J.: Prentice-Hall, 1983), 143–47; see also Bruce A. Ackerman and William T. Hassler, *Clean Coal/Dirty Air* (New Haven, Conn.: Yale University Press, 1981), esp. chaps. 4, 7.

16. John Locke, *Two Treatises of Government,* 2d ed., ed. Peter Laslett (Cambridge: Cambridge University Press, 1967), II: 87–89, 120–22, 123. See also Adam Smith's caveat about business collusion: "People of the same trade seldom meet together, even for merriment and diversion, but the conversation ends in a conspiracy against the public, or in some contrivance to raise prices." *An Inquiry into the Nature and Causes of the Wealth of Nations,* ed. Edwin Cannan (New York: Modern Library, 1937), book 1, chap. 10, pt. II, 123–32ff., at 128.

17. Grant McConnell, *Private Power and American Democracy* (New York: Alfred A. Knopf, 1966), 51–52.

18. For American possessive individualism, this would be analogous to G. D. H. Cole's objectives. See the discussion in Carole Pateman, *Participation and Democratic Theory* (Cambridge: Cambridge University Press, 1970), 37–40.

19. For a somewhat different approach, see Robert A. Dahl on the appeal of "inalienable" property rights in *A Preface to Economic Democracy* (Berkeley: University of California Press, 1985), 62–83; cf. his *Dilemmas of Pluralist Democracy* (New Haven, Conn.: Yale University Press, 1982), 198–202. The parenthetical quotations are from Locke, *Two Treatises*, II: 138, 88, 40; see also, II: 131, 134–35, 140.

20. See the concluding section of chapter 7 and the penultimate section of chapter 8.

21. Lowi, *End of Liberalism*, 2d ed., 124.

22. Contrast Robert N. Bellah, Richard Madsen, William M. Sullivan, Ann Swidler, and Steven M. Tipton, *Habits of the Heart* (New York: Harper and Row, 1985), with Bertram Gross, *Friendly Fascism* (Boston: South End Press, 1982).

23. See David Held, *Models of Democracy* (Stanford, Calif.: Stanford University Press, 1987); C. B. Macpherson, *The Life and Times of Liberal Democracy* (New York: Oxford University Press, 1977).

24. For one effort to deal with the first of these but not sufficiently with the second, see Benjamin Barber, *Strong Democracy* (Berkeley: University of California Press, 1984).

25. Cf. Eric A. Nordlinger, *On the Autonomy of the Democratic State* (Cambridge, Mass.: Harvard University Press, 1981); Theodore J. Lowi and Alan Stone, eds., *Nationalizing Government* (Beverly Hills, Calif.: Sage Publications, 1978), editors' preface.

Index

ROBERT C. GRADY is a professor of political science at Eastern Michigan University. He received a B.A. from Centre College and a Ph.D. from Vanderbilt University.